Future History

Future History

Global Fantasies in Seventeenth-Century American and British Writings

Kristina Bross

OXFORD
UNIVERSITY PRESS

OXFORD
UNIVERSITY PRESS

Oxford University Press is a department of the University of Oxford.
It furthers the University's objective of excellence in research, scholarship,
and education by publishing worldwide. Oxford is a registered trade mark of
Oxford University Press in the UK and certain other countries.

Published in the United States of America by Oxford University Press
198 Madison Avenue, New York, NY 10016, United States of America.

Library of Congress Cataloging-in-Publication Data
Names: Bross, Kristina, author.
Title: Future history : global fantasies in seventeenth-century American and
British writings / Kristina Bross.
Description: New York : Oxford University Press, 2017. | Includes
bibliographical references and index.
Identifiers: LCCN 2017002198| ISBN 9780190665135 (hardback) | ISBN
9780190665159 (epub)
Subjects: LCSH: English literature—Early modern, 1500-1700—History and
criticism. | American literature—Colonial period, ca. 1600–1775—History
and criticism. | Comparative literature—English and American. |
Comparative literature—American and English. | English
literature—American influences. | American literature—English
influences. | Literature and globalization. | BISAC: HISTORY / United
States / Civil War Period (1850-1877).
Classification: LCC PR129.A4 B76 2017 | DDC 820.9/35873—dc23 LC record available at
https://lccn.loc.gov/2017002198

1 3 5 7 9 8 6 4 2

Printed by Sheridan Books, Inc., United States of America

For Steve, Gracie, Katie. It's off the dining table, finally!

I sing the Mariner who first unfurl'd
An eastern banner o'er the western world,
And taught mankind where future empires lay
In these fair confines of descending day;
                    —*The Columbiad*, Joel Barlow

October 12 their dream came true.
You never saw a happier crew!
"Indians! Indians!" Columbus cried;
His heart was filled with joyful pride
But "India" the land was not;
It was the Bahamas, and it was hot.
                    —*In 1492*, Jean Marzollo

CONTENTS

ACKNOWLEDGMENTS

How to thank the many people who supported me in the long gestation of this project? I owe a debt of gratitude to the staff of the British Library, particularly the Asian and African Studies Reading Room, the Bishopsgate Library staff, the Newberry Library, and the Huntington Library. Thanks as well to Elyssa Tardif, formerly of the Rhode Island Historical Association and now director of the Carpenter Museum in Rehoboth, Massachusetts, and to Jennifer Madden, of the Heritage Museums and Gardens, for helping to track down baskets. Thanks also to Purdue Libraries' Special Collections and Archives, whose knowledgeable staff members were always enthusiastic collaborators in my research, with an especial debt to Neal Harmeyer for lightning-quick digital scans.

Oxford University Press has been an enthusiastic backer of this project, and I want to recognize especially the excellent comments that the anonymous readers provided to me, which truly gave a stronger focus and a better shape to my analyses. I especially want to thank my editor, Sarah Pirovitz, and production editor Gwen Colvin for responding so quickly and efficiently to all challenges, as well as Martha Ramsey for her stellar work copyediting the rough (too rough) manuscript.

Individual colleagues lifted up the project and lifted me personally over the last several years, sometimes with just the right word at the right time— theirs is a consistent generosity and kindness that is such a part of their collegial natures that I'll bet they won't even remember the particulars: in particular, Linda Gregerson, Tom Hallock, Tom Krise, Meredith Neuman, Cassie Smith, Tim Sweet, Theresa Toulouse, and Phil Round (thanks, Phil, for all your work for the conference in the summer of 2015). The Society of Early Americanists has been my intellectual home for many years—I am grateful for the opportunities to present my work at our meetings, to bat ideas around over dinner and drinks, and to renew my excitement and interest in the field by absorbing the great and good ideas of so many talented scholars. Gratitude beyond words to Laura Stevens and Hilary Wyss, who are steady collaborators and ready commiserators and who continue to inspire me with their dedication and smarts.

Closer to home, I have benefited so much from the generosity of my Purdue colleagues who endlessly talked through my ideas, encouraged the project, and read early—and I fear, ugly—drafts of the chapters. My appreciation to Nancy Peterson and to Kris Ratcliffe, who both spurred me to finish it up already, and Clayton Lein for encouraging me in the last push. Thanks to Aparajita Sagar, Shaun Hughes, Emily Allen, Shannon McMullen, and especially to Susan Curtis, who has read far too many drafts of far too many parts of this book and who has offered me unstinting support throughout. Many thanks to Stacey Dearing, who took on the Herculean task of double-checking my quotations.

This project simply would not have been possible without the support of those who helped care for hearth and home—Suzie Tomlinson, Lisa Harmon, and Laurie Hermundson. Thanks to Linda Wereley for being soccer home base week in and week out. And love and thanks to JoAnn Bross and Billy Bross, who never, ever said no, not even when they probably should have.

To Gracie and Katie for putting up with it all, and more for cheering me on; and especially to Steve, for stepping into the breach time and time (and time) again: love.

Part of chapter 2 previously appeared in "Coda: Animating Absences," in *Journeys of the Slave Narrative in the Early Americas*, ed. Nicole N. Aljoe and Ian Finseth (Charlottesville: University of Virginia Press, 2014). Part of chapter 3 was published as "From London to Nonantum: Mission Literature in the Transatlantic English World," in *Empires of God: Religious Encounters in the Early Modern Atlantic World*, ed. Linda Gregerson and Susan Juster (Philadelphia: University of Pennsylvania Press, 2011), 123–142. The original version of chapter 4, "'Why Should You Be So Furious?': Fantasies of Violence in Seventeenth-Century Writings," was published in *American Literature* 88.2 (2016): 213–240. Copyright 2016. Included by permission of the publisher, Duke University Press.

A NOTE ON TRANSCRIPTIONS

I have silently exchanged *u* and *v*, *i* and *j*, when quoting seventeenth-century printed texts. I have left these characters in place when quoting manuscript materials.

PREFACE

Sheltering Violence

This book would not exist—or at least would have taken a very different shape—had my lens on the past not been ground by the terrible events of my own moment, events such as the abuse of prisoners at Abu Ghraib prison, the records of which are even now being preserved in the archives of my government. Such archival "sheltering," as Jacques Derrida observes in *Archive Fever*, is an act that is as much about forgetting as it is about preservation.[1] It may be surprising to find references to Abu Ghraib in the first paragraph of a book written by a colonial American literature scholar, a book analyzing English and American works of the seventeenth century. But as I will argue—and as I discovered as I researched and wrote this book—the texts that are the focus of my analysis are the literature of an early moment of globalization that in many ways parallels our own, right down to debates about the legality of torture.

That my scholarship reflects my own time as much as it does the past seems a commonplace observation. My background is primarily early American studies, and we in the field have long commented on present-day inspiration for our work, even if the results of that inspiration are most clearly visible in hindsight. See, for instance, the preface to Perry Miller's *Errand into the Wilderness*, which Randall Fuller has described as "the opening chapter of American studies's book of Genesis."[2] In it, Miller credits his experiences in Africa with defining his scholarly vocation, experiences determined by postwar economic and political circumstances. And because of his prominence in the field of early American studies, that vocation was shared by many. As my field has changed, Miller's motivations have been

1. "The concept of the archive shelters in itself, of course, this memory of the name *arkhē*. But it also *shelters* itself from this memory which it shelters: which comes down to saying also that it forgets it." Jacques Derrida, *Archive Fever: A Freudian Impression*, trans. Eric Prenowitz (Chicago: University of Chicago Press, 1995), 2.

2. Randall Fuller, "*Errand into the Wilderness*: Perry Miller as American Scholar," *American Literary History* 18.1 (Spring 2006), 103.

challenged and have become subjects of analysis themselves.[3] Most recently, increased interest such as my own in large-scale geographic contexts for early modern literature can surely be mapped onto new-found political and economic interests in (or fears of) globalization, sparked by a new-media or a post-9/11 sense that in our time we lean toward postnationalism. In early American studies, such interests are met by the realization that state configurations in the seventeenth and early eighteenth centuries can teach us about our own, and that the period produced literature that speaks to us today in ways we couldn't imagine a few decades ago.

Suspicion of presentist motivation is commonplace among most scholars of the past. We want our work to have long shelf life and so present our findings as independent of our own moment as much as possible. Moreover, many of us have a knee-jerk reaction to the quest for "relevance"; in U.S.-based work especially it smacks of insupportable American exceptionalism or simply callow narcissism.[4] But of course, we all indulge in it, and at times to good effect. After all, our immersion in the archives of the past is only productive if in the midst of our wading through ledgers, poems, letters, reports, and so on, something can stop us in our tracks—a rough edge that disrupts the stream of narrative, records, figures, and propaganda and snags our attention. To be sure, we literary historians are generally most comfortable when that something comes from formal or contextual considerations of our sources and their own times, considerations for which we are disciplined through literary and historical study. In a commentary on her book on the origin of the Royal Society and its American interests, Susan Scott Parrish describes how repetition in her sources snagged her attention: the recurrence of the possum in the Royal Society papers. In considering the little marsupial trooping across the pages, Parrish was prompted by her archive to ask particular questions and trace additional sources.[5] For literary historians, such a pause in our archival meanderings depends on deep or

3. For a discussion of Miller's preface and the challenge it presents to later early American scholars, see Jane Tompkins, "'Indians': Textualism, Morality, and the Problem of History," *Critical Inquiry* 13.1 (Autumn 1986): 101–119. For a defense of "one of the most eminent practitioners of American history," published just a few years before Tompkins's essay, see Francis T. Butts, "The Myth of Perry Miller," *American Historical Review* 87.3 (June 1982), 666.

4. For instance, I often teach about New England Puritans and their writings. But despite my investment in the past qua past in order to counter naïve teleological analysis of colonial America, I shamelessly divide my time between the notion that "the past is a foreign country; they do things differently there" and assuring students that Puritans "are us" to help motivate them to stick with the most difficult, strange, or even off-putting elements of the literature and culture.

5. Parrish describes this process in "Rummaging/In and Out of Holds," *Early American Literature* 45.2 (2010): 261–274. The result of her quest to follow the possum is her book *American Curiosity: Cultures of Natural History in the Colonial British Atlantic World* (Chapel Hill: University North Carolina Press, 2006).

long immersion in our textual and historical materials—*this* seems unusual for the time, *this* out of place in the text, *this* part of a pattern.

On the other hand, our attention can be snagged by elements that are for us overdetermined, that depend less on learned considerations and more on our particular situations as individuals embedded within countless systems and institutions—personal, familial, national. In addition to whatever historical, formal, or cultural understanding we bring to bear on our sources, sometimes our gaze is caught for other reasons. In his *Camera Lucida*, Roland Barthes argues that a photograph carries its *studium*, that is, a photograph encodes meaning that can be accessed through conventional analysis—its ostensible subject. But a viewer may also encounter *punctum*, that which "pierces," "pricks," or "bruises" the viewer and is particular and personal to that viewer.[6] The *studium* depends on "my knowledge, my culture," an "*average* affect, almost from a certain training."[7] By contrast, "In order to perceive the punctum, no analysis would be of any use to me (but perhaps memory sometimes would)." The punctum, then, "is an intense mutation of my interest."[8] Archival materials seem to work in much the same way as Barthes's photographs.[9] Like a photograph, the Archive can masquerade as a repository of objective truth.[10] Like photographs, archival materials are created by particular technologies that make them seem complete or even "objective." I am thinking here of Enlightenment technologies of organization

6. Roland Barthes, *Camera Lucida: Reflections on Photography*, trans. Richard Howard (New York: Hill and Wang, 1981), 26, 27. Parrish's use of Barthes's notion of *stadium* and *punctum* in "Rummaging/In and Out of Holds" pointed me toward this use of the theory: "instead, if the design of the archive is something like a *studium*—a socially fixed meaning of the collection, or an ordering concept, the *punctum* designates that which can be stumbled upon by people working within an archive. The *punctum* is what is stowed away in the hold, an accidental passenger or bit of cargo, from the past. No originary collector or latter-day archivist particularly took note of it, or bothered to exclude it" ("Rummaging/In and Out of Holds," 291).

7. Barthes, *Camera Lucida*, 25, 26.

8. Barthes, *Camera Lucida*, 42, 49.

9. And of course, archival collections may include photographs. Although I find that image and text often sustain parallel modes of analysis, Barthes differentiates between a photo and text as between a static and a dynamic medium: "the Photograph is pure contingency and can be nothing else (it is always *something* that is represented)—contrary to the text which, by the sudden action of a single word, can shift a sentence from description to reflection." *Camera Lucida*, 28.

10. Here and throughout the book, I differentiate "the Archive" (singular noun, capitalized), which is a theoretical concept, from "the archives" (plural noun, not capitalized), which is the actual repository of unique records and papers that scholars consult. This split in terminology is not unique to me, but few researchers address the differences directly in their published work, and not all fields view the distinction as in play. My use of the terms depends on the theories of knowledge creation or the organization of information in works such as Michel Foucault's *Archaeology of Knowledge* and especially Jacques Derrida's *Archive Fever*, in which the concept of what I'm calling "the Archive" is concomitant with the wielding of authority—of institutionalized power—that gives shape and even meaning to the collection of materials we traditionally call "the archives."

and order as well as recent innovations in preservation technology, from calendars and indices to acid-free folders and the sealed, argon-filled chambers that contain our most fragile and precious papers, and assure us of their intrinsic value.[11]

This project began when I read anew a midcentury tract celebrating Dutch missionary efforts and comparing them to English missionary work in America. The author, Henry Jessey, praised Dutch colonial evangelism, and his enthusiasm persuaded me to learn more about Anglo-Dutch relations in the mid-seventeenth century (the *studium* of his text as it were, which I had imagined as I began this project would be my own). But at that same moment, U.S. mainstream media began reporting on the torture of prisoners in Abu Ghraib prison. Journalists focused especially on the practice of waterboarding, or simulated drowning. Thus, I experienced quite a shock of recognition when I encountered another seventeenth-century pamphlet that included a detailed and graphic description of the abuse of English prisoners at the hands of the Dutch on the spice-factory island of Amboyna in 1623 (a description I analyze in detail in chapter 4): "Then they bound a cloth about his necke and face so close, that little or no water could go by. That done, they poured the water softly upon his head until the cloth was full, up to the mouth and nostrills, and somewhat higher; so that he could not draw breath."[12] The *punctum* for me is the word "softly," a word that suggests nothing so much as the disavowal of violence that we witness in U.S. torture memos, the U.S. administration defense of them, and continuing debates over the definition of torture and the closing of Guantánamo. Water is being poured "softly"; interrogation is "enhanced." My shock upon encountering this passage was then immediately met by "my knowledge, my culture." Thus *punctum* shades into *studium*, into understanding that early modern forms of torture are being applied to prisoners today. My shock of recognition illuminates the resonances between twenty-first-century networks of information, political and military action, and aesthetic responses with such networks, actions, and responses nearly 400 years earlier.

As they flashed around the world, the Abu Ghraib photographs, ostensibly taken as un-self-conscious trophies of war by victorious U.S. troops, were made to illustrate arguments quite opposed to the mindset and moti-

---

11. See Mary Lynn Ritzenthaler and Catherine Nicholson, "A New Era Begins for the Charters of Freedom," *Prologue* 35.3 (Fall 2003), http://www.archives.gov/publications/prologue/2003/fall/charters-new-era.html, accessed 11 March 2015. Consider, too, Derrida's reminder that "there could be no archiving without titles (thus without names and without the archontic principle of legitimization, without laws, without criteria of classification and of hierarchization, without order and without order, in the double sense of the word)"; *Archive Fever*, 40.

12. *A True Relation of the Unjust, Cruell, and Barbarous Proceedings Against the English at Amboyna in the East-Indies* (London, 1624), 10–11.

vations of those who first captured and shared them. Judith Butler talks about such circulation as the breaking of the "frames of war" that circumscribe the meaning of such images, enabling them to speak within and for different contexts and causes.[13] The photos from Abu Ghraib broke their "frame" as they became part of global news cycles and were used to support arguments against the actions of the U.S. military and its treatment of prisoners. So, too, engravings and descriptions of naked, tormented Englishmen being abused in 1623 by their Dutch captors circulated quickly and continued to circulate for decades (even centuries) after the events they depicted took place, coming to signify in ways unimaginable to their first creators. I'm not the first to make such connections, but I have been struck by how few scholars who have previously worked on the violence in Amboyna have not revisited it, given the possibilities for insight produced when we assume a stance that is "deliberately anachronistic," in Ayanna Thompson's words, at least when it comes to considering the chilling consanguinity of such early modern and contemporary scenes of violence.[14] Taken together, theories of the archive and theories of violence, such as Butler's exploration of media, war, and the limitations of discursive control, provide a powerful means to unpack the figures and description of warfare and torture that we find in the early modern archive and that continue to resonate so powerfully today. While scenes of violence are not the only ones that I consider in this book, they are perhaps the most compelling, and if I had not been so struck by the bloody parallels between the early modern literature of globalization and our own today, I might never have been led to my larger Archive of American-English global fantasies.

One of the essential tasks of journalists, historians, humanistic researchers of all disciplines—including literary history—is to grapple with and challenge the immurement of the past (even the very recent past) in institutions that shelter to forget. This book is meant as a modest contribution to that effort. We often imagine that ours is the most connected, the most globalized time. From a contemporary perspective, it can be easy to assume that people in earlier times were atomized, isolated, professing at most local allegiances. One goal of this book is simply to puncture that assumption by tracing a rather idiosyncratic literary history that encodes the personal and discursive connections among early modern English writers and travelers. In this book, I analyze how seventeenth-century writers saw themselves in the world, and how in their works they navigated the changing political,

---

13. Judith Butler, *Frames of War: When Is Life Grievable?* (reprint, London: Verso, 2010); see especially 9–12.

14. Thompson is one of those scholars who has read the Amboyna incident through the lens of Abu Ghraib—and vice versa. See Ayanna Thompson, *Performing Race and Torture on the Early Modern Stage* (New York: Routledge, 2007), 122.

economic, and above all religious systems in which they were enmeshed, systems that connected them from the West to the East Indies. By tracing the contexts of early modern global fantasies in English cultural productions, we are reminded that all such imaginative work is always contingent on its contexts, even our own.

Introduction

"America is as properly East as China"

In 1641, pamphleteer and revolutionary Henry Parker outlined a point of cartographic relativism that seems only common sense today. In his *Altar Dispute* he dismisses the notion that Christian altars should be placed in the most easterly location in a house of worship because Christ had been crucified in the East. We need not adhere to such a seemingly arbitrary rule, he reasons, since there is no absolute "East": "we know that the East is named so from the rising of the Sunne, and wee know the Sunne has neither rising nor setting, but comparative, and so *America* is as properly East, as *China*, for if *America* lie West to us, yet it lies East to *China*; which lies East to us."[1] "*America* is as properly East, as *China*": Parker's geographic sensibilities speak to the ways that religious speculation prompted expansive thought in an age of European travel, trade, exploration, and colonization. For Englishmen at the mid-seventeenth century, certainly for the radical Protestants in this study, the world was their stage. Enthusiastic believers in England and its colonies looked to a time—coming soon—in which everyone around the globe would be united under the rule of Christ. Some millennialists, especially the militant Fifth Monarchists, believed that the "Fifth Kingdom," Christ's kingdom, was imminent, and they directed their sometimes violent efforts toward that hoped-for end of history.[2] In numerous publications, English missionaries and their supporters turned to biblical texts describing God's rule spreading over the whole world as proof that their efforts were part of God's plan, suggesting that their work to convert "gentiles"—

---

1. Henry Parker, *The Altar Dispute, or, A Discourse Concerning the Severall Innovations of the Altar* (London, 1641), 35.
2. Bernard Capp, *The Fifth Monarchy Men: A Study in Seventeenth-Century English Millenarianism* (London: Faber and Faber, 1972).

indigenous people of all sorts—was biblically sanctioned and tied to millennial prophecy: "from the rising of the sun even unto the going down of the same my name shall be great among the Gentiles; and in every place incense shall be offered unto my name."[3] Merchants, traders, explorers, and natural philosophers might have been less exalted in their discussions, but they too saw the world as connected from the rising to the setting sun as they sought to make good on Columbus's voyages, to find and establish routes of exchange from the Spice Islands in the Pacific to the sugar islands in the Atlantic.

The global imagination of English writers was given urgency by economic and political competition. In the East, Chinese power and influence in this period was extensive, so much so that Andre Gunder Frank argues that the period was "Sinocentric": "from a global perspective Asia and not Europe held center stage for most of early modern history." Robert Markley terms the period "Asian-dominated."[4] But of course, however powerful Eastern power may have been, the English found threats closer to home especially troubling. In its global ambition and reach, England was seriously outpaced not only by Asian powers but also by the Netherlands, Portugal, and especially Spain. European competition was driven in part by a voracious appetite for Eastern trade goods and luxury items, such as silks, porcelain, and above all, spices.[5] Despite England's desire for such goods, it lagged behind other European powers in setting up regular, effective trade relationships and routes. And everyone lagged behind Spain. As Karen Ordahl Kupperman explains, despite the possibilities for trade and travel in "the interconnected ocean system," only Spain "came closest to realizing the dream with which Columbus first set out: find a route to the rich Asian trades."[6] Spain, considered by many to be England's direct competitor for both wealth and souls, established regular routes and systems of global trade, which linked Spain

3. Malachi 1:11.

4. Andre Gunder Frank, *ReOrient: Global Economy in the Asian Age* (Berkeley: University of California Press, 1998), xv. Robert Markley, *The Far East and the English Imagination, 1600–1730* (Cambridge: Cambridge University Press, 2006), 2. For a discussion of Elizabethan views of England and the world, especially as compared with Spain's global empire, see Richard Helgerson, *Forms of Nationhood: The Elizabethan Writing of England in the Early Modern Period* (Chicago: University of Chicago Press, 1992).

5. Scholarship on the history and significance of European spice trading and consumption is plentiful. A selection of helpful work is Wolfgang Schivelbusch, *Tastes of Paradise: A Society History of Spices, Stimulants and Intoxicants*, trans. David Jacobson (New York: Vintage Books, 1992); John Brewer and Roy Porter, eds., *Consumption and the World of Goods* (New York: Routledge, 1994); Jack Turner, *Spice: The History of a Temptation* (New York: Vintage, 2005); Anne E. C. McCants, "Exotic Goods, Popular Consumption, and the Standard of Living: Thinking about Globalization in the Early Modern World," *Journal of World History* 18.4 (December 2007): 433–462.

6. Karen Ordahl Kupperman, *The Atlantic in World History* (London: Oxford University Press, 2012), 124.

to American mineral wealth and to Asian goods. English envy of Spain's success helped shape England's version of the "Black Legend," an anti-Catholic tradition of bashing Spain that England inherited from the Dutch and that held sway from the sixteenth century on.[7]

However vilified, Spanish tactics were also grudgingly admired by pragmatic Englishmen. In his Commonplace Book, Thomas Bowdler recommended that England focus its overseas expansion on America rather than Asia. Settlement in America "would 'raise another England to withstand our new Spain.'" And John Smith, in his *Advertisements for the unexperienced planters of New England* (1631), enjoined his countrymen to follow the example of Spanish soldiers and so win the world for King James: "I...could wish every English man to carry alwaies this Motto in his heart; Why should the brave Spanish Souldiers brag. The Sunne never sets in the Spanish dominions, but ever shineth on one part or other we have conquered for our King...but to animate us to doe the like for ours, who is no way his inferior."[8]

We in Anglo-American studies are more accustomed to attaching Smith's "sun never sets" phrase to a later British empire. During the mid-seventeenth century, however, England was hardly a global power, while Spain indeed spanned the earth, with its Manila galleons in the Pacific and its West Indian fleet of the Atlantic.[9] England would not inherit the motto until later, but English writers in the seventeenth century laid anxious claim to that future by fantasizing about English ascendancy and encouraging active steps toward England's appropriation of Spain's holdings, influence, and trade, especially in the Americas.

7. For an extended treatment of England's version of the Black Legend, see William S. Maltby, *The Black Legend in England: The Development of Anti-Spanish Sentiment, 1558–1660* (Durham: Duke University Press, 1971), and Margaret R. Green, Walter D. Mignolo, and Maureen Quilligan, eds., *Rereading the Black Legend: The Discourses of Religious and Racial Difference in the Renaissance Empires* (Chicago: University of Chicago Press, 2007). Benjamin Schmidt treats the Dutch invention of the Black Legend in detail in *Innocence Abroad: The Dutch Imagination and the New World, 1570–1670* (Cambridge: Cambridge University Press, 2001).

8. Thomas Bowdler, Commonplace Book, 1635–1636, quoted in Nicholas Canny, "The Origins of Empire," in *Oxford History of the British Empire*, vol. 1, ed. Nicholas Canny (Oxford: Oxford University Press, 2001), 19. John Smith, *Advertisements for the Unexperienced Planters of New England, or Any Where* (London, 1631), 37.

9. On the Manila galleons' route and influence, see William Lytle Schurz, *The Manila Galleon* (New York: Dutton, 1939); M. N. Pearson, "Spain and Spanish Trade in Southeast Asia," *Journal of Asian History* 2 (1968): 109–129; Schell Hoberman, *Mexico's Merchant Elite, 1590–1660: Silver, State and Society* (Durham: Duke University Press, 1991); Dennis O'Flynn and Arturo Giráldez, "Born with a 'Silver Spoon': The Origin of World Trade in 1571," *Journal of World History* 6.2 (Fall 1995): 201–221. Javier Ruescas and Javier Wrana, "The West Indies and Manila Galleons: The First Global Trade Route," paper presented at seminar The Galleon and the Making of the Pacific, Asociacio'n Cultural Galeo'n de Manila (Madrid), Manila, 9 November 2009, http://www.galeondemanila.org/images/stories/The_West_Indies__Manila_Galleons_Ruescas__Wrana_-_Revised_March_2010_con_cabecera.pdf, accessed 11 March 2015.

This book examines such writings, works written and published from the 1620s to the 1670s that imagined England on a global stage in the Americas and East Indies just as—and in some cases even before—England occupied such spaces in force. Indeed, to some extent the texts I analyze here drove England's ambition to expand overseas. To be sure, England's East-West networks had their start earlier in the seventeenth century. The English East India Company had begun sponsoring voyages in the early 1600s. In America and the Atlantic, English settlers and investors began colonization with Jamestown in 1607. By the 1620s, however, trade and colonization in the East and the West were firmly established, the pace of both increasing. Of course, England's expansion did not go unchallenged. In the East, English trade was severely tested by Dutch competitors, and in the Americas, the resistance of Native peoples to the English incursion could be devastating.[10] But the foothold the English had established in Eastern trade would prove permanent, and in the 1620s the English presence in America began truly to consolidate. New colonies were planted in rapid succession: Plymouth in 1620, Barbados in 1627, the Massachusetts Bay Colony in 1629. Moreover, English and American writers began to imagine the Eastern and Western enterprises as connected in some way—if not yet quite as an empire, certainly as linked networks of faith and trade from the rising to the setting sun.

At the other end of my period, the 1670s mark a concerted shift in England's foreign policies and ambitions, changes driven by the Restoration and coinciding with the Third Anglo-Dutch War. The span of years I consider in this book encompasses the extraordinary transformation of England from a nation with little global significance to a soon-to-be-powerful nation with growing worldwide influence. As Alison Games notes, in the late sixteenth century, England was a state "too weak to intrude effectively on European affairs," but it "grew to become a powerful kingdom with global reach by 1660."[11] Despite the changes that she notes over this period, the texts that I consider from the 1670s arguably belong as much to an earlier moment as to the beginnings of the long eighteenth century and the flourishing of a true English empire. Dryden's *Amboyna* (1673), for instance, may be seen as transitional: looking forward to a realized empire but still

10. For a comparative study of this period, see Alison Games, "Violence on the Fringes: The Virginia (1622) and Amboyna (1623) Massacres in Comparative Perspective," *History* 98.336 (2014): 505–529.

11. Alison Games, *The Web of Empire: English Cosmopolitans in an Age of Expansion, 1560–1660* (Oxford: Oxford University Press, 2009), 7. Carla Pestana notes the profound effects of European extension into the world more generally: "The expansion of Europe from its peninsula into other parts of the globe was one of the most significant events to shape the modern world." *Protestant Empire: Religion and the Making of the British Atlantic World* (Philadelphia: University of Pennsylvania Press, 2011), 1.

reflecting older ways of viewing England in the world, and drawing on fifty-year-old narratives and records to do so.

Other periodization is certainly possible. Like Games, I am interested in the period of English trial and experimentation on a global scale, though I am more interested in the effect on the imaginations of those involved than on the how and why of that transformation. I could therefore follow Games and consider the English global imagination from 1560 to 1660. Another way to parse this period is to treat the "short seventeenth century," which stretches from 1608 to 1660, from the ascension of King James to the throne through the Interregnum and to the Restoration. Or I might date the start of this book to the first East India Company voyage or the first permanent English settlement in the Americas, both in the first decade of the 1600s. But as a literary history, the endpoints of this study are publication dates, not events, determined by the first reports of the execution of Englishmen by Dutch traders on the island of Amboyna and by the dramatization of that same event fifty years later. This book is thus anchored by works that describe and dramatize a particularly explosive event of international colonial competition, an event that sparked interest among English readers worldwide.

Historical endpoints aside, the center of gravity of this book is writings at the midcentury, that is, writings coincident with the Interregnum, a time when England hatched and launched ambitious (often violent) schemes to conquer, colonize, or otherwise appropriate other lands, driven by both mercantilist and religious desires. It was a time when such political ambitions were met by religious enthusiasm about biblical prophecy, a moment of heightened political speculation about the chronology of God's divine plan to rule, judge, and end the world. The title of this book is borrowed from the midcentury publication *A Brief Description of the Future History of Europe* (1650), a work that plots a coincidence of human events with divine drama, yielding a means by which readers could locate their moment in a cosmic calendar extending to 1710, when Christ's kingdom was expected to commence. Writings such as *A Brief Description of the Future History*, Thomas Gage's *English-American* (1648), and Henry Jessey's *Of the Conversion of Five Thousand and Nine Hundred East Indians* (1650), all of which I analyze in the following chapters, helped convince rulers and a wider reading public that England's move onto a global stage was both viable and desirable, that it was divinely ordained and would result in temporal gains. At the same time, London publishers did a thriving business in reprints of earlier accounts of English travel, exploration, settlement, and trade. Midcentury reissues of Sir Francis Drake's travel narratives, or a 1650s return to the "news" of the execution of English traders by their Dutch rivals in the spice islands some thirty years earlier, helped construct a revisionist history that included, in the one case, a legacy of English glory and, in the other, an excuse for failure.

The thumbnail literary history that I have just sketched, and that I elaborate through the rest of the book, suggests that these writings are (proto) national, focused on England as a future empire. Indeed, one way to understand seventeenth-century print discussions of England's place in the world is as a predominantly metropolitan discourse. Most of the texts that I take up in this book were productions of London printers, published in London for an English readership. As such, they might seem properly to be the purview of a British historian or an English Renaissance scholar. But if they were *published* on Pope's Head Alley, in Cornhill, or in Little Britain in London, such texts were *conceived* at the margins (or even outside) of English control—in New England or the Dutch East Indies—by colonial, creole, enslaved, or indigenous actors, some of whom had never been to, nor indeed even imagined, a place called London. English global fantasies of the seventeenth century were thus born colonial.

Although they were published in London and were adopted and adapted by readers and writers there, their "Englishness" was a result of processes similar to those that Benedict Anderson describes in his essay "Exodus," a New England application of his ideas of "imagined community." When the colonial captive Mary Rowlandson describes a cowpath cutting through the Massachusetts landscape as English," Anderson argues, she is experiencing a "nationalizing moment" made possible by her "fearful exile."[12] Or we might apply Leonard Tennenhouse's analysis of eighteenth-century colonial and early national writings as a literature of diaspora to this earlier period and ask what effect new conceptions of the world and of England in the world had on English imaginations.[13] Anibal Quijano offers another, sweeping articulation of the ways that early modern Europe was a colonial construct. In his study of the role of Latin America in the history of globalization, Quijano argues that "America was constituted as the first space/time of a new model of power of global vocation." Europe may have been "the center of global capitalism," but even as Europe embraced a "new model of power" that developed in the sixteenth and seventeenth centuries, as Quijano argues, it was ordered by "coloniality."[14] My research suggests that one result of these processes was the creation of global fantasies centered on England but profoundly influenced by colonial and other overseas experiences and agents. As Anderson asserts, the colonists' "unstable

---

12. Benedict Anderson, "Exodus," *Critical Inquiry* 20.2 (Winter 1994): 316.
13. Leonard Tennenhouse, *The Importance of Feeling English: American Literature and the British Diaspora, 1750–1850* (Princeton: Princeton University Press, 2007).
14. Anibal Quijano, "Coloniality of Power: Eurocentrism, and Latin America," in *Nepantla: Views from South* 1.3 (2000): 533, 540. Walter D. Mignolo said: "There is no modernity without coloniality and that coloniality is constitutive, and not derivative, of modernity." *Local Histories/Global Designs: Coloniality, Subaltern Knowledges, and Border Thinking* (Princeton: Princeton University Press: 2000; reprint, 2012), ix.

Englishness" is shared with England itself. Paradoxically, English nationalism emerges from "the essential nexus of long-distance transportation and
print capitalist communications" from and about England's colonies and trading posts.[15] Such technologies were important means by which early modern
people began, as Alison Games persuasively argues, "to perceive in its en-
tirety a world once experienced only in fragments," and more, to understand themselves as being "English" in that world.[16]

In her important challenge to the insularity of New England studies,
Michelle Burnham turns our attention to such forces not just in Europe but
also in the study of early America. In her *Folded Selves*, she describes New
England as "a criss-crossed site engaged in uneven negotiations with European
core states and their peripheries, and marked also by its own unequally developed colonial centers and colonial peripheries."[17] As Burnham argues, if
we are to understand colonial American culture, we must deploy new spatial orientations, to recognize how and why colonial subjects (in American
and elsewhere) placed themselves in the world. Her analysis depends on
the macrohistorical world-systems theory of Immanuel Wallerstein because
of her particular interest in shifting our analyses of America/New England
from a purely religious framework to one that takes economics and capital
exchange as much into account.[18] Similarly, Alison Games turns to the "overlapping and intersecting worlds of commercial and colonial enterprises" in
her study of England's rise to global prominence in the seventeenth century.[19] The world-systems approach and other economic analyses have been
instrumental in directing our attention to the global horizon in the seventeenth and eighteenth centuries.

Trade, mercantilism, and capitalism certainly must be considered in any
analysis of an interconnected world in the seventeenth century, but these
cannot be easily separated from other influences, and a world-systems perspective on the period should be complemented by a continued interest in
forces apart from the economic. Lynn Hunt, in her *Writing History in the
Global Era*, urges us to take a "middle ground" in our approach to globalization as "a series of transnational processes in which the histories of diverse
places can become connected and interdependent." Hunt's discussion of
historical approaches to globalization eschews analysis from "above," which

15. Anderson, "Exodus," 316.
16. Games, *Web of Empire*, 6.
17. Michelle Burnham, *Folded Selves: Colonial New England Writing in the World System*
(Hanover: University Press of New England, 2007), 15.
18. Immanuel Wallerstein has helpfully provided an overview of his theories in *World-
Systems Analysis: An Introduction* (Durham: Duke University Press, 2004). See also Walter
Goldrank, "Paradigm Regained? The Rules of Wallerstein's World-System Method," *Journal of
World-Systems Research* 6.2 (2000): 150–195.
19. Games, *Web of Empire*, 7.

she identifies with Wallerstein's and similar approaches. She argues that the world-systems approach to globalization is necessarily "destined to draw historians' attention to macro-historical and systemic process," thus taking "the modern dominance of the West" as a given.[20] While I agree that we should be on our guard against such assumptions, Burnham's and Games's books present fine-grained analyses with careful attention to local manifestations of and lives within an economic world system.[21] And a focus on the local does not necessarily inoculate against Western exceptionalist fallacies. Especially in the case of New England, smaller-scale religious and intellectual histories can result in—and traditionally have resulted in—descriptions of the United States' or the West's dominance as destiny. A shift in our understanding at/of the macro level, as Burnham's work demonstrates, can positively affect our methods of analyzing history and culture more locally.

Trade and mercantilism are important to all the works I consider in this book. Indeed, economic exchange is the enabling condition of the texts I analyze, even when it is not treated overtly. Nevertheless, in Burnham's important call to "abandon our tendency to define dissent in the colonial New England context exclusively in terms of religious forms of difference," I stress her world "exclusively." Even as I rely on the findings of scholars such as Burnham and Games (and Benedict before them) that depend on economic analyses for a more expansive perspective, it seems to me that we must follow an iterative process to unpack the seventeenth-century imagination.

English and American writers had frames of reference other than capitalism and nationalism to locate themselves in the early modern world. Christian theology, especially millennialism, provided ready-made images and a language with which they could articulate global interconnection. While not all English Christians believed in a literal millennium—a thousand-year rule of Christ that would presage the end of time—and even millennialists differed in their beliefs about when and how that rule would be manifested, all Christians were familiar with the Bible's global imagery, with descriptions of Christ and his saints ruling over all the earth.[22] Indeed, some English enthusiasts believed that human action could work with God's will to hasten—or forestall—the end-times. These believers worked on a national stage, certainly, but they also saw these prophecies at work on a global scale. As a result, on the one hand they infused reports of new mercantile

20. Hunt, *Writing History in the Global Era*, 60, 62.
21. See Burnham's discussion of Wallerstein and his critics, 17.
22. Such images are numerous. In other work, I have traced the significance of Malachi 1:11 and its global imagery to the English mission in New England. See Kristina Bross, *Dry Bones and Indian Sermons: Praying Indians in Colonial America* (Ithaca: Cornell University Press, 2004), 28–51. The prophecies of Daniel and the Book of Revelation were even more widely cited in English texts discussing millennial possibilities.

endeavor with global-millennial justification and on the other Christian theology took a decidedly colonial turn.

Analysis of early modern religious frameworks has much yet to teach us, especially in conjunction with other methods.[23] Such work is essential if we are to understand how seventeenth-century English and American writers connected themselves across the world and the ways that they disciplined indigenous and other marginalized people into their social, economic, and political systems. As Carla Pestana argues, "more than any other cultural practice, religion had a far-reaching impact on the very process of colonization and the world that resulted."[24] In terms of a global perspective on the seventeenth century, I am particularly interested in how the old Christian model of a "world system"—millennial rule—was instantiated in local contexts and translated into polemical literature at midcentury, works that sought to understand the connections among the peoples of England, America, and Asia. Thus in this book I employ a religiospatial framework that yields a new understanding of faith and culture as well as the political and economic valence of literature in the seventeenth century English world.

Millennial beliefs, of course, took many forms. But while believers may have disagreed about the timing of the millennium or the particulars of prophecy, they generally agreed that England and its saints had important roles to play in the cosmic drama. At midcentury, London was the center of colonial and religious networks that began to produce texts describing and dreaming of England at the center of a coming empire. England's needs and desires motivated migration and trade. The metropole regulated property, controlled the circulation of capital, and collected, published, and read colonial narratives. Religious enthusiasts brought their claims to colonial lands to the English Parliament for adjudication.[25] And England's armies issued forth to suppress dissent or conquer lands in Ireland, Scotland, and the West Indies. But for all its claims to centrality, the national and discursive links between England, America, and the East Indies that I examine in the pages to follow suggest just how powerfully the margins created that center: intercolonial competition launched Cromwell's fleet to Hispaniola; the promise of colonial evangelism in New England opened English purses and inspired prayer; an incident of extrajudicial torture—of just nineteen Englishmen on an island thousands of miles from London—sparked a diplomatic crisis and created new English martyrs.[26] Throughout, we find

---

23. Bross, *Dry Bones and Indian Sermons*, 7.

24. Pestana, *Protestant Empire*, 6.

25. See Jonathan Beecher Field, *Errands into the Metropolis: New England Dissidents in Revolutionary London* (Lebanon, NH: Dartmouth University Press, 2009).

26. Others were killed in this incident as well, most notably a group of Japanese men. But their suffering and death was largely ignored by the London press.

records, narratives, court testimony, "true relations," letters, sermons, and plays that insist on the connections between the East and the West. The maps—both real and discursive—produced by such English writings centered not on London but on Guadalupe and Vera Cruz, Amboyna and Jakarta, Boston and Nonantum.

UP FROM THE ARCHIVES

In an essay included in "Globalizing Literary Studies," a special issue of *PMLA*, Edward Said asks: "Can one formulate a theory of connection between part and whole that denies neither the specificity of the individual experience nor the validity of a projected, putative, or imputed whole?"[27] While this book does not attempt to outline such a theory of global studies, my methodology suggests that we may be able to answer Said's question in the affirmative. To do so, rather than drilling down from the systems within which the works were produced, I propose an archives-up approach. This book relies on the unifying fictions of a roughly chronological structure and of a focus on writings in English but combines them with speculative criticism and asynchronous archival representation and analysis so as to better understand the worlding of the English imagination in the seventeenth century.

As an example of my methods, consider the text that launched me on this study and to which I give extended attention in chapter 4: Henry Jessey's *Of the Conversion of Five-thousand Nine-Hundred East Indians*. It was published in 1650, edited and introduced by Jessey, a well-known and well-connected (in Interregnum terms) Baptist minister. The tract gives a summary account of Dutch evangelism in Taiwan, which the English at that time knew as Formosa, followed by an edited version of several works previously published in London describing efforts in New England to Christianize Algonquian peoples. Jessey's work has received almost no critical attention, and the tract's neglect is not hard to understand. For scholars interested in New England, the tract is a recapitulation of previous publications, an edited work of dubious authorship that doesn't provide historians with fresh details about American evangelism. The tract seems merely to repeat some descriptions of the Eliot mission that had been published in greater detail elsewhere. For those concerned with the Dutch or with Dutch expansion into Asia, it seems even less useful, a secondhand (or even thirdhand) account with overly general and highly suspect details. Moreover, as a work of comparative evangelism, it seems an utter failure. It yokes two disparate

27. Edward Said, "Globalizing Literary Study," in "Globalizing Literary Studies," special issue, *PMLA* 116.1 (January 2001), 68.

missionary fields, New England and Formosa—endeavors that shared neither evangelists nor local constituents, national sponsors, or even geographic boundaries. Thus the English and Dutch missions resist easy (or even logical) comparison, and the resulting publication seems eccentric at best, pointless at worst.

But if we shift our attention when reading Jessey's tract away from elements that might seem protonational or even protoethnographic and ask why Jessey was so interested in linking evangelism in the East Indies with that in America, we can better understand its significance. Jessey was an ecumenical thinker, a theologian who looked forward to the global rule of Jesus Christ. As such, he was not writing another English mission tract when he penned *Of the Conversion* but rather was collecting evidence of a worldwide shift to Protestant Christianity. We should look at his work not as a history of evangelism in New England or Taiwan but as a "True Relation," an example of that expansive, flexible, early modern genre that, as Frances Dolan has explained, readers might accept as "fictions without assuming them to be untrue." Rather than conveying certain fact, true relations prescribed a "relational reading practice." Such a "text presents itself as a true one, defined by its ability to transact a relation between event and representation, between relator and reader."[28] The seventeenth-century true relation aims to describe current events in order to spur readers to act. If we adopt Dolan's approach, we must read through the lens of the literary rather than the straight historian. If we do, *Of the Conversion* will be more accurately understood as a work that does not document as much as construct global currents of faith and action. Writing from London, Jessey follows Protestants to the ends of the earth. He has read the breaking news accounts of evangelism in New England, and he has heard grand claims of thousands of new Christians in Dutch-controlled colonies in Asia. As a theologian committed to a near future in which Christ would rule the entire earth, he seeks corroboration of those claims. He interviews secondhand witnesses to that Dutch evangelical success, men and women who had recently been among the English expatriate community in Amsterdam. He pursues his investigation by corresponding with the missionaries and eyewitnesses to conversion. He then packages his Findings in a portmanteau of globalized Christian reporting: the forty-five-page *Of the Conversion*. The result is a promise of a unified, worldwide evangelism movement stretching from the East to the West Indies, as well as from the North to the "Land of Sinum," as his title page declares. This movement is destined, he believes, to fulfill biblical prophecy "that the Earth may be so fill'd with the knowledge of *Jehovah*,

---

28. Frances Dolan, *True Relations: Reading, Literature, and Evidence in Seventeenth-Century England* (Philadelphia: University of Pennsylvania Press, 2013), 14, 18.

that *all his people* may be one visibly, and serve *Jehovah* with one shoulder; and all *differences and envies amongst them may be removed farre away.*"[29]

Jessey's global vision is one reason I've reconsidered his work. Equally important are the research methods he describes in his brief preface. Having heard rumors of mass Protestant conversions in Asia, he excitedly tracks down sources—jogging off to Chelsea to consult with a corroborating witness, writing to sources in Yorkshire and Delft, collecting letters and publications that back up the story. His resulting account certainly gives the lie to the notion that early modern people were separated by impassable gulfs of distance or culture. Jessey saw himself as embedded in a network of believers who spanned the globe and who—in this tract alone—spoke at least five languages. In his world, the East and West Indies were not antipodes but parallel mission sites in a unified Protestant effort. His archives include an astonishing array of voices, represented in the testimonies of Dutch missionaries and the reported speeches of Formosan "inchanters" and of Algonquian Christian converts living in the newly created praying Indian town of Nonantum in the Massachusetts Bay Colony.

I imagine his research experiences as something akin to those described by Susan Scott Parrish in her meditative essay on early American and transatlantic research methods, "Rummaging/In and Out of Holds." Parrish recommends (or at least benefited from) a kind of generative aimlessness to which Jessey would certainly have reacted in horror (his aims are always clear and present: to know and glorify God). But he would have recognized the directive, which she adapts from the work of Marcus Garvey, to follow actors and ideas "across multiple social and communicative nodes in the Atlantic World" and to let the resulting Archive teach us about the "particular spatial linkages and mentalities of this period.[30] In 1650, Jessey took it upon himself to follow the missionary—or more likely he would have seen his task as following Jesus Christ—across the multiple social and communicative nodes of his time, a network that included Amsterdam's expatriate English community, the East Indian Dutch and New England missionaries, the Formosan and Algonquian converts, and an English group of cosmopolitan Christian contacts.

GLOBAL-COLONIAL FANTASIES

One linkage Jessey's quest—and mine—uncovers is proclaimed in the very title of his tract and is key to my own work: the connection of the East

29. Henry Jessey, *Of the Conversion of Five-thousand Nine-Hundred East Indians* (London, 1650), A2r.

30. Susan Scott Parrish, "Rummaging/In and Out of Holds," *Early American Literature* 45.2 (2010), 267, 272.

with the West Indies. As a result, the global fantasies that I consider in this book are organized along an East-West axis, "from the rising to the setting of the sun." As I discuss in chapter 2, seventeenth-century English writers knew that the "Asia in the West" theory was incorrect. That is, English writers were well aware that Columbus's claims to have reached China were wrong. Nonetheless, they had compelling reasons to capitalize on the error, continuing to search for a passage through North America to the Pacific and, more tellingly for my purposes, continuing to insist on the parallels and commonalities between the terms "East Indies" and "West Indies." At times, this insistence inadvertently leads to new geographic errors—one midcentury broadside touts the "East Indian" origins of the American co-mestible chocolate.[31] But in the works I bring together in this book, the writers often *intentionally* mistake, collapse, or parallel East and West Indian goods, peoples, and events in order to construct a particular vision of England in/and the world. Seventeenth-century writers were not as naïve about the world's geography and their place in it as we sometimes imagine. In his study of Asia in the English imagination of the seventeenth and eighteenth centuries, Robert Markley argues that Europeans' encounters with Asia served as a "catalyst for their recognition that the discourse of European empire was an ideological construct."[32] The works I consider in this book betray the degree to which English writers at midcentury understood their work to be imagining empire in the absence of successful conquest or colonization.

Seventeenth-century interest in networks of East-West exchange was motivated by a variety of concerns. Greed, national rivalry, fervent religious belief, racism, desire, pride: at times these concerns bleed into one another. The writings of most interest to me are those that insist on connections of all sorts between the East and West Indies in the early seventeenth century, and those particularly that engage in what we today might call revisionist history or presentist exaggeration to assert England's or America's place in global networks of faith, information, and power. Moreover, works that describe an English presence in colonial and trading outposts in the West or East Indies inevitably imagine indigenous people as subjects of those networks, controlled—at times violently—by English agents. As such, the works I take up in this study should be termed "colonial" as well as global fantasies.[33]

The terms "fantasy" and the allied "desire" have been applied to colonial texts most often in psychoanalytic terms. The fantasies of early exploration

31. *The Vertues of Chocolate; the Properties of Cavee* (Oxford: Henry Hall, 1660).
32. Markley, *Far East and the English Imagination*, 9.
33. Markley sees the Far East as having a particular hold on the early English imagination. It "serves as a fantasy space for mercantile capitalism. *Far East and the English Imagination*, 4.

Figure I.1. Jan van der Straet, "Discovery of America: Vespucci Landing in America," c. 1587–1589. The Metropolitan Museum of Art. Gift of Estate of James Hazen Hyde, 1959. www.metmuseum.org.

travel narratives, for instance, are often understood as unconscious, as revealing some of the colonial writer's pathologies or hidden desires as he struggles to come to terms with and to dominate the fearsome New World or the Orient and the Others who reside there.[34] Following this understanding, we can see works such as the sixteenth-century drawing of Amerigo Vespucci discovering America (c. 1587–1589; see fig. I.1), Thomas Harriot's turn-of-the-century illustrated descriptions of Native Carolina peoples, and John Smith's early seventeenth-century descriptions of Pocahontas as different expressions of European colonial fantasy.[35]

While such postcolonial approaches are often quite useful in unpacking colonial texts, I am here more interested in using the term "fantasy" in a generic sense, closer to the sense that we employ today in discussions of

34. Examples of this approach are numerous, but because I am exploring East-West connections, Edward Said's powerful work in *Orientalism* is perhaps most salient. Said explains that the notion of "Orientalism" takes several meanings, but his book is most concerned with the definition of Orientalism as "a Western style for dominating, restructuring and having authority over the Orient." *Orientalism*, 25th anniversary ed. (New York: Vintage Books, 1979), 3. Of the European consideration of the Orient, he argues that "the imaginary examination of things Oriental was based more or less exclusively upon a sovereign Western consciousness out of whose unchallenged centrality an Oriental world emerged... by a battery of desires, repressions, investments, and projections" (8).

35. Thomas Harriot, *A Brief and True Report of the New Found Land of Virginia* (1588); a 1590 edition included illustrations based on John White's watercolors. John Smith described Pocahontas in his 1608 "A True Relation" and in his later *A Generall Historie of Virginia* (1624).

fantasy as a literary genre. Scholars agree that modern fantasy dates, at the earliest, to the eighteenth century, emerging most clearly as Romanticism takes hold.[36] Michelle L. Eilers defines fantasy as "a post-Enlightenment prose fiction genre composed of narratives in which an extranatural power plays a fundamental role and that aim to create an illusion of reality."[37] Although she links the development of the genre to the Enlightenment, Eilers takes issue with the commonplace assumption that the emergence of fantasy literature was coincident with "a cultural disbelief in the supernatural," arguing instead that fantasy writers and readers took seriously the possibility of the supernatural explanation. In *The Fantastic*, Tzvetan Todorov sees fantasy as emerging from "an uncanny phenomenon which we can explain in two fashions, by types of natural causes and supernatural causes. The possibility of a hesitation between the two creates the fantastic."[38] We might think of seventeenth-century writers, those inhabitants of what David D. Hall calls an "enchanted universe," as living in a state of permanent hesitation, or—perhaps better, given the rise of new scientific modes of analysis and approaches to theology, alchemy, natural philosophy, and more—as living in a state of heightened excitement about the possibilities of that hesitation.[39] If we think then of the history of fantasy writings less as formulaic genre and more as what Brian Attebery calls "fantasy-as-mode," we can see protofantastic and even science fiction elements in play much earlier.[40] The genre that emerged in the seventeenth century that is closest to such definitions of the fantastic is the Utopia, and I do talk about utopian works in the chapters to follow. But I am interested in less political works, even in works that eschew utopianism but employ other modes of the (proto)fantastic. And so in this book, I explore a range of writings whose authors seem knowingly to be hesitating between natural and supernatural explanations of events, or even to be knowingly manipulating the received history of their time in order to open their narratives to the divine—the "supernatural"—and to convince their readers of the right course of action and to shape a possible better future.

I've chosen to use the term "colonial fantasy" here, though scholars of speculative fiction might argue (if they concede to me the anachronism at all) that what interests me is "alternate history," a generic term usually seen as a subgenre of science fiction. But of course, the realms of "science" as we

36. See Brian Attebery, *Strategies of Fantasy* (Bloomington: Indiana University Press, 1992), 10.

37. Michelle L. Eilers, "On the Origins of Modern Fantasy," *Extrapolation* 41. 4 (2000), 318.

38. Tzvetan Todorov, *The Fantastic: A Structural Approach to a Literary Genre* (Cleveland: Case Western Reserve University Press, 1973), 26.

39. David D. Hall, *Worlds of Wonder, Days of Judgment: Popular Religious Belief in Early New England* (Cambridge, MA: Harvard University Press, 1990), 71.

40. Attebery, *Strategies of Fantasy*, 2.

know it today and "supernatural," which is a key component of the fantasy fiction genre, overlapped thoroughly in the seventeenth century. In the works I read closely in this book, we can see a mid-seventeenth-century understanding of history and of narrative, one that encompasses new scientific-objective approaches to understanding the past yet embraces divine or supernatural interpretations of the patterns evident in past and present events or in predictions of the future. In this way, the writers who interest me in this book created false or, more accurately, counterfactual pasts not in order to fool their readers or because they themselves were deluded but rather because they hoped to use such stories to shape the future.

Part of the challenge in unpacking these notions of time and the imagination lies in understanding early modern notions of time and history. Walter Mignolo argues that European Renaissance Christians thought of themselves in terms of space rather than time, noting that "Christians did not classify the world in terms of a point of arrival in time, the point of arrival in History, but in space. The point of arrival was the final judgment, not the present as in secular history."[41] It is this deeply held understanding of humanity, of the past and the future as bound together in a set pattern, that we must grasp in order to analyze the midcentury proliferation of historically oriented texts and the fantasies that they encode. The contemporary Western thinker likely considers the future malleable (or at least undetermined), examining events of the past and present to predict likely outcomes in order to make decisions about the best personal or political action. Early modernists, by contrast, saw the future as fixed and obsessively read and reinterpreted the events of the past and present to chart their place on the path to that future.

Although, as Daniel Woolf explains, "there is a noticeable swing in the 1640s toward granting greater priority to causation, contingency, and contiguity," many midcentury writers were still invested in, still held deeply to the notion of, a fixed future that was not a product of past events: "The deeply rooted Christian view of human time, *chronos*, was of a set of this-worldly events and persons related allegorically to eternal qualities in divine time, or *kairos*, and related typologically to future earthly events and persons that 'fulfilled' the promise of the past without being an 'effect' of that past."[42] For most of the people I consider in this book, events could be evaluated for what Reinhart Koselleck calls "eschatological status." Once an event was identified as having that status, it could be understood as timeless, "as the prelude, figure, or archetype of the final struggle between Christ

41. Walter Mignolo, "The Enduring Enchantment: Or the Epistemic Privilege of Modernity and Where to Go from Here?," *South Atlantic Quarterly* 101.4 (Fall 2002), 933.
42. Daniel Woolf, "From Hystories to the Historical: Five Transitions in Thinking about the Past, 1500–1700," *Huntington Library Quarterly* 68.1–2 (March 2005), 48, 44.

and Antichrist; those participating in it were contemporaries of those who lived in expectation of the Last Judgment."[43]

Debate over eschatological status could be quite heated, as in the pamphlet exchange I examine in chapter 1. The strength of such disagreements may reflect the pressure brought to bear on such ways of thinking—still dominant at midcentury but soon to be challenged by new epistemologies and new approaches to the past. Koselleck calls the 1650s in England "the last great predictive struggle conducted on a political plane." The result was an unusual moment in English letters. In his study of seventeenth-century utopianism, James Holstun argues that "never in England before or since the Interregnum have the barriers between literary form, political rhetoric, and social practice seemed so permeable."[44] To his formulation I would add theology. The result is a wonderfully complex, highly charged body of work that grapples with—as I've jokingly put it in the title of chapter 3—the space-time continuum.

Once we understand this early modern sense of millennial time, we can expand our methods of close reading. We need not analyze these writings only against the grain, assuming that the writers (or readers) were unconscious of the effects they wrought. I suppose that in making this statement I borrow some traditional approaches to historical literature as reflecting "the writer's controlling consciousness."[45] I do not mean to argue that the language of the works in this book is not discursive but that in order to analyze it, we have to take into account the possibility that early modern writers at times *knew* themselves to be playful, that seventeenth-century writers did not naively understand themselves as describing real facts about life, the universe, and everything but as representing Truth—whatever its relation to documented "reality."

As Frances Dolan suggests, seventeenth-century writers and readers were far more sophisticated in their analyses of truth claims than we often credit. Although "true relations" were to "connote supposedly true textual relations or accounts," the word "supposedly" is the crux of the matter for her study: "In many seventeenth-century texts, we find the supposedly postmodern claim that truth is a product or effect of narrative, that the story is not the opposite of reality, or the trope the opposite of truth, but the only means by which truth can be *related* both in terms of 'conveyed to another'

43. Reinhart Koselleck, *Futures Past: On the Semantics of Historical Time*, trans. Keith Tribe (New York: Columbia University Press, 2004), 12.

44. Koselleck, *Futures Past*, 16; James Holstun, *Rational Millennium: Puritan Utopias of Seventeenth-Century England and America* (Oxford: Oxford University Press, 1987), 14.

45. The phrase is Holstun's following J. G. A. Pocock in "State of the Art," in *Virtue, Commerce, and History: Essays on Political Thought and History, Chiefly in the Eighteenth Century* (Cambridge: Cambridge University Press, 1985), 14.

and in terms of 'engaged with.'"[46] This doubling of the truth effect can be traced in seventeenth-century genres other than the true relation. Millennialists engaged with the idea of truth in both senses. The doubled sense of truth was especially important to those who believed that by intervening in current events, sometimes violently, they were helping to usher in the end-times. Supernatural and natural explanations were mixed and messy in the seventeenth-century world. One bled into the other as natural philosophers, theologians, and astrologers developed heuristics and technologies to better understand and predict the times to come.

Thus I find the term "colonial fantasy" useful because it implies elements of nationalism, prophecy, and utopianism, all important flavors of early modern English writing. Moreover, the term suggests the ways that the genre is underpinned by desire—economic, religious, embodied. In the chapters that follow, I take up texts that mix these elements together in different proportions, but all of them have this in common: they imagine the past, present, and future, at times counterfactually, to construct a glorious time to come for England or its people around the world, insisting on a brilliant future despite a record of destruction and tragedy that seems counter to every bright prediction.

*   *   *

I have defined the endpoints of this study by publication dates. In the pages that follow, I consider a variety of texts: records, manuscripts, visual images, travel narratives, drama. And I analyze them through several disciplinary lenses. I examine the ways that global fantasies are present in a variety of works that demonstrate the broad reach of such protoimperial fantasies. Each chapter is anchored by a key text in which the links of East and West are significant, in which the millennial global horizon is both subject and theme. The Archive for this study lends itself to a bit of formal experimentation, and this book alternates between full chapters that progress chronologically and extended codas that function like fugues in a musical composition, allowing new voices to enter successively, to amplify, repeat, or develop the themes of the main chapters.

I hit on this structure as a means to represent in part my method of following archival threads, which do not always lead in a tidy linear fashion from point A to point B but take turns, fork, and turn in on themselves. This approach allows me to construct a historicized analytical framework in the main chapters, while the codas show how the frame is, to paraphrase Judith Butler, made to be broken.[47] The codas explore the research path that I took, analyzing the archival scaffolding that makes early modern materials available—the indexes and their often-ignored creators, the digital databases,

---

46. Dolan, *True Relations*, 1, 6.
47. Judith Butler, *Frames of War: When Is Life Grievable?* (reprint, London: Verso, 2010).

the finding aids. This organization also allows me to consider inscriptions of the global imaginary that are hard to categorize or fit into a literary history and that depend heavily on critical speculation: marginalia, material objects, state papers.

The result is a web of meaning—not in the Geertzian sense, in which structures exist and humans spin significance out of them, but in the sense that nodes on the web are endlessly interconnecting, and structures and agency are mutually constitutive. And while the movement of the whole book is roughly chronological, the codas allow for an asynchronous examination of the archive. This approach makes visible the constructed nature of both archival collections and the scholarly narratives—my own included— that depend on them. By acknowledging and analyzing the limitations of the archives and texts that make such narratives possible, the structure of the book opens up a space for speculation and for the recovery of voices and experiences that have often been overwritten or ignored by more traditional methodologies of research and representation. Whereas the chapters taken together describe a particular global (East Indies–West Indies) literary history, the codas, taken as a separate sequence, demonstrate how a "slant" view on the literary history of the main chapters—a view through the particular lens of archival theory and the history of the book—affords us a reading of English global fantasies that is precluded when we approach the main texts directly.

Chapters 2 and 3 take up works that are marked throughout by a politico-religio-geographic sensibility and that trace an East-West axis to spin fantasies of England in the world. In chapter 2, I examine a midcentury pamphlet exchange that pits one interpretation of prophecy against another. The two texts, one Royalist and Presbyterian, one Parliamentarian and Independent, map England's Civil Wars, Regicide, and Interregnum rule onto millennialist prophecy and debate its global implications. In chapter 3 I consider the writings of Thomas Gage, which were instrumental in setting the Cromwell government on its quest to wrest control of the West Indies and America from Spain. Gage, who had served for twelve years as a Catholic priest in New Spain, apostatized and returned to England in 1642 to take up the mantle of Puritan reformation. He advised the Cromwell government that New Spain was ripe for godly English conquest, encouraging the invasion of Hispaniola and Jamaica in 1655 (he served as chaplain on the campaign). This invasion force was the vanguard of the ill-fated Western Design.[48] What

---

48. For studies of the Western Design see Carla Pestana, "English Character and the Fiasco of the Western Design," *Early American Studies* 3.1 (Spring 2005): 1–31. David Armitage, "The Cromwellian Protectorate and the Language of Empire, *Historical Journal* 35.3 (September 1992): 531–555. For a popular historical account, see James Robertson, "Cromwell and the Conquest of Jamaica," *History Today* 55.5 (May 2005): 15–22.

interests me in Gage's works is the way he imagines England as a global leader. In 1654, he rewrites the history of European exploration in America, casting himself as a new Columbus and imagining Cromwell as a wiser King Henry, ready to support Columbus and so make England the true discoverer of the "new world."[49] With the invasion of America, Gage argues, England will right the historical record and inherit Spain's mantle as the empire on which the sun never sets.

Chapter 4 returns to Henry Jessey's *Of the Conversion*. As I have explained, when Jessey edited this work, he yoked together an account of Dutch missions in Asia with accounts of Puritans in America, presenting the fruits of the mission field as harbingers of an unfolding cosmic drama—signs that Christ's kingdom on earth was imminent. If Gage's writings fantasize an alternative history that gives birth to an English imperial future, Jessey spins fantasies of the present. The result is a tract that—although perhaps a failure on several counts (aesthetically and in terms of its influence)—nevertheless is valuable as a window onto England's global aspirations at midcentury. And an essential aspect of those aspirations, of English fantasies, is control over indigenous or enslaved peoples, an aspect of Jessey's text that I explore in the coda that follows through my speculation about the life story and experiences of a Christian Algonquian woman.

In taking a speculative turn, I am aware of the challenges it poses to my "up from the archives" methods. Quite often the archival threads that I follow end abruptly. There is only silence. Such is certainly the case with some of the subjects of this study—particularly women—and I have taken it as a part of my task to connect my own narrative threads to such foreshortened archival strands. Such work, as Saidiya Hartman notes, "can be described as straining against the limits of the archive to write a cultural history of the captive, and, at the same time, enacting the impossibility of representing the lives of the captives precisely through the process of narration."[50]

The "limits of the archive" that Hartman invokes are created, as I've suggested, by the silencing of historical subjects. But sometimes the colonial print Archive is not silent. Rather, it is filled with a noisy busy-ness that can mislead the researcher into imagining it as full and complete. Derrida's term "archival violence" is borne out of that noise and our response to it. In *Archive Fever*, he describes the Archive as being subject to a power that "at once posits and conserves the law" and in so doing creates the past even as it seems a

49. Thomas Gage, "Some Brief and True Observations Concerning the West-Indies" (December 1654 Memorial to Oliver Cromwell), in *A Collection of the State Papers of John Thurloe*, vol. 3, December 1654–August 1655 (London: Fletcher Gyles, 1742), ed. Thomas Birch, British History Online, http://www.british-history.ac.uk/, accessed 12 March 2015.

50. Saidya Hartman, "Venus in Two Acts," *Small Axe* 26 (June 2008), 11.

mere pointer to it. As Carolyn Steedman argues, citing Ann Laura Stoler, cultural theory has used Derrida's idea of the Archive and "forged a powerful metaphor for the processes of collecting traces of the past, and for the forgetting of them."[51] Steedman goes on to argue that "the grammatical tense of the archive is thus the future perfect, 'when it will have been.'" Or as Derrida puts it: "The archive: if we want to know what that will have meant, we will only know in times to come."[52] Operating in the future perfect, the Archive inscribes the subject of the past into a meaning not of his or her own making, a process—a noisy business—that is enabled by what Derrida terms *"communal* dissymmetry" and is by definition an act of violence.[53]

This may all seem just so much eggheaded philosophizing, unless one remembers the real-world implications of the archival function. Consider U.S procedures for awarding federal recognition of tribes or tribal membership; court cases worldwide dealing with water and mineral rights on indigenous lands; or endangered language revitalization. All such efforts depend on extant archival sources.[54] Although the vocabulary differs, Hartman's project resonates with Gayatri Spivak's approach to archival analysis, the creation of a "postcolonial archive."[55] The task of the scholar, Sandhya Shetty and Elizabeth Jane Bellamy argue, is "'measuring silences,' a task, in Spivak's words, of 'attempting to recover a (sexually) subaltern subject ... lost in an institutional textuality at the archaic origin.'"[56] My use of the phrase "archival violence" is a reminder that archival studies—as dusty and safe as such work might seem to a researcher sitting placidly in a reading room in a library—may well be the quiet contemplation of blood-soaked pages. Cromwell's invasion of Hispaniola, encouraged by Thomas Gage, was the conclusion of violent, even genocidal incursions into Ireland and Scotland, and was made possible by Spain's decimation of America's indigenous population and importation of enslaved Africans. Even texts seemingly dis-

---

51. Carolyn Steedman, *Dust: The Archive and Cultural History* (New Brunswick: Rutgers University Press, 2002), 4.

52. Steedman, *Dust*, 7. Jacques Derrida, *Archive Fever: A Freudian Impression*, trans. Eric Prenowitz (Chicago: University of Chicago Press, 1995), 36.

53. Derrida makes this point in discussing a moment when Yerushalmi directly addresses Freud in his book *Freud's Moses*. Because, as Derrida notes, "he is dead and thus incapable of responding, Freud can only acquiesce. He cannot refuse this community at once proposed and imposed." *Archive Fever*, 41. So too are the subjects of the past forced to acquiesce to the researcher's questions-and-answers.

54. For a wide-ranging discussion of the real-world implications of archival theory in a non-U.S. setting see Carolyn Hamilton, Verne Harris, Michele Pickover, Graem Reid, Razia Saleh, and Jane Taylor, eds., *Refiguring the Archive* (Norwell, MA: Kluwer Academic, 2002).

55. Sandhya Shetty and Elizabeth Jane Bellamy coin this term to describe Spivak's work in their analysis of the neglected parts 3 and 4 of Spivak's foundational essay "Can the Subaltern Speak?" "Postcolonialism's Archive Fever," *Diacritics* 30.1 (2000), 32.

56. Quoted in Shetty and Bellamy, "Postcolonialism's Archive Fever," 32.

tant from violence are really only a short remove from bloodshed. Jessey's celebration of worldwide Protestant brotherhood elides the violent wars and other incursions—the Pequot War, the Banda war, the enslaving of indigenous peoples in the East and West Indies—that made conversion efforts possible.

In chapters 3 and 4, I discuss some of these violent moments, but bloody deeds take center stage in chapter 5, in which I analyze the uses to which overseas and metropolitan writers put vivid descriptions of torture, state-sanctioned murder, and massacre. Chapter 5 continues the focus on Anglo-Dutch relations from Asia to America, but in contrast to Jessey's hopeful views of Anglo-Dutch Christianity, the texts of this chapter are written against the background of Anglo-Dutch war. I analyze midcentury reprints of accounts of a 1623 incident in Amboyna that describe the torture and execution of English spice traders by their Dutch rivals in the East Indies and treat the "martyrdom" of Englishmen that occurred decades earlier as news. Drawing on Susan Sontag's theories of violence in *Regarding the Pain of Others*, I compare the visual representation of that East Indian violence with an image of violence in New England: John Underhill's "figure" of the Mystic Fort massacre of the Pequot War. I argue that these images anchor a history of torture that suggests how representations of violence were key elements of colonial fantasies and made (and make) real atrocities possible.

In chapter 6, I turn to speculation and fictions of power and powerlessness, both in (and of) the early modern world and in (and of) the archival record today. I offer a kind of historical fiction myself, speculating on the stories of the women that are suggested by fleeting, seemingly incidental references in the manuscript and print record of the Amboyna incident. I construct their experiences not only by distilling information about them from the print record but also by taking an interdisciplinary approach to inform my speculations about their experiences, by reading the Archive through the lenses of ethnography, archival theory, oral history, art history, cartography, and even architecture, as well as through historical and literary analysis. The chapter contrasts my speculative fantasy of the women's experiences with John Dryden's version in his 1673 play *Amboyna*. Dryden's rewriting of the women's actions and experiences suggest that even the most seemingly marginalized or powerless of women could capture the imagination of the colonial men and their metropolitan counterparts who controlled information about European incursion in American and the East Indies. Taken together, the fictional "wives' tales" of chapter 5 and my final coda illustrate the ambition of the European overseas companies, East and West, English and Dutch—and of their governments—to extend their reach into people's lives, from their pocketbooks to their bedrooms. But these women's stories also suggest the limits of that power and the limits of the archival function to control the stories of marginalized people. It is clear from both the archival record and Dryden's dramatic fiction that women, especially, figure in unexpected ways in colonial history and literature. Their direct appearance in the record, or even the archival gap that suggests the outline of a historical presence, was not always in the Company's control. In this way, some figures and events of the past may escape Derrida's sheltering Archive, an Archive that has worked so hard to forget them.

CHAPTER 1

"A Universall Monarchy"

Millennialism, Translatio, and the Global Imagination

S pend time reading the polemical tracts that flooded the English market in the 1640s and 1650s, and it's easy to see that global sensibilities—the perceived connections of England and the world—were everywhere in play: booksellers flogged world histories, stocked descriptions of Africa, Russia, and the Levant along with maps of all sorts, and sold eyewitness narratives by the employees of the East India Company. in 1652, Royalist Peter Heylyn published the first edition of his *Cosmographie,* which promised to provide a description of "the whole world," as a means to make ends meet during his lean years in the Interregnum. The work was well received, going through eight editions before the end of the century.[1] Heylyn's compendium may have been "better organized and larger in scope" than those of his predecessors, but Richard Hakluyt's and especially Samuel Purchas's compendiums were still available and well read.[2] Missionary tracts, travel narratives, dramas, and poems described, celebrated, analyzed, and criticized England's place in global politics, trade, and religion.

The midcentury pamphlet exchange that I examine in this chapter illustrates the keen interest English writers took in these ideas and demonstrates the way that East-West connections mattered even in works that had little direct concern with English experiences in America or Asia. Here I closely

1. On the politics and religion of Heylyn's work, see Robert J. Mayhew, "Geography Is Twinned with Divinity': The Laudian Geography of Peter Heylyn," *Geographical Review* 90.1 (January 2000): 18–34; and Peter Craft, "Peter Heylyn's Seventeenth-Century World View," *Studies in Medieval and Renaissance History,* 3rd ser., 11 (2014): 325–344.

2. Peter Craft, "Peter Heylyn's Seventeenth-Century World View," *Studies in Medieval and Renaissance History,* 3rd ser., 11 (2014), 235.

examine two works that are primarily concerned with a Christian prophetic vision of England in the coming millennium. Given the ubiquity of such beliefs in early modern England, these two tracts and their debates about history and the future can help us better understand the ideological background against which other global visions of England, Asia, and America were written.

The first tract was published in 1650. Its title—a short version of which I have borrowed for this book—indicates its investment in calculating a prophetic timetable: *A Brief Description of the Future History of Europe, from Anno 1650 to An. 1710.*[3] Brought to press by an anonymous author, it promises to forecast world events, including the ruin of pope and Turk, the Christianization of global Jewry and the final earthly empire (the Fifth Monarchy), the establishment of which presaged the end of time according to Christian millennial theology. All in a forty-eight-page tract. The work is purportedly a summary of the prophecies of Paul Grebner, a Saxon whose prophecies were collected in the 1570s and 1580s. Grebner, according to Jonathan Green, was little regarded by his fellow Germans but reached a wide audience through translation.[4] His prophecies were conveyed to Queen Elizabeth I, and eventually the Latin manuscript was deposited in the Bodleian Library. Political and religious visionaries had recourse to the manuscript for decades, but summaries and transcriptions of it were first published in the 1640s and 1650s.[5] *Future History* was one such work, published the year after King Charles's execution, just as the Interregnum government was consolidating its power. The tract predicts a royal Restoration, presenting evidence that King Charles II was the "King of the North" from the Book of Daniel and thus a key figure in apocalyptic prophecy.

Not surprisingly, *Future History* provoked a response. The pro-Parliamentary Christian astrologer William Lilly published *Monarchy or No Monarchy in England* in 1651, which included a point-by-point rebuttal of

---

3. *A brief description of the future history of Europe, from Anno 1650 to An. 1710. Treating principally of those grand and famous mutations yet expected in the world, as, the ruine of the Popish hierarchy, the final annihilation of the Turkish Empire, the conversion of the eastern and western Jews, and their restauration to their ancient inheritance in the Holy Land, and the Fifth Monarchie of the universall reign of the Gospel of Christ upon Earth. With principal passages upon every of these, out of that famous manuscript of Paul Grebner, extant in Trinity-Colledge Library in Cambridge. Composed upon the occasion of the young Kings arrival into Scotland, to shew what will in probability be the event of the present affairs in England and Scotland* (London, 1650).

4. Jonathan Green, "Translating Time: Chronicle, Prognostication, Prophecy," *Renaissance Studies* 29.1 (2015), 174.

5. See Charles Webster, *Paracelsus to Newton: Magic and the Making of Modern Science* (Cambridge: Cambridge University Press, 1982; reprint, Dover, 2005), 45; and Harry Rusche, "Prophecies and Propaganda, 1641 to 1651," *English Historical Review* 84.33 (October 1969): 752–770.

Future History.[6] To this occasional argument, Lilly added his established in-terpretation of another prophecy, that of the "Wite King," a medieval proph-ecy attributed to Ambrose Merlin, traceable to Geoffrey of Monmouth, in which Lilly had long been interested.[7] By the time he published his attack on *Future History*, Lilly was a popular and influential player in English poli-tics and popular culture. Though born to a family with modest means—he could not afford a university education—he found patrons and scrabbled together instruction in both practical magic and "judicial astrology," for which he exhibited especial talent. Lilly's astrology was a science of obser-vation and interpretation. Practitioners of judicial astrology held that the stars did not influence worldly events but could be studied for evidence of God's plan. Thus, judicial astrology "decoded human conditions and events from celestial patterns."[8] Lilly worked to popularize astrology, taking in students and, more important, publishing explanations of astrology in the vernacular. As Ann Geneva notes, until Lilly published his enormously popular *Christian Astrology* in 1647, "astrological works had been written almost exclusively in Latin."[9] Patrick Curry views the work as a political act. Publishing an accessible text was "deliberate, part of the demotic and dem-ocratic programme he shared with other astrologers on the side of parlia-ment and the army."[10] Lilly laid the ground work for that publication by is-suing almanacs that "mixed eschatological prophecy, judicial astrology, and gritty politics."[11] These were insanely popular. He issued the first in 1644 to modest but encouraging sales. In 1647, he sold 17,000 copies; in 1649, 30,000.[12]

The year 1644 was especially auspicious for Lilly in terms of his author-ship. He stormed onto the publishing scene with several works. In addition to his first almanac, *Merlinus Anglicus junior*, he also published *Supernaturall Sights and Apparitions Seen in London, June 30. 1644*; *England's Prophetical Merlin*; and *A Prophecy of the White King*. The latter work compiles and translates (Lilly's term: "paraphrases") cryptic national prophecies, ranging from several versions of the headlining "Prophecy of the White King" to the

6. William Lilly, *Monarchy or No Monarchy in England* (London, 1651), copy in Virginia Kelly Karnes Archives and Special Collections, Purdue University, West Lafayette, Indiana.

7. My thanks to Shaun Hughes for explaining the provenance of the prophecy. *Future History* also discusses Merlin and prophecy but is much more interested in the white king and in Grebner.

8. Ann Geneva, *Astrology and the Seventeenth Century Mind: William Lilly and the Language of the Skies* (Manchester: Manchester University Press, 1995), 9.

9. Geneva, *Astrology and the Seventeenth Century Mind*, 63.

10. Patrick Curry, "William Lilly (1602–1681)," in *Oxford Dictionary of National Biography* (Oxford: Oxford University Press, 2004), http://www.oxforddnb.com/view/article 16661, ac-cessed 12 July 2016.

11. Curry, "William Lilly."

12. Curry, "William Lilly." See also Keith Thompson, *Religion and the Decline of Magic* (New York: Scribner's, 1971), 294.

Prophecie of Sibylla Tiburtina and to a prediction by Kepler prompted by "the fiery Trygon," and "A Prophecie found in a Wall."[13] For Lilly in the mid-1640s, all these prophecies point in the same direction: centuries of prophetic tradition had predicted the violence that the English were experiencing in the seventeenth century, from the Thirty Years War to the Civil Wars. But Lilly was loathe, so early in the conflict, to identify positively prophetic symbols or characters with specific events and individuals. Indeed, he tells the reader early on that in order to "avoid all misconstruction, that my intentions might point out any particular man living (as some may knavishly surmise, I will keep close to the letter of the words."[14] Rather, his interpretation of the words was meant to rally popular support to Parliament's cause and to assure the reader of the providential return of peace.[15]

By 1651, Lilly had no such hesitation. By then, he had determined that the white king's prophecy applied directly to the very recent history of Charles I, his regicide, and the Commonwealth, and so when *Future History* interpreted it very differently, Lilly intervened. He used his tract to counter vigorously *Future History*'s claim that a Scottish king, identified by *Future History* as Charles II, would ascend England's throne and bring the English revolution to an end. Rather, Lilly reports that his astrological calculations confirmed a different interpretation of ancient prophecies. Any readers who might remember his more general—if not tentative—paraphrases of 1644 encountered a much more confident and detailed explication of the prophecies and a more ambitious publication in general.[16] Obviously, in the intervening half decade Lilly's star had been on the rise, and he does not hesitate to make political points. In *Monarchy or No Monarchy*, he ties the prophecy of the white king directly to Charles I, going so far as to describe the prophecies he compiles in the tract as *"relating to the life and death of* Charles Stuart, *late King of* Brittain, *and unto the finall* extirpation *and rooting up of* Monarchy *in* England."[17] And he offers several astrological charts, particularly the "Figure of that Moment" for the beheading of Charles on 30 January 1649. By 1651, in short, he had no difficulty definitively identifying Charles I as the "white king" doomed to destruction by an ancient prophecy. By so doing, Lilly constructed a reading of prophecy that—at odds with the nationalist eschatology of *Future History*—rejected the notion his

13. William Lilly, *Prophecy of the White King; and Dreadfull Dead-man Explaned* [sic] (London, 1644), 27, 29.

14. Lilly, *Prophecy of the White King*, 11.

15. See Lilly's prefatory letter, "To All Well Affected Englishmen," in *Prophecy of the White King*, 6.

16. Indeed, his title plays off of one of his own earlier works: *Anglicus: Peace or No Peace* (London, 1645).

17. Lilly, *Monarchy or No Monarchy*, 33.

opponent put forward that England would lead the world and help to establish a literal millennial rule. By rejecting *Future History*'s global vision of an imminent end of time, Lilly embraced a more pragmatic world vision that was appropriate for a partisan writer convinced that the best of all possible worlds had already arrived.

NEW WORLD MILLENNIUM

Millennialism can be broadly defined as the belief that Christ's return, prophesied to coincide with the end of the world and divine judgment of humanity, would be accompanied by a thousand-year reign of saints on earth, a worldwide Christian kingdom. Of course, there were—and are— many varieties of millennial belief. Andrew Escobedo contrasts the forward-thinking millennialism of the seventeenth century to "Early-Elizabethan apocalypticism" that, believing the millennium to be in the past, "appears unable to conceive of Christ's return as anything other than the annihilation of the English future, of any earthly future whatsoever."[18] By contrast, he argues that seventeenth-century enthusiasts looked forward to a coming millennium.[19] Some believed that Christ would personally return as head of this kingdom (premillennialists), others that Christian rule would precede Christ's return (postmillennialists). Still others thought of the millennium in metaphorical rather than literal terms. But in its broadest strokes, millennial beliefs were widely held among English Christians, and William Lilly and the anonymous author of *Future History*, whatever their differences, both look forward to an unfolding and progressive future in both human and cosmic time.

The European colonization of America turned millennialism colonial. Indeed, Escobedo argues that "the development of English colonialism in the New World, moving from abysmal failure in the sixteenth century to only moderate failure in the early seventeenth century" was one of the factors that pushed millennial thinking away from a view of history as closed and over to the idea of history as "novelty and progress."[20] By the midcentury, fairly mainstream publications were debating the identity of indigenous America within millennial time. Although several theories of the origins of Native Americans were proffered, by far the most exciting and controversial was the idea that they were the remnants of the lost tribes of

18. Andrew Escobedo, "The Millennial Border between Tradition and Innovation: Foxe, Milton, and the Idea of Historical Progress," in *Anglo-American Millennialism, from Milton to the Millerites,* ed. Richard Connors and Andrew Colin Gow (Leiden: Brill, 2004), 14.
19. Escobedo, "Millennial Border between Tradition and Innovation," 2.
20. Escobedo, "Millennial Border between Tradition and Innovation," 22, 2.

Israel.[21] If they were, and if these lost Jews were indeed turning Christian, biblical prophecy would seem to be fulfilling. But even those who didn't subscribe to the lost tribes theory included the European "discovery" of the Americas in their prophecies and speculations. If nothing else, millennialists believed that at some point in history, all the world would be under Christian rule—including, necessarily, the people of America, whether gentile or Jew. Millennialism was a thread running throughout ideas of expansion and of English empire building.

In the seventeenth century, millennialism was intertwined with a second important concept: *translatio imperii.* The notion of *translatio*—the movement of government (*imperium*), faith (*fides*), and learning (*scientia*) from the East to the West is related to, though not congruent with, millennialism. In works that dealt with Christianity in historic time, *translatio* was described as the mechanism that would prepare the way for the Christian millennium. For the writers I consider, *translatio* was traceable in human history; they tracked the transfer of empire, faith, and learning from Asia to Rome as successive empires rose, fell into sin, degenerated, and lost their leading place in human and divine history.[22] Theologians in the seventeenth century began to correlate the European discovery of the Americas with such theories. Some saw the *translatio* as necessarily continuing the geographic movement that had brought culture and religion from Asia to Europe in America; others used the theory to call for reform in order to hold off the transfer. George Herbert famously encoded the notion in verse in 1633: "Religion stands on tip-toe in our land / Readie to pass to the *American* strand"—predicting that in America Native people would "have their times of Gospel, ev'n as we." The notion of *translatio imperii, fidei, scientiae* structured the imaginations of kings, humanists, and Christians of all sects. Belief in *translatio* produced in seventeenth-century literature the kind of spatial relativism evident in Henry Parker's *Altar dispute* and depended on a notion of history that was both linear and cyclical. Herbert's verse describes a chase across the globe, with sin following the Gospel until the church returns full circle to its starting place, triggering the apocalypse:

21. On the debate in England, see Richard Cogley's work, especially "'Some Other Kinde of Being and Condition': The Controversy in Mid-seventeenth Century England over the Peopling of Ancient America," *Journal of the History of Ideas* 68.1 (January 2007): 35–56.

22. David A. Boruchoff offers a detailed comparison of Catholic and Puritan ideas and uses of the notion of *translatio* in his "New Spain, New England, and the New Jerusalem: The 'Translation' of Empire, Faith, and Learning (*translatio imperii, fidei ac scientiae*) in the Colonial Mission Project," *Early American Literature* 43.1 (2008): 5–34. His essay provides an excellent definition and description of the ideas of *translatio* at work in New Spain in the late sixteenth century and in New England throughout the seventeenth centuries. See also Zachary Hutchins, *Inventing Eden: Primitivism, Millennialism, and the Making of New England* (New York: Oxford University Press, 2014).

> *But as the Sunne still goes both west and east;*
> *So also did the Church by going west*
> *Still eastward go; because it drew more neare*
> *To time and place, where judgment shall appeare.*[23]

As government, culture and faith translate to new lands, the Occident becomes the Orient.

Or it doesn't. Of course, there was nothing like universal agreement on whether America would inherit the power and prestige of Europe or when and where the events triggering the end of the world would begin. Just as some looked to America for its promise, others firmly identified it as the devil's territories. Even as some writers imagined the "Danger of Desertion," that is, the horrors that would be visited upon England as a nation after God and the true church had left it behind for America, others sought to reform themselves and so remain at the center of cosmic events, or eschewed such apocalyptic predictions altogether and simply worked toward new, productive relations in the East-West networks that missionaries and merchants alike were establishing in the seventeenth century.[24] For instance, in 1650, Edward Williams and John Ferrar published their *Virgo Triumphas, or, Virginia in Generall*, which argued the case of the Virginia colony's value to England in part by doubling down on the old idea—the "Asia in the West" theory—that the riches of Asia could be found by sailing West. They promised readers that Virginia offered a "most compendious passage" to the "more opulent Kingdomes of China... [and the] East Indies," but they also argued that even if Asian trade did not result from England's "nursing" of Virginia into a going concern, Virginia could simply produce the goods of the East itself: "*it will admit of all things producible in any other part of the World, lying the same Parallel with China, Persia, Japan.*"[25]

It's one thing to note East-West connections or a millenarian understanding of time and history generally in the seventeenth-century literature, but we can see these shattering ideas laid out in succinct prose in *A Brief Description of the Future History of Europe*. Unlike most of the other works I consider in this book, *Future History* is written from a Royalist, Presbyterian perspective rather than from a Puritan or Independent Parliamentarian point of view. Nonetheless, it articulates the themes that I'm tracing in midcentury

23. George Herbert, "Church Militant," in *New World Metaphysics: Readings on the Religious Meaning of the American Experience*, ed. Giles Gunn (New York: Oxford University Press, 1981), 36.
24. "The Danger of Desertion" is the title of a 1641 sermon by Thomas Hooker.
25. Edward Williams and John Ferrar, *Virgo Triumphans, or, Virginia in Generall* (London, 1650), n.p. For a broader discussion of this text, see Nicholas K. Mohlmann, "Corporate Poetics and the Virginia Company of London, 1607–1655," Ph.D. diss., Purdue University, 2014, 126–154.

English literature in crystalline miniature: a Christian global sensibility and faith in *translatio* as the way that history will unfold. Specifically, the author of *Future History* is a postmillennialist. Early in the tract he declares himself against the notion of the personal reign of Christ.[26] And contra the hopes of leaders such as Oliver Cromwell himself, he agrees with prognosticators who place England in a subordinate rather than leading position, "as *England* ever was a Monarchy within it self... so shall it continue and remain, even then when all other Kingdomes and States in Europe are swallowed up of the FIFTH MONARCHY."[27] England will remain an insular kingdom unto itself. By contrast, the author's Fifth Monarchy, his millennialism, will be realized in a dispersed kingdom of Christian saints and converted Jews, presently invisible but living among all the peoples of the earth. The catalyst of these momentous changes and the establishment of a universal Christian monarchy will be the ascendance of the "Lion of the North," whom the author identifies as Charles II, whose restoration will trigger the rise of the Fifth Monarchy even as he consolidates an enduring English monarchy. Clearly the tract is polemical and provocative. Yet no matter how contested the particulars were of the global fantasy that *Future History* laid out, its staunchest opponents agreed with its central premise that at the midcentury, human history was enacting cosmic drama.

Of course, such millennial and apocalyptic ideas were not new in the seventeenth century, but they took on a distinct flavor of the times. The European encounter with America sparked a reassessment of long-held beliefs and prompted questions: what role was America to take in cataclysmic events? What role Americans? Even authors who weren't deeply concerned with European colonies in America or with their indigenous inhabitants had to contend with the bare fact of America. *Future History* promised a "universall Monarchy of the Gospel of Christ upon Earth."[28] For the authors of sentiments such as these, there was no denying that such a kingdom encompassed the new-to-them peoples and lands of America and that the discovery of America had prompted a new understanding of the world's geography and human history. Consider *Future History*'s listing of the reach of the Gospel as it spread around the world: "[God] shall transferre his Gospel from Europe, as he hath done from Asia, and raise up and inspire godly Ministers, after his own will, who shall implant his holy word in all and every of the Kingdomes and Provinces of America, and in all the countries of the Southern and Eastern India, China, Tartaria, and in all the regions of the North unto the worlds end, and make it shine in as great purity

26. *Future History* (London, 1650), A2.
27. *Future History*, A4r.
28. *Future History*, A2r.

and glory as ever it hath done in England or Germany."[29] Here, the author seems to suggest that as the Gospel is transferred from Europe all parts of the world will share equally and at once in the "purity and glory" of the millennial world. But in fact, *Future History* understands the movement to be accomplished through *translatio*, in which one part of the world loses its monopoly on the Gospel, and truth and light move elsewhere. The English civil wars, the author contends (not to mention the Thirty Years War, concluded just two years earlier by the Peace of Westphalia), are a clear sign that "Our Western Sun is set."[30]

CYCLES OF HISTORY

If the sun has set in the West, where will it rise? Paradoxically, according to the author of *Future History*, farther West—so far West as to become East. In a colonial version of *translatio*, the author traces the movement of earthly and divine authority to America and parts beyond. Ignoring Catholic missions (of course) and even the recent efforts of the English in New England, he projects an evangelical movement yet to come. In 1699, he avers that "the kingdom of salvation [shall] be preached by the Ministry of the Saints of the most High, to those immense and unknown *American Coasts....* And that people, who from Creation till that time were the Empire of Satan, shall be called the specious and spacious Church of God."[31] Lest English readers lament the setting of Europe's "Western Sun," the author assures them that this translation of the Gospel to America is part of a natural cycle:

> this is the eternal Law of Creatures.... that the Birth of one thing should be the Death of another.... Cities, Republiques, Empires and Families are as mortal as men, have their states of Birth, Infamy [*sic*; surely "infancy"], Growth and Old-age as well as they. Glory, Majesty, Arts and Soveraignty began in *Asia* by the *Assyrians*; from them departed to the *Medes* and *Persians*; and from there (before they had well tasted the sweetnesse of them) translated to the *Grecians*, and next to the *Romans*: The Glory of the Roman Empire was eclipsed and humbled.[32]

Future History's views on *translatio* also depended on a third key English imperial concept, one adapted from the Dutch: the Black Legend. This discourse vilified Spain and Spanish Catholicism and was the rationale for some English writers to promote English colonial schemes over those of

---

29. *Future History,* A1v (repeated on A2r).
30. *Future History,* A1.
31. *Future History,* 36. "Specious" in this context means "pleasing."
32. *Future History,* 36.

the Spanish and even to advocate military action against Spain in the Americas.[33] *Future History*'s understanding of *translatio* had particular implications for earthly powers, especially for England and Spain. The "ruin" of the Popish hierarchy" foretold in the very title of this tract could bring with it, logically, the downfall of one of the pope's greatest earthly allies, Spain. As Rome's glory was translated to more westerly parts, including America, Catholic and Spanish power in American would be usurped. As evidence, the author points to present Spanish atrocities and the resulting revolt of oppressed Indians against Spain, commonplace tropes of the Black Legend. He claims that the Spaniard "is for his inhumane cruelty so generally hated of Christians, all men avoiding him and flying from him, as the Serpent from the Ash: His Indian Plantations both thrive not, and likewise for their barbarousnesse are so detested of the savages worse than vipers, and upon opportunities are accordingly massacred."[34]

Despite this rhetorical takedown of Spain and its colonial enterprise, the future of *Future History* is meant to transcend nation. Because the tract relies so heavily on the idea of *translatio,* in which no earthly kingdom is permanent, even England is represented as wielding conditional power. England might make some successful conquests, the tract argues, but only to secure its borders: "If it chance that she make war upon any neighbour Enemy, and enlarge their Dominions by Conquest, it is more to secure her self...then any greedinesse of extending her Bounders [sic] by the Conquest and ruine of others."[35] But if not England, who is prophesied to lead the Fifth Monarchy? The tract's gnomic answer: "a Nation which at this day is hid invisibly within the bowels of *Europe,* which seeing are not seen, and living are not known."[36] The answer to the riddle is twofold: "All the godly in every Kingdom and State in *Europe*" will be met by "converted Jews."[37] The author dates the spread of this invisible nation's dominion over the rest of the world to 1699, the year when *Future History* predicts that the effects of the turning tide of human events will be felt in America and indeed, around the world. Sparked in part by the "encreasing Idolatry of Western and Eastern Indians," the Fifth Monarchy will take hold, and the prophecy "shall begin to operate upon *Europe* and the Eastern Coasts of *America*."[38] *Future History* thus fantasizes a dispersed, global Christianity just at the moment when

33. See William S. Maltby, *The Black Legend in England: The Development of Anti-Spanish Sentiment, 1558–1660* (Durham: Duke University Press, 1971); and Margaret R. Green, Walter D. Mignolo, and Maureen Quilligan, eds., *Rereading the Black Legend: The Discourses of Religious and Racial Difference in the Renaissance Empires* (Chicago: University of Chicago Press, 2007).

34. *Future History,* 33

35. *Future History,* 34.

36. *Future History,* 34.

37. *Future History,* 34.

38. *Future History,* 16, 34.

England's Commonwealth leaders were consolidating power and imagining their next steps, a moment when, for instance, England had set its sights on Ireland and calls to invade Hispaniola were circulating in secret and in print.[39] The Royalist analysis of *Future History*, then, tries to circumscribe the Commonwealth's colonial or protoimperial aspirations, making English aggression merely defensive.

We can see in this text a parallel to the "political geography" of other Royalist writers of the time. Consider Peter Heylyn's *Cosmographie*, first published a year after Lilly's *Monarchy or No Monarchy*. The book's subtitle asserts that it contains "the chorographie and historie of the whole world." Compare *Cosmographie*'s claims to describe the space-time continuum of the whole world to the more modest ambition of Heylyn's first book of global geography, *Microcosmos*, first published in 1621. To be sure, its title page promised to treat the world through lenses "Historicall, Geographicall, Politicall, Theologicall." But still, according to its subtitle, it was "a Little Description of the Great World."[40] Robert J. Mayhew, the most recent editor of *Cosmographie*, notes that the book's grand scale has served to camouflage its politics: "the enormous bulk of information contained in the *Cosmographie* tends to anesthetize a casual reader to the book's polemical argument."[41] And lest we think that Mayhew means that early modern readers were better able to sift through the more than a thousand pages of Heylyn's geographical observations than we are today, Mayhew likens the thick descriptions to an "intellectual priest hole" in which Heylyn could hide what were, in the 1650s, actionable beliefs.[42]

Indeed, the attentive reader might see evidence of his politics very early in the text. On the third page of his prefatory letter "To the Reader," Heylyn notes that "*In the pursuance of this Work, as I have taken on my self the parts of an* Historian *and* Geographer; *so I have not forgotten that I an* [sic] *English-man, and which is somewhat more, a* Church-man." At the time he wrote these sentiments, Heylyn was a displaced Church-man. A supporter of Bishop Laud, chaplain to Charles I, and as the author tapped as the first editor of *Mercurius Aulicus*, the Royalist newsbook published during the war, Heylyn found himself without a settled living during the Interregnum, and one

---

39. Not to mention the First Anglo-Dutch War just beginning. On England's international affairs in these years, see Timothy Venning, *Cromwellian Foreign Policy* (New York: St. Martin's Press, 1995). Steven Pincus treats Anglo-Dutch relations in *Protestantism and Patriotism: Ideologies and the Making of English Foreign Policy, 1650–1658* (Cambridge: Cambridge University Press, 1996).

40. Peter Heylyn, *Microcosmos* (London, 1621).

41. Robert J. Mayhew, "'Geography Is Twinned with Divinity': The Laudian Geography of Peter Heylyn," *Geographical Review* 90.1 (January 2000), 32.

42. Mayhew, "'Geography Is Twinned with Divinity.'"

project he took up in his free time was the revision of *Microcosmos* into the much larger *Cosmographie*.[43] The book was well received, it seems, despite the fact that, as Peter Craft argues, it encodes a particular worldview that is an explanation and apology for Royalist ill fortune. The work comprises four "books," one each on the history and geography of Europe, Asia, Africa, and America. As Heylyn recounts the rise and fall of empires in other parts of the world, Craft argues, he establishes a "cycle of victory and defeat on a massive scale," particularly in his observations on the history of military might in India, which "dwarfs the Commonwealth."[44] The work as a whole serves to "place recent events in England within a biblical narrative of providential history" in which Royalists take "the role of God's people in the midst of a temporarily painful test that would eventually lead them to unprecedented prosperity."[45] This point of view is parallel to that of *Future History,* in which suffering is part of God's plan, and God's people—notably Charles II and his followers—will triumph in the end.

Heylyn's prefatory letter "To the Reader," while it could be read by Parliamentarians as unobjectionable English partisanship, suggests the kind of "grander perspective" in which Cromwell's victories need not seem so overwhelming or permanent. Heylyn has taken every opportunity *"of recording the heroick Acts of my native Soil, and filing on the Registers of perptuall Fame the Gallantrie and brave Atchievements* [sic] *of the People of* England. *Exemplified in their many victories and signall services in* Italie, France, Spain, Scotland, Belgium, *in* Palestine, Cyprus, Africk *and* America, *and indeed, where not?"*[46] Heylyn goes on to list more of England's particular interventions on a global stage, notably the nation's claims to France and Scotland, not to mention its right over "discoveries" such as "New-Found-land," Novum Belgium, Guiana, the Cape of Good Hope, and even Estotiland, an island that was presumed to lie near Greenland.[47] England's right to the far corners of the world, Heylyn argues, is wrapped up in the country's royal rule: *"as I have been zealous to record the Actions, so have I been as carefull to assert the Rights of the* English *Nation: inherent personally in their Kings, by way of publick interess* [sic] *in the Subject also; as the whole body doth partake of that sense and motion, which is originally in the Head."*[48] That the literal head of the most

43. See Anthony Milton, "Heylyn, Peter (1599– 1662)," in *Oxford Dictionary of National Biography* (Oxford: Oxford University Press, 2004), http://www.oxforddnb.com/view/article/13171, accessed 14 July 2016.

44. Craft, "Peter Heylyn's Seventeenth-Century World View," 335.

45. Craft, "Peter Heylyn's Seventeenth-Century World View," 331.

46. Heylyn, *Cosmographie,* A4r.

47. Heylyn, *Cosmographie,* A4r. On Estotiland, see John Dee's description in John Dee, *John Dee: The Limits of the British Empire,* ed. Ken MacMillan and Jennifer Abeles (Westport: Praeger, 2004).

48. Heylyn, *Cosmographie,* A4r.

recent king had lately separated from his literal body was lightly papered over by Heylyn's invocation of England's kings—plural and past, not singular and just lately executed. But if the point is that power ebbs and flows, that history witnesses cycles of victory and defeat, the implication is surely that England's inevitable return to global prominence needs must be accompanied by a Restoration and a return to power of men like Bishop Laud, not to mention Peter Heylyn himself.[49] In this way, as Craft argues, Heylyn's worldview is "a kind of consolation fantasy."[50]

ARCHIVAL PROPHECIES

William Lilly's treatment of *Future History* suggests that he sees its author's interpretation of ancient prophecy and recent astrological signs similarly, as compensatory fantasies for Royalist losses. But he takes the anonymous author directly to task for trying to disguise fantasy as fact. A good bit of Lilly's criticism of the author of *Future History* is evidentiary—even archival. Lilly's own reputation had been built upon two points: his ability to make astrology respectable (Christian) and accessible, and his virtuoso interpretation skills.[51] In *Monarchy or No Monarchy*, he eschews unverified prophetic revelations, preferring predictions that can be correlated with or corroborated by historical or other strong evidence, especially—of course—astrological predictions. And he leans on his own reputation— fairly recently achieved—to promote his interpretation of events over that of *Future History*.

Significantly, Lilly presents his evidence in such a way as to evince reasoned assent among his readers, and he criticizes *Future History* for demanding blind submission to authority. Richard Popkin, in his history of English prophetic traditions, describes a division in prophetic methodologies later in the century: "two kinds of prophesying occur in the late seventeenth century, one 'scientific,' worked out by Sir Isaac Newton and his disciples, the other 'activist,' offered by various religious enthusiasts."[52] In *Future History* and *Monarchy or No Monarchy* we see the distinction being worked out even earlier. Lilly promotes prophecy based on astrological observation and other "scientific" evidence as opposed to what he sees as suspect: direct

49. If a return to preferment was Heylyn's personal hope, he was disappointed. As Anthony Milton notes in his *Dictionary of National Biography* entry on Heylyn, he did not receive a promotion after the Restoration.

50. Craft, "Peter Heylyn's Seventeenth-Century World View," 336.

51. Lilly was especially well known for his 1659 publication *Christian Astrologer*.

52. Richard H. Popkin, *The Third Force in Seventeenth-Century Thought* (Leiden: Brill, 1992), 295.

revelation that lacks such corroboration. The debate is theological to be sure, but also epistemological. Lilly suggests an approach to the writing of prophecy based on archival sources that are not arcane and secret, accessible only to the initiated, but held in well-known libraries, open to the scrutiny of any interested party. His is a Protestant astrological or historical heuristic that parallels new scientific methods by privileging shared, reproducible findings and reporting them in detail, thereby engaging readers in "virtual witnessing" and verification of experiments.[53] It's worth remembering that his *Christian Astrologer*, which presented astrological instruction in English rather than Latin, was one of his early, great successes. In *Monarchy or No Monarchy*, he lambasts *Future History* for failing to lay down a traceable archival trail. He charges that the anonymous author "quotes strange Authors and Bookes, and such as are not to be seen in every *Library*.... his *Authors* I conceive lived in *Utopia*, and their Bookes... are no where to be seen or heard but in *Terra incognita*."[54] In this attack, he affirms what Robert Appelbaum says of Utopian discourse in the seventeenth century, that although English people were concerned with ideal order, the word "'utopia' was more often a term of disparagement than encouragement; it signified hopeless impracticality.... Utopia could thus be assumed to be a location of idle dreams."[55] His reference to Utopia indicates that he wishes to ground his methods and findings in scientific principles. By associating *Future History* with More's imagined land, Lilly labels his opponent's analyses unworkable fantasies. In his view, *Future History* promulgates idle dreams in the guise of prophetic interpretation dependent on unverifiable texts.

Lilly accuses *Future History* of being a purely partisan effort relying on elite privilege—access to private libraries—to yield conclusions that must be taken on faith and cannot be tested independently. He charges the author with making deliberate errors in transcription, relying on obfuscation, and fabricating evidence outright. His own methods, he asserts, depend on open, "public" calculations of the future history of England and the world that others may test for accuracy. By contrast, he sees the future he forecasts as attainable, a vision that yields to investigation and analysis, from the archival to the astrological.

Lilly is best known as a juridical astrologer, and astrological calculations are clearly important to his arguments in *Monarchy or No Monarchy*. But the text musters other technologies of prognostication as well. One of the most

53. Stephen Shapin uses the idea of virtual witnessing to describe the effects of the "literary techniques" of early modern writers and scientists such as Robert Boyle. See "Pump and Circumstance: Robert Boyle's Literary Technology," *Social Studies of Science* 14.4 (1984): 481–520.
54. Lilly, *Monarchy or No Monarchy*, 6.
55. Roger Appelbaum, *Literature and Utopian Politics in Seventeenth-Century England* (Cambridge: Cambridge University Press, 2004), 4.

important that he employs to persuade his readers is chronology, a necessary tool for accurately tracking millennial prophecies. English authors created scores of chronologies in the seventeenth century. As a genre of history
writing, the seventeenth-century chronology stands between the medieval
chronicle, which emphasized strict chronological order and presented
events as discrete and noncausal, and later innovations in narrative history.[56]
As seventeenth-century writers adapted older forms of history writing to the
needs of their present, the chronology as a genre was haled into new scientific and religious practices. Kevin Killeen defines the chronology as "the
millenarian mathematics that sought to discern the historical timetables from
Eden to the second coming."[57] We can see the blending of science, math,
and faith in the technologies Lilly encodes in his tract's pages. He provides
astrological charts as well as the archival evidence needed to calculate the
predictions he has made, but it all depends on his readers' shared understanding that God's providential design rules history and time and can be
discerned by the careful observer tracing events historically.

It is perhaps difficult at this remove for us to separate Lilly's methods,
relying as they do on specious prophetic texts and astrological prediction,
from those that, as he charges, rely on "secret" sources and what seem to us
equally specious texts, however clearly he sees the differences between
them. It is difficult to see his work as "scientific."[58] But we can perhaps better
understand his methods by considering a specific, traceable example of the
historic evidence on which he relies. After taking apart *Future History*'s use
of Grebner's prophecies—even challenging the version of Grebner on
which *Future History* depends, calling it "counterfeit" in a marginal note,[59]
Lilly turns to a different text, "A Prophecy of the *Wite King*, wrote by
Ambrose Merlin 900. years since."[60] Whereas Lilly has treated the mistakes
of his opponent in fairly broad strokes in previous sections of *Monarchy or
No Monarchy*, this section of the tract is detailed and slow. Lilly parses the
prophecy line by line, offering a point-by-point gloss of each mysterious
pronouncement and, as proof of the accuracy of his interpretation, pointing
to evidence showing which elements of the prophecy have already been fulfilled. The margins helpfully label each line of Merlin's statements "Prophecy"

56. See Joseph H. Preston, "Was There a Historical Revolution?," *Journal of the History of Ideas* 38 (1977), 356, and Daniel Woolf, "From Hystories to the Historical: Five Transitions in Thinking about the Past, 1500–1700," *Huntington Library Quarterly* 68.1–2 (March 2005), 42.

57. Kevin Killeen, *Biblical Scholarship, Science and Politics in Early Modern England: Thomas Browne and the Thorny Place of Knowledge* (Farnham, UK: Ashgate, 2009), 90.

58. Indeed, Ann Geneva argues that it is misguided to judge Lilly's work against such a standard.

59. Lilly, *Monarchy or No Monarchy*, 11.

60. Lilly, *Monarchy or No Monarchy*, 38.

and the paragraphs that contain Lilly's explanations and proofs "Verification." So the rhythm goes for some ten pages: prophecy and verification, prophecy and verification.

Among the evidences brought to bear is the fate of Scots prisoners of war. Amid the prophetic symphony of kings ascending, armies marching across Europe, and cataclysmic battles between the forces of Christendom and those who oppose Christ's rule sounds a considerably more humble note: "And there shall bee Merchandise of Men, as of an Horse or an Ox."[61] In Lilly's 1644 treatment of the white king's prophecy, this moment is treated fairly generally, as the expected aftermath of battle: "here seems to be insinuated a fight or battell... wherein many prisoners are like to be taken on both sides, and they againe as frequently exchanged, viz. man for man, as formerly men chaffered for Horse and Oxe.... when such a general exchange of prisoners is, the people will have hopes of better times."[62] But in 1651, he sees things differently and is able to bring the ancient prophecy into his own moment by mapping the prophecy onto the transportation of Scottish prisoners of war to Barbados following their defeat by Cromwell's troops at the Battle of Preston. The evidence is simultaneously a worlding of events in England and of English plantations in America, and it is no less a fantasy than the readings of prophecy by the author of Future History or the consolation for loss that Peter Heylyn was busy working into his Cosmographie.

Lilly's recourse to contemporary "verification" for ancient prophecy results in a curious mix of concrete detail and fluctuating tone. He begins by placing the verification specifically into human chronological time: "This part of the prophecy was exactly verified in King Charles or the White Kings time, for in 1648, after the defeat of the wretched Scots in Lancashire, the English Merchants did give money for as many of the common Soldiers as were worth anything, and sent them for Barbados and the forraigne Plantations."[63] This opening moment of the verification suggests the dizzying pace of events in revolutionary England. As Lilly looks back just a couple of years to the Battle of Preston, he can see from his vantage point the clash of Parliamentary and Royal armies, the defeat and capture of the king, his execution in 1649, and the English campaign in Ireland. The pace of events must have seemed vertiginous.

The switch in register from the phrase "King Charles, or the White Kings time" to "English Merchants," "common Soldiers," and "forraigne Plantations" is notable. In a single sentence Lilly moves from invoking royal medieval prophecy that is being enacted in his own time to indirect political and

61. Lilly, Monarchy or No Monarchy, 43.
62. Lilly, Prophecy of the White King, 12.
63. Lilly, Monarchy or No Monarchy, 43.

economic commentary. And when he maps the ancient prophecies onto present-day events, he strays, at least briefly, into open partisanship. He sees the fulfillment of the White King's prediction that "There shall bee a Merchandise of Men, as of an Horse or an Ox," in the shipping of Scottish prisoners of war to the West Indies. To be sure, such a "merchandise of men" had been in place in England for some time. By the 1650s, indentured servants were being shipped to the Caribbean islands regularly, but these were drawn—at least ostensibly—from the criminal classes, from the prison populations of Newgate or Bridewell. Their indentures, then, were part of their legal punishments. As the Civil Wars unfolded, new practices, including prisoner exchanges, were put in place. As Lilly himself describes, these prisoner-of-war exchanges merged with the treatment of civilian criminal prisoners and turned into a new practice of selling men at arms into indentures: "There was in 1644, 1645 &c. exchanging of Soldiers and Prisoners, but in 1648, absolute Merchandising of Mens Bodyes, and not before."[64] Following the Battle of Preston, the Society of Merchant Venturers out of Bristol (Lilly's "English Merchants") arranged to take advantage of a ready market in laborers and began transportation of prisoners whose only crime had been fighting for the losing side. Hundreds if not thousands of Scottish prisoners were shipped to Barbados. As Jill Sheppard notes, by 1655, "the Planters of Barbados estimated that they were employing a total of 12,000 prisoners of war." While she believes that number was exaggerated, laborers did include transported prisoners of war from several major Parliamentarian (New Model Army) victories: Preston and Colchester, Dunbar and Worcester.[65]

At first glance, Lilly's discussion of how "this part of the Prophecy was exactly verified" suggests, if not protoabolitionist sentiments, at least a distaste for the "absolute Merchandising of Mens Bodyes." He calls the men sold into service "wretches," a word that at the time carried the connotations we might think of first today—miserable, unhappy, sorrowful. An earlier meaning recorded by the Oxford English Dictionary seems even more on point: "wretch" could also mean "exile." But read a bit further in Lilly's explanation of the prophecy, and we see that what he really means to say—unsurprisingly—is that a Scottish prisoner is a "vile, sorry or despicable person."[66] He concludes the section with a short assessment of market value: "what price the Scots were sold for I know not, hee that gave but twelve pence a peece for any of that nasty people, gave too much."[67] One can only

64. Lilly, Monarchy or No Monarchy, 43.

65. Jill Sheppard, "A Historical Sketch of the Poor Whites of Barbados: From Indentured Servants to 'Redlegs,'" Caribbean Studies 14.3 (October 1974), 73.

66. See the Oxford English Dictionary's third definition of the term.

67. Lilly, Monarchy or No Monarchy, 43.

imagine the reception that the anonymous, pro-Scotland author of *Future History* would have given Lilly's statement, particularly given reports of the terrible conditions under which the transported laborers suffered. Just a few years later we find a petition written by men sold to Barbados in 1654 that challenges such unfeeling assessments. Marcellus Rivers and Oxenbridge Foyle recount their deprivations and suffering as "Englands slaves." They describe how they were sold for "15 50. pound weight of Sugar apiece" and put to hard labor: "generally grinding at the Mills attending the Fornaces, or digging in this scorching Island, having nothing to feed on (notwithstanding their hard labour,) [*sic*] but Potatoe Roots, nor to drink but water, with such roots masht in it . . . being whipt at their whipping posts, as Rogues, for their masters pleasure, and sleep in styes worse then hogs in *England*."[68] For his part, Lilly articulates the classic defense of slavery—it's good for, even welcomed by, the enslaved themselves: "It is reported, that many of those miserable wretches, since their being at the *Barbados*, do say, they have left *Hell*, viz. *Scotland*, and are arrived into *Heaven*."[69]

Because of their different political allegiances—the author of *Future History* to the dream of Charles II's restoration to the throne and Lilly to Parliament and the Interregnum government—their understandings of millennial time and their articulations of the future have different registers. *Future History* places its faith (as does Peter Heylyn's *Cosmographie*) in a future period of peace and prosperity. And so its interpretation of prophecy takes a grander scale and employs the future perfect tense to describe the inevitability of a Fifth Monarchy brought about by a future king of England. For Lilly, the future is now. Indeed, he recognizes that his 1644 understanding of the prophecy of the white king doesn't match his 1651 version, but he excuses the change on the grounds that "*The* White Kings *Tragedy is now acted, it was then on the Stage*" and "Later Counsels ever correct the former."[70] For Lilly there will be "no fifth universal Monarchy," and his task is not to predict sweeping changes but to document, in as many ways as he can, the future stability of the England brought into being by the Civil Wars. To that end, in his multivalent *Monarchy or No Monarchy* he says that he has "in Types, Formes, Figures, Shapes, Etc. delivered very significantly the severall changes of *England*," whose foundations have now been firmly established, and for which one can project the future "for many hundreds of years yet to come."[71]

But if his is a prosaic fantasy, it is a fantasy nonetheless. Whatever the historic suffering suggested by Lilly's gloss of this part of the prophecy, for

68. Marcellus Rivers and Oxenbridge Foyle, *Englands slavery, or Barbados merchandize; represented in a petition to the high court of Parliament* (London, 1659), 5.

69. Lilly, *Monarchy or No Monarchy*, 43.

70. Lilly, *Monarchy or No Monarchy*, A4v.

71. Lilly, *Monarchy or No Monarchy*, A3v.

Lilly, and presumably for his readers, the realities of indentured life on Barbados are subsumed in God's plan. In one copy of the text, held in the Purdue University archives, marginal notes suggest that readers took seriously Lilly's methodology and considered historic evidence themselves. In this much-thumbed and annotated copy a reader has commented on elements of Lilly's prophecy. Next to Lilly's discussion of whether the merchandise-of-men prophecy refers to Scots prisoners transported to the Caribbean, a reader has jotted the phrase "now fulfilling." The observation suggests that reader's agreement that one element of the prophecy, at least, has come to pass.[72]

72. Lilly, *Monarchy or No Monarchy*, 29, 43. To my mind, the phrase "now fulfilling" reads like agreement with Lilly's own claims that the merchandise of men had occurred shortly before he published, suggesting that this hand in the margin is near contemporary with publication. But the emphasis could be on the "now," meaning that the prophecy of the merchandise of men, not yet complete in 1651, was being fulfilled later.

Coda: "'Tis Done!"

I was surprised, skeptical even, when a title search for William Lilly's *Monarchy or No Monarchy* in my university library's catalog suggested that we had a copy—a physical, leather-and-paper copy—in the holdings of the Purdue University libraries. After all, Purdue is a technologically focused land-grant university in the U.S. Midwest. Purdue's library is not particularly known for its early modern holdings. Yet if one types "Monarchy or No Monarchy" into the online catalog, one sees the message "multiple versions found." That message leads to a list of editions, beginning with the expected: the digital facsimiles provided by Early English Books Online, to which, fortunately for the local researcher, Purdue subscribes. It contains copies of the tract from both the Huntington Library and the British Library. Nothing startling in those results. A quick check in the catalog of those illustrious collections of early modern imprints reveals they both hold copies of the 1651 and 1655 editions of the tract, as well as the 1683 reprint of its "hieroglyphics," the series of symbolic pictures with which Lilly concluded the original.

But the next entry in the Purdue catalog says the patron can also choose to "find in print." How did Purdue come to join the ranks of the British Library in collecting William Lilly's obscure text? More, Purdue owns a particularly interesting version of the tract, as its copy is annotated, filled with manuscript marginalia that promises to offer a glimpse into the way the ordinary reader read the debate between Lilly and the author of *Future History*, the way the theologically inclined layperson experienced the millennial impulses that motivated the two authors. While drawing conclusions from marginalia always involves speculation, a triangulated reading of Lilly's 1651 work, the anonymous *A Brief Description of the Future History of Europe*, and the marginal notes contained in Purdue's copy of Lilly's work illustrates the fervor with which millennial ideas were being discussed throughout the seventeenth century. At the same time, as a result of the vicissitudes of book collecting and the particular mission of one of Purdue's special collections, this copy was archived at Purdue as a work of economic history. Before the advent of the electronic catalog, a researcher like me, interested in the theology of Lilly and his tractarian adversary, had little chance of discovering a local ink-and-paper copy.

Monarchy or No Monarchy came to Purdue in the mid-twentieth century as part of a purchase for the Krannert School of Business's history of economics collection. Along with over 100 other sixteenth- and seventeenth-century tracts (and about 3,000 total items), the tract was originally housed in a reading room for rare materials in the School of Business (see fig. 1.1).

Figure 1.1. Special Collections materials on display in Management and Economics Library, c. 1960s. Courtesy of Purdue University Libraries, Karnes Archives and Special Collections.

In recent years that reading room was repurposed, and the tract is now housed with the general holdings of Purdue's archives and special collections, but it is still marked in the catalog as part of the original Krannert collection. Such an identification confirms the importance of recent scholarly attention to the mercantilist structures that knit together the early modern world. The accession information for the tract gives no indication that it records a mid-seventeenth-century interest in global forces beyond capitalism: that it is a tract primarily concerned with debating the meaning of ancient religious prophecies and charting end-times events.

The primary faculty mover in the building of this special collection was Nathan Rosenberg, a Purdue economist who wrote extensively on the ways technology drives economic history. As Judith Nixon explains, he found this copy of *Monarchy or No Monarchy* among a collection of books that had been assembled by Herbert S. Foxwell, a noted English economist, who over the years amassed several libraries' worth of books and ephemera that documented the history of economics in the West. The bulk of his collection was purchased by the Worshipful Company of Goldsmiths in 1901 and donated to the Senate House Library at the University of London (now the Goldsmiths' Library of Economic Literature) and by Harvard in the 1920s and late 1930s (now the Kress Collection of Business and Economics).[73]

73. On the economics collection at Purdue, see Judith M. Nixon, "Krannert Special Collection: The Story of Treasures in Economics at Purdue University and How They Found

Foxwell seems to have had a flexible intellect, perhaps nurtured by the state of his discipline at the time. One biographer remarks that in his early career, Foxwell "had the whole range of economics as his field" and was inclined toward historic as opposed to analytic analysis of economics.[74] Just after his death, C. E. Collet, his student and longtime colleague, summed up his career, noting that his publications had been focused on "financial and monetary topics, with a special reference to Bimetallism" but his true contribution to the field had been "his study and classification and collection of every fragment of printed economic argument and record from the seventeenth to the nineteenth centuries."[75] As for why *Monarchy or No Monarchy* might have attracted his attention, Foxwell was a proto-cultural studies scholar: "Foxwell was one of the pioneers in attaching great significance to what is now called Institutionalism as a necessary subject for study by economists, and he was often to be found protesting against the falsification of facts involved in theories which regard society as merely a congeries of discrete individuals."[76] Foxwell's own account of his collecting practices suggests why he classified *Monarchy or No Monarchy* as economic literature. Of his criteria for inclusion he writes: "If any partiality has been shown, it has been in the desire to put in evidence the scanty and obscure literature which gives a clue to the opinions of the almost inarticulate masses of the people."[77]

Rosenberg apparently stumbled across the rump of Foxwell's collection in a London bookstore that was looking to unload it.[78] At that time, the Krannert School of Business—then called the School of Industrial Education—was just establishing its reputation. With this purchase, its library would gain more than 3,000 items of economic literature.[79] *Monarchy and No Monarchy*'s continued housing within an economics special collection, then, largely depends on the coincidence of a young, topnotch economics scholar working in a fledgling school of business that was "hungry for recognition and acclaim."[80] Rosenberg recognized the value of the col-

---

Their Way to Indiana," *Journal of Business and Finance Librarianship* 8.1 (2002): 3–25. Neither library contains a copy of Lilly's work, so this text is not one of the theorized "duplicates or triplicates" of the original collection. See Nixon, "Krannert Special Collection," 9.

74. See A. L. Bowley, "Foxwell, Herbert Somerton (1849–1936)," rev. Richard D. Freeman, in *Oxford Dictionary of National Biography* (Oxford: Oxford University Press, 2004), http://www.oxforddnb.com/view/article/33239, accessed 22 September 2016.

75. C. E. Collet, "Herbert Somerton Foxwell," *Economic Journal* 46.184 (December 1936), 599 and 603. Clara Collet founded (or helped to found) two economics clubs in the 1890s, both of which counted Foxwell among their members. See Deborah McDonald, *Clara Collet 1860–1948: An Educated Working Woman* (London: Woburn Press, 2004) 82–83.

76. Collet, "Herbert Somerton Foxwell," 609.

77. "Economic Libraries," in *The Palgrave Dictionary of Political Economy*, vol. 1, ed. Henry Higgs, 870–872, quoted in Collet, "Herbert Somerton Foxwell," 606.

78. Nixon gives an overview of the collection's acquisition, "Krannert Special Collection," 4–8.

79. Nixon, "Krannert Special Collection," 5.

80. Nixon, "Krannert Special Collection," 3.

lection, and the school was willing to take the leavings of more prestigious institutions in order to ramp up its holdings.[81]

Rosenberg's decision to collect titles that reflect a global understanding of economics was of a piece with the cutting-edge scholarship of the day. It is noteworthy that Immanuel Wallerstein first began publishing his world-system theory monographs a decade later and that Rosenberg himself published *How the West Grew Rich: The Economic Transformation of the Industrial World* in 1986. These projects were born out of a sense that large-scale Western innovations in trade, mercantilism, and technology had profound effects not just on the West but the world.[82] The projects argue (implicitly at least) that we can understand Western history and culture as we know it by tracing the rise of capitalism.[83] Read through the lens of its institutional home, we can see Lilly's attention to the prophecy of a "Merchandise of Men" as one element that fits the tract into a business school's special collection. That prophecy predicted—and the tract reported the enactment of—a protocapitalist, mercantile system of unfree West Indian labor at the beginning of the Caribbean's transformation into an economic engine producing luxury goods, especially sugar, for a metropolitan market.

Lilly's tract lurks with other early modern materials in the Krannert special collections. Yet on its face, *Monarchy or No Monarchy* has little to do directly with the fields of business or economics, the Krannert collections' primary focus; it is surely more valuable to historians, cultural critics, and literary scholars. Indeed, Foxwell's interest in the "opinions of the almost inarticulate masses of the people" suggest a prescient sense that his collection would reach beyond his immediate colleagues, as he thought that the scanty and obscure literature that particularly interested him would "probably have for future ages a very special and pathetic interest."[84] Yet until recently the institutional home of this copy of Lilly's work rendered it

81. Moreover, the school's librarian, John Houkes, determined that the value of the collection was more than double the asking price. See Nixon, "Krannert Special Collection," 5.

82. Nathan Rosenberg and L. E. Birdzell, Jr., *How the West Grew Rich* (New York: Basic Books, 1986). Sadly, I write this note just three days after Professor Rosenberg's death, so I will not be able to confirm the reasons why he advocated purchasing early modern religious texts.

83. This categorization of the tract as properly belonging to the field of economics rather than (say) religious studies, history, or even physics by way of its astrological calculations is confirmed by a recent archival development. In 2013, Kwansei Gakuin University purchased an extensive collection of Herbert Foxwell's papers. Their rationale for the purchase was that it helped meet the university's new goal to become "a world center of research." See "On the Foxwell Papers at Kwansei Gakuin University Library," http://library2.kwansei.ac.jp/e-lib/keizaishokan/foxwell/english.html, accessed 21 September 2016. Specifically, the university's description of the acquisition claims that the Foxwell papers are "part of the world heritage that testifies to the 'global exchange of knowledge' centering on England in the late nineteenth through early twentieth centuries."

84. Quoted in Collet, "Herbert Catalogue," 606.

invisible to, or at least less likely to be discovered by, such researchers. Moreover, one of this copy's features, perhaps its most "obscure," yet arguably its most important—is its manuscript marginal comments. These, like most other early modern manuscript resources, are only apparent upon personal inspection of this particular copy; Purdue's records do not note the annotations.[85]

Moreover, even if the tract had originally been subject to more extensive indexing, the marginalia are easy to overlook; so disciplined am I to the primacy of print that it took me several readings before I made any real note of the messages scrawled alongside Lilly's arguments. When I did, I discovered that the margins of Lilly's tract, which are often a direct challenge to Lilly's beliefs, are also a challenge to the original identification of the work as a specimen of economic literature that led to its immurement in the Krannert special collections. The marginal comments are archival stowaways that remind us of the work's significance beyond the economic. This particular copy was read and inscribed by readers because it encoded a divine calculus that engaged readers eager to encounter a different kind of world system. It promised, as an anonymous reader noted in the margins on one of the opening pages of Purdue's copy, to locate "Christ upon Earth."[86] In short, the marginal notes in this copy constitute a third voice in the debate and dialogue about millennialism initiated by Lilly and the author of *Future History.*

To this point, I've been following archival threads to discover the architecture of the collecting practices, special collections, and archives that ensured the preservation of this copy of Lilly's tract and recorded its presence at Purdue. But those threads do not connect specifically to the marginal comments. We will likely never know who was interested enough to track in this way the events and prophecies that Lilly's tract relates. There seem to be three or maybe four hands traceable in the margins, inscribing notes that range from direct commentary on the text to scribbles and even an accounts list totting up small purchases.[87] There are several signatures. And Purdue

85. I in no way mean this description of the tract's archival history to disparage the excellent work of my colleagues in libraries and special collections. On the contrary, because they have continued to care for and develop the collection, the tract's information was brought into the digital system, the tract itself was rehoused in Purdue's special collections, and I was able to discover it among Purdue's holdings and request it. I've since consulted the physical copy regularly, and my colleagues have kindly provided me with digital copies of the most important marginal notes.

86. Lilly, *Monarchy or No Monarchy,* 7.

87. In addition to the marginalia that most interest me, several end pages in both the front and back of the copy are covered in what seems to be a Latin index to another work. These pages appear to have been used to bulk out the binding of the pamphlet and were likely recycled. My thanks to Meredith Neuman for consulting with me on the physical makeup of this copy of the work.

has no record of this work's specific provenance. Foxwell's typical practice, according to Christine Riggle, special collections librarian at Harvard Business School's Baker Library, was to take note of his sources: "Foxwell had a habit of recording in pencil the name of the bookseller and the year of the purchase on the inside front cover or in the case of pamphlets on a piece of paper he used as a wrapper."[88] If such a note ever existed, it is no longer extant.

Yet even though we cannot know their authors, the comments have substance; they have heft, and despite our incomplete knowledge of whence and wherefore they came, some accounting of them is revealing.[89] In order to move forward, I am left to construct an "imaginary record" for the identities of the readers of this tract, conjured within an "impossible archival imaginary." As Anne J. Gilliland and Michelle Caswell define it, an "impossible archival imaginary" builds on Caswell's earlier notion of the "archival imaginary," which can enable communities to "creatively and collectively re-envision the future through archival interventions in representations of the shared past."[90] Often through partnerships with activist archivists, such work depends on new approaches to extant archival materials. With the addition of the "imaginary," they extend the concept to include such interventions even through nonexistent, "impossible" archival records, that is, in "situations where the archive and its hoped-for contents are absent or forever unattainable."[91]

I take such a concept of the imaginary record as my rhetorical warrant to turn to the affective quality of these marginalia for the contemporary reader today and to read them closely as a whole and for the way they respond to and steer the dialogue of *Future History* and *Monarchy or No Monarchy*. I have not yet been able to identify any specific individual who read and commented on this copy of the tract, though several names are inscribed on its pages and covers. Looking through the margins, one encounters several colors of ink, stroke width, and handwriting styles. Internal textual evidence suggests that the notes (at least some of them) date to after the Restoration, but there's no way to set a date range for them or even to tell in what order they were written. All we really have are the comments themselves.

88. Christine Riggle, e-mail message to author, 21 July 2016. For a fuller description of his bibliographic practices, see John Maynard Keynes, "Herbert Somerton Foxwell," in *The Collected Writings of John Maynard Keynes*, vol. 10, *Essays in Biography* (Cambridge: Macmillan St. Martin's Press, 1971), 283–292.

89. "While such records do not actually exist, their weight, as manifestations of affect, as symbols of collective grief and aspiration, as evidence of the capacity of records to imagine impossible futures, is immeasurable." Anne J. Gilliland and Michelle Caswell, "Records and Their Imaginaries: Imagining the Impossible, Making Possible the Imagined," *Archival Science* 16 (2016), 72.

90. Quoted in Gilliland and Caswell, "Records and Their Imaginaries," 61.

91. Gilliland and Caswell, "Records and Their Imaginaries," 61.

What follows, then, is an analysis of what feels like a three-way discussion of England, prophecy, and millennialism. It is a "critical fabulation," following Saidiya Hartman's definition, that "play[s] with and rearrang[es] the basic elements of the story, by re-presenting the sequence of events in divergent stories and from contested points of view."[92] Hartman employs the method "to jeopardize the status of the event, to displace the received or authorized account, and to imagine what might have happened or might have been said or might have been done." The stakes of her work are much higher than my own here, as she is working with the events and (non)accounts of individuals who endured the Middle Passage and slavery. Yet, as Foxwell himself suggests, we may posit the manuscript marginal writer(s) to be "obscure," "almost inarticulate," if not necessarily "pathetic." And maybe—just maybe—one of them was a woman who otherwise does not appear in the early modern print archives. This move from archival certainty to speculation doesn't always result in a perfectly satisfying fabulation, but if we refuse to exercise our imaginations in this way, we simply consolidate a view of the past that is dominated mostly by powerful men and ignore other possibilities that rob us of a richer heritage upon which to draw our sense of possibility.[93]

My approach has been to read the marginal comments in order as they appear in the text (though of course I have no way of knowing in what order they were inscribed). Whereas some notes are obviously simply making use of white space in the margins as waste paper for other purposes, the notes that most interest me comment directly on the main text and attend to the ways history and millennial prophecy intertwined in the seventeenth century. So I have traced a thread of commentary through these notes that is all the same color and seems to be in a similar hand. I have named the imagined writer behind that thread of comments "Elizabeth Wilcocks," a signature that appears inside the back cover in a similar style and ink to those of the marginal notes and that seems the most likely candidate for an ownership mark.[94] It's impossible to know if the inscription is meant to indicate authorship or is really just some daydreaming doodle, but I have chosen to name my unknown author after it because it helps make concrete the widespread popular engagement with the ideas that Lilly and his anonymous opponent debate. Even though my fantasy of a female reader may be entirely

92. Saidiya Hartman, "Venus in Two Acts," *Small Axe* 26 (June 2008), 11. Cassander Smith first drew my attention to the critical and pedagogical possibilities of using *fabula* critically. She grapples with the issues of mediation and the limitations of the archive in *Black Africans in the British Imagination: English Narratives of the Early Atlantic World* (Baton Rouge: Louisiana University Press, 2016).

93. My thanks to Susan Curtis for helping me to articulate this point.

94. Again, my thanks to Meredith Neuman for lending me her expertise on seventeenth-century handwriting and marginalia.

wrong, the fact of Elizabeth Wilcocks's name inside the cover is a reminder to us that many people—celebrated or obscure, powerful and not, men and women alike—approached prophecy with seriousness and passion.

And perhaps they approached it with a touch of sarcasm, if not downright snarkiness. Certainly Lilly's arsenal of rhetorical flourishes includes acerbic comments on his interlocutor's perceived shortcomings and any among his readers who might be inclined to accept his opponent's claims. Lilly remarks that *Future History*'s claims about Charles II "want sufficient matter, to make even a Jury of Ideots [*sic*] to beleeve [*sic*] any such matter of the present King their Master."[95] But debates about the coming millennium seem to bring out a certain level of asperity in Wilcocks as they do in him. Lilly's work reproduces long passages of *Future History*'s version of Grebner's prophecies, part of which, the anonymous tractarian argues, concerns the fate of Charles I and the Restoration. But Lilly cannot simply let *Future History*'s version of Grebner stand. He adds printed marginal comments, and at one key juncture points out to his readers language that reveals, in his view, the anonymous author's true purpose. Lilly quotes *Future History*'s injunction to resolve the Civil Wars peacefully: since Restoration is inevitable, why not end the conflict "by an happy agreement and composition, than by Sword and Musket, and the King placed on his throne rather with the hands of his loving and rejoycefull Subjects."[96] Lilly thinks the author reveals himself in this moment, suggesting that this call for a peaceful restoration of Charles II identifies him as a partisan hack, his "intentions discovered." But just below the printed marginal comment by Lilly, Elizabeth Wilcocks has penned: "& Twas prov'd Truth," the early modern equivalent, perhaps, of "told you so!"[97]

When Lilly gets deep into the weeds of theological dispute with *Future History*, Wilcocks keeps pace. At one point Lilly counters *Future History*'s interpretations of the prophetic language in the Book of Daniel by opposing them with his own readings, which are spiritual, not literal—what Reiner Smolinski identifies as an Augustinian strain of millennialism that understands early stages of the millennial process as allegorical.[98] His opponent, Lilly argues, makes unsupportable interpretive leaps. *Future History* maps scripture onto the dissolution of the Roman empire, then the rise and fall of Austria, which in turn will make way for a "Lyon of the North"—whom he identifies as Charles Stuart—to lay the groundwork for a Fifth Monarchy,

---

95. Lilly, *Monarchy or No Monarchy*, 5.
96. Lilly, *Monarchy or No Monarchy*, 12.
97. Lilly, *Monarchy or No Monarchy*, 12.
98. Reiner Smolinksi, "Caveat Emptor: Pre- and Postmillennialism in the Late Reformation Period," in *Milleniarianism and Messianism in Early Modern European Culture: The Millenarian Turn*, ed. J. E. Force and R. H. Popkin (Dordrecht: Kluwer Academic, 2001), 155.

led by "the Church of God upon Earth," invigorated and inspired by the pure faith and practices of the converted "Universal Nation of the Jews."[99]

Lilly dispenses with these predictions as so much wish fulfillment, based on flimsy or even fabricated evidence. He notes that *Future History* at this point moves away from the unassailable evidence of scripture and the established prophecies of Merlin and instead "tells us of a rare *Scotish Merlin*."[100] Lilly believes this source is not only wrong but proves the anonymous author's identity as a Scottish Presbyterian. Of the "rare Merlin," Lilly scoffs, "No Prophet pleaseth his [the author of *Future History*] humour but a *Scotish* Rimer.... Who beleives [*sic*]what this Relator writes must have above three grains of *Scotish* Faith... you must know he dares quote no Authors but invisible ones, and Manuscripts of his owne in *Utopia* to aver this *Scot Merline*."[101]

Three grains or not, Wilcocks does believe him, and sees Lilly's arguments as by turns shortsighted and stupid. To Lilly's skepticism about an actual Fifth Monarchy on earth, Wilcocks simply notes, contra Lilly: "True."[102] A bit later, as Lilly professes to be confused by *Future History*'s explanation of the coming millennium, Wilcocks intervenes. Lilly suggests that he has caught his opponent in a contradiction: "I cannot understand how this Lyon of the North, or this man greater than *Charles* the great, can burn Cities, Men, Cattel, &c. devoure all with the Sword, and yet after that be said to perform the workes of God in righteousness." In the margin Wilcocks glosses the "Lyon of the North" in a rather straightforward way, refusing to engage in the ill-mannered tone, at least at this instance, and simply identifying the lion of the north as "The Lyon of the Tribe of Judah."[103]

It's hard to read tone in such small notations. A few pages later Wilcocks again seem to correct Lilly, who has returned to the confession of ignorance in the face of *Future History*'s incredible claims. *Future History* has explained that the Fifth Kingdom will be ruled by "all the godly in every Kingdom and State in *Europe*, [and] the converted Jews conjoyned and united with them in spirit and habitation, shall (as I said before) root out all manner of Iniquity, and be this Monarchy."[104] Lilly claims that he simply cannot understand this prediction: "I know not, or how it can be verified or beleeved [*sic*], that the Saints in every Nation of the World can be gathered together into one Body without a mixture of some fleshly, prophane or carnall people, I understand not." In response to this profession of ignorance Wilcocks explains: "no—

99. *Future History*, 12.
100. Lilly, *Monarchy or No Monarchy*, 15.
101. Lilly, *Monarchy or No Monarchy*, 15
102. Lilly, *Monarchy or No Monarchy*, 14.
103. Lilly, *Monarchy or No Monarchy*, 14.
104. *Future History*, 34.

good people god will raise up." This time the tone could be read as patient, patronizing, or exasperated.

I have accused Lilly of getting into the theological weeds as he disputes the claims of *Future History*; it is difficult at our remove from such beliefs to understand how a debate such as this between William Lilly and whoever authored *Future History* can be more than just pedantic. But once we admit the author of the marginalia into the debate—Elizabeth Wilcocks or whoever she may be—we can perhaps see more clearly the passion that these believers invested in their prophecies and calculations. One more example: as Lilly parses the many claims of *Future History*, he argues that his opposite is completely wrong about the fate of the Austrian empire. In order for the "Charles" in Grebner's prophecy to come to power, Lilly writes, "the House of Austria must be over thrown." But common sense proves his opposition's calculations wrong: "This is the year 1651. and yet we know the Emperour hath not lost his Dominion." What might seem tedious detail and contestation to us is obviously read differently by our commentator, writing from a future vantage point. Wilcocks corrects Lilly, emphatically penning a rebuttal: "'tis done!"[105] Here she obviously has thrilled to the debate, the exclamation point the only mark of punctuation in any of her notes.

There are other comments, other hands marking up the margins. There's a list of accounts—so much for gloves, so much for buttons—written in a faint ink quite distinct from that of the notes that have most interested me. Someone has colored in the rivers of blood and the Turks' hats in the symbolic pictures at the end of the book. Even among the comments I have identified as belonging to a single reader there are less passionate notes, words from the text copied out as an aid to memory; sketches of little hands pointing to interesting moments. I've named the voice in my head that speaks these words in the margins Elizabeth Wilcocks, though I readily admit that I've no evidence that she wrote any of them, not even her name. The marginal comments may not have been written by the same person, but by imagining them as connected, they create a compelling dialogue that gets us out of the closed print conversation between Lilly and the author of *Future History*. In other words, it allows somebody else the last word and reminds us that the economics library is not the only context for this early modern tract. The marginal comments, even if they're not written by Elizabeth Wilcocks or even by a single reader-writer, extend the conversation that took place in print between 1650 and 1651 into the future. *Monarchy or No Monarchy* and *Future History* form a closed dyad. But if we attend to the comments, Lilly doesn't get the last word.

---

105. *Monarchy or No Monarchy*, 29.

CHAPTER 2

"Of the *New-World* a new discoverie"

Thomas Gage Breaks the Space-Time Continuum

O ne of the challenges to a study of global currents of thought and belief is that field- or discipline-specific approaches often can't account for the complexities of works, genres, and individuals who crossed borders of time and place in the early modern world. Consider the case of Thomas Gage, aka Tomás de Santa Maria, subject of England, Spain, New Spain, the pope's Rome, and the archbishop's Canterbury; sometime resident of Artois, Valladolid, Guatemala, Kent, Kingston—and for a time hopeful citizen of Manila. His life and writings embody connections between the West and East Indies that are both literal and metaphorical. For scholars of English history he is perhaps most significant as the author of a midcentury Spanish-bashing tract detailing his travels in America or as the chaplain of the fleet sent by Cromwell to invade Spanish-controlled Hispaniola and Jamaica in 1655. From such an angle, he seems notable as an English national and religious enthusiast. Indeed, his writings influenced Cromwell as he made the decision to invade, and they were popular among a wide readership in England.[1]

---

1. There are few scholarly considerations of Gage in English or American studies, though he is sometimes mentioned in general histories of England at midcentury or of the Atlantic world. Two twentieth-century editions offer introductory material: A. P. Newton's edition, *Thomas Gage, The English-American: A New Survey of the West Indies, 1648* (London: Routledge, 1946); and J. Eric Thompson's edition, *Thomas Gage's Travels in the New World* (Norman: University of Oklahoma Press, 1958). More recent studies include Edmund Valentine Campos, "Thomas Gage and the English Encounter with Chocolate," *Journal of Medieval and Early Modern Studies* 39.1 (Winter 2009): 183–200. See also Cassander Smith, "*Washing the Ethiop Red*": Black Africans

Gage's arguments in favor of invasion were authoritative because he had spent his young adulthood as a Dominican friar in America under the protection of the Spanish Crown. He was born Catholic and took holy orders in the 1620s. In his travels he gained a wide circle of allies and made a fair number of enemies, including creoles, Spanish immigrants, indigenous believers, "blackamoors," and maroons. Scholars of New Spain mine his works, despite their anti-Spanish, Black Legend bent, for their vivid descriptions of the Spanish colonies. Seen from this angle, he is most significant as a chronicler of the many peoples, goods, and terrains of Spanish-American colonies.[2]

While he has received some historical attention, he has largely been ignored by literature scholars, despite the fact that his major work, the more than 200-page travel narrative *The English-American his Travail by Sea and Land: or, A New Survey of the West-India's* [*sic*], first published in 1648, is anecdotal, detailed, and relatively entertaining (see fig. 2.1). That he and it have been largely neglected may be attributable to his neither-fish-nor-fowl identity as seen from one or the other purely nationalist perspective. He is one of those figures Alison Games calls an early modern "cosmopolitan," an identity that in her analysis is manifest by a willingness "to adapt and to learn from the examples of rivals and predecessors."[3] Alternatively, we might turn to Karen Kupperman's formulation, and define him as an early modern "expert." That is, he was one of a cadre of individuals with specialized skills or, as in Gage's case, specialized knowledge on which the English depended in the sixteenth and early seventeenth centuries as they sought to modernize, expand their territories, and enrich themselves. As Kupperman points out, "for the English skilled knowledge was foreign knowledge," a state of affairs that was "galling" and often caused resentment on the part of English nationals toward the foreign experts on whom they relied.[4] The title of

and English Anti-Spanish Sentiment in the Early Atlantic World (Baton Rouge: Louisiana State University Press, 2016); Julie Chun Kim, "Chocolate, Subsistence, and Survival in Early English Jamaica," in *Caribbeana: The Journal of the Early Caribbean Society* 1.1 (2016): 4–33.

2. See Roćio Olivares Zorrilla, "Chiapas a través de los viajeros del siglo XVII: Aspectos narrativos e historia descriptiva en Thomas Gage y Antonio de Espinosa," in *Homenaje a Alejandro de Humboldt: Literatura de Viajes desde y hacia Latinoamérica, Siglos XV–XXI*, (Oaxaca: Universidad Autónoma Benito Juárez de Oaxaca, 2005), 234–241. Fernando Polanco Martínez, "Las ciudades de la Nueva España en Motolinía y Thomas Gage," in *Villes réelles et imaginaires d'Amérique Latine: Actes des Premiéres journées américanistes des Universités de Catalogne 19 et 20 mai 2000*, ed. Pierre-Luc Abramson, Marie-Jeanne Galera, and Pierre Lopez (Perpignan: Université de Perpignan, 2002), 63–76. My thanks to Sandra Usaga for bringing these works to my attention. See also Jean-Pierre Tardieu, "Los negros de Hispanoamérica en la vision predestinacionista del inglés Thomas Gage (1648)," in *Culturas y escrituras entre siglos (del XVI al XXI)*, ed. Alain Bégue, María Luisa Lobato, Carlos Mata Induráin, and Jean-Pierre Tardieu (Pamplona: Servicio de Publicacaiones de la Universidad de Navarra, 2013), 257–273.

3. Alison Games, *Web of Empire, 1560–1660* (Oxford: Oxford University Press, 2009), 10.

4. Karen Ordahl Kupperman, "The Love-Hate Relationship with Experts in the Early Modern Atlantic," *Early American Studies* 9.2 (Spring 2011), 247–248.

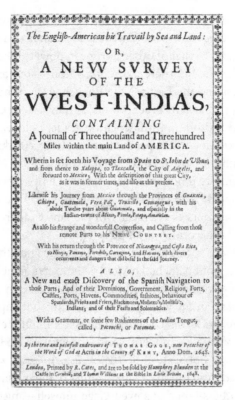

The *English-American his Travail by Sea and Land :*

O R,

A NEW SVRVEY
OF THE
WEST-INDIA'S,

CONTAINING

A Journall of Three thoufand and Three hundred
Miles within the main Land of A M E R I C A.

Wherin is fet forth his Voyage from *Spain* to *S^t. Iohn de Ulhua;*
and from thence to *Xalappa,* to *Tlaxcalla,* the City of *Angeles,* and
forward to *Mexico ;* With the defcription of that great City,
as it was in former times, and alfo at this prefent.

Likewife his Journey from *Mexico* through the Provinces of *Guaxaca,*
Chiapa, Guatemala, Vera Paz, Truxillo, Comayagua ; with his
abode Twelve years about *Guatemala,* and efpecially in the
Indian-towns of *Mixco, Pinola, Petapa, Amatitlan.*

As alfo his ftrange and wonderfull Converfion, and Calling from thofe
remote Parts to his Native C O U N T R E Y.

With his return through the Province of *Nicaragua,* and *Cofta Rica,*
to *Nicoya, Panama, Portobelo, Cartagena,* and *Havana,* with divers
occurrents and dangers that did befal in the faid Journey.

A L S O,

A New and exact Difcovery of the Spanifh Navigation to
thofe Parts ; And of their Dominions, Government, Religion, Forts,
Caftles, Ports, Havens, Commodities, fafhions, behaviour of
Spaniards, Priefts and Friers, Blackmores, Mulatto's, Meftifo's,
Indians ; and of their Feafts and Solemnities.

With a Grammar, or fome few Rudiments of the *Indian* Tongue,
called, *Poconchi,* or *Pocoman.*

By the true and painfull endevours of T H O M A S G A G E, *now Preacher of*
the Word of God at Acris *in the County of* K E N T, Anno Dom. 1648.

London, Printed by *R. Cotes,* and are to be fold by *Humphrey Blunden* at the
Caftle in *Cornhil,* and *Thomas Williams* at the Bible in *Little Britain,* 1648.

Figure 2.1. Title page, Thomas Gage, *The English-American,* 1648. Photo Courtesy of The Newberry
Library, Chicago. Call # Graff 1470.

Gage's best-known work suggests that he was aware of these difficulties. By
styling himself an "English-American," he at once claims the specialized
knowledge of the foreigner ("American" at this time was a term reserved for
Native peoples) and reassures his readers that his knowledge has been domesticated—it's English, and it is therefore safe.[5] Even better, his knowledge
can be put to particular English ends. These complexities can make Gage
and others like him by turns uninteresting, invisible, or opaque to scholars
working within nationalist traditions. But Gage's status as a man who moved
among and between national, religious, and geographic identities makes him
the ideal figure for a study of global fantasies in early modern English writings.

Gage's career and his experiences as a world traveler allow us to discern
how linked the East and West Indies were for Europeans at midcentury. While
such a claim is unsurprising for the Spanish, the Portuguese, and the Dutch,
all of whom had a presence in the Atlantic world and successful trading enterprises in Asia, most scholars of England's global experiences in the early

5. Campos sees the appellation as testament to "the difficulty of asserting stable identities
in both Europe and abroad" for recusants; "Thomas Gage and the English Encounter with
Chocolate," 188.

seventeenth century characterize England's Atlantic powers as developing and its Pacific connections as more wished-for than real.[6] In the main, they are right. Compared to that of other European powers, England's presence in Asia was negligible. But there *were* connections—real and imaginary—between the West and the East for the English, even if those connections were sometimes mediated by other powers, as they were in Gage's case. Such connections had a profound influence on trade, politics, foodways, and technologies, as well as written productions. In Gage's works we can see one strategy for writing American and England into a global identity, into the anticipation of empire if not an actual period of empire building. In short, Gage wrote compelling colonial fantasies between 1648 and 1654, offering himself and his experiences as a means for England to appropriate the holdings and status of the worldwide empire of Spain.

One of his most interesting strategies is to reimagine the course of history as if England, not Spain, had backed Columbus's gamble to sail west in order to find the East. More than any other work I consider in this book, Gage's fantasies of England in the world come closest to contemporary genre fiction. In *English-American his Travail*, he fantasizes about breaking the space-time continuum of the early modern world. The invasion of Hispaniola within a decade of the first publication of *The English-American* suggests that his offer was accepted. And the spectacular failure of the mission indicates that Cromwell and others—perhaps even Gage himself—mistook his fantasy for history.

AMERICA BY WAY OF ASIA

Born about 1603 to a Catholic family in Surrey, Thomas Gage was educated on the Continent and joined the Dominican order against the wishes of his father, who had hoped he would become a Jesuit.[7] He set sail in 1625 under the Spanish flag, intending to immigrate to the Philippines and become a missionary there. As did all who sailed with the Spanish fleet, he disembarked in the Americas for rest and to replenish stores, but rather than continuing on to the East Indies, he jumped ship and stayed for twelve years in New

---

6. Games notes that England was "on the sidelines of…major global trends" until roughly 1660. *Web of Empire*, 6. According to Karen Ordahl Kupperman, "the interconnected ocean system was experienced especially by the Spanish in the early modern period.… Spain's presence on the Americas' western shore meant that it came closest to realizing the dream with which Columbus first set out: find a route to the rich Asian trades." *The Atlantic in World History* (Oxford: Oxford University Press, 2012), 124.

7. Allen D. Boyer, "Gage, Thomas (1603?–1656)," *Oxford Dictionary of National Biography* (Oxford: Oxford University Press, 2004), http://www.oxforddnb.com/view/article/10274, accessed 6 November 2015.

Spain. In 1637, he returned to England, professing himself a convert to Protestantism, and in a move likely calculated to silence critics (whatever his feelings toward the lady), he married.[8] Eventually, he took a rectorship in Kent and set about cementing his new Protestant reputation by publishing journal-travel-unofficial-spy reports for England, in which he advised that England invade and conquer New Spain. In his career as a Protestant, he devoted himself to envisioning the plan that has come to be known as Cromwell's "Western Design." Gage composed two key works promoting this invasion: *The English-American* in 1648, reprinted in 1655, and a 1654 letter to Cromwell detailing his recommendations for the conquest of Spain's holding in America. More, he offered his life to the cause; he served as chaplain to the fleet that attempted to conquer Spanish colonial holdings, beginning in 1655 with the invasion of Hispaniola and Jamaica. He died of disease soon after his arrival.

In his writings, Gage positions himself and his works as instrumental to England's appropriation of Spain's place in the Americas, and indeed the world. During his time as a friar in Mexico and Guatemala, Spain was the envy of Europe. Its fleet connected the East to the West by transporting Spanish silver that was mined in America and minted with the king's likeness to Spain and to the Philippines, where it was traded for luxury goods such as porcelain, spices, tea, and silks. The Manila galleons traversed the globe in regular, annual runs, creating linkages that can be traced through the circulation of capital and goods. Gage determined to get himself on board one of these ships for reasons both practical and high minded. His father had disowned him, so he considered removal from Europe a prudent notion and a means of securing his living without familial financial support. He also describes himself as inspired by reports from the far-flung reaches of the Church's mission, balancing his praise of America and Asia in his recollections: "well considered I ... the increase of knowledge natural by the insight of rich *America* and flourishing *Asia*, and of knowledge spirituall by a long contemplation of that new planted Church, and of those Church Planters lives and Conversations."[9] But he reserves his most vivid descriptions for sensual knowledge. His clerical recruiter to the Spanish mission to the Philippines vividly describes the East Indies as a new paradise on earth, but the Eden he imagines is an amalgamation of Eastern and American delights, well sweetened with sugar. Gage is promised that the Indies will be "paved

8. He preached *Tyranny of Satan, Discovered by the Teares of a Converted sinner ... By Thomas Gage, Formerly a Romish Priest, for the Space of 38 Yeares, and Now Truly Reconciled to the Church of England* in 1642 to demonstrate his new orthodox Protestant faith.

9. Thomas Gage, *The English-American, his Travail by Sea and Land, or, A New Survey of the West-India's* (London, 1648), 13. All citations of this work hereafter are to this edition unless otherwise noted.

with tiles of gold and silver, the stones to be Pearls, Rubies, and Diamonds, the trees to bee hung with clusters of nutmegs bigger then the clusters of grapes of *Canaan*, the fields to be planted with Sugar Canes, which should so sweeten the *Chocolatte*, that it should farre exceed the milke and hony of the land of promise."[10] Note the biblically allusive language, which Spanish and English conquistadores searching for El Dorado had tapped for decades. This image includes a specific, creole American recipe of chocolate sweetened with sugar, a nod to the emerging European plantation colonies of the Atlantic world certainly, but also—at least implicitly—to the notion of American chocolate as a commodity in a global system of trade. Indeed, the recruiter has recourse to fantasies as he paints a picture of all the riches of the world's trade emerging from the same ground: "There should the Gold and Silver, which here are fingered, in the growth in the bowels of the earth be known; there should the pepper be known in its season, the nutmeg and Clove, the Cinnamon as a rine or bark on a tree; the fashioning of the Sugar from a green growing Cane into a loaf; the strange shaping the Cochinil from a worme to so rich a Scarlet die; the changing of the Tinta which is but grasse with stalk and leaves into an Indigo black dye, should be taught and learned; and without much labour."[11] Suffice to say, Gage is susceptible to global fantasies—and the fantasy spun by his recruiter is heavily indebted to "golden age" classical as well as biblical visions.

He decides to sail to the Philippines, a route to the East that necessarily takes him first to the Americas. Once landed on the mainland he travels, during which time he hears bad reports of the Philippine mission. He determines that he will jump ship—against his orders and against Spain's strictures against foreign residents in their colonial holdings—and remain in America rather than continue to the Philippines.[12] His activities and choices may seem unusual to us, at a remove from his moment and not familiar with the possibilities for young adventurers with means in the early seventeenth century. Yet the particulars of Gage's stay were, while rare, not unique; he was part of a group of young, ambitious friars who were persuaded by tales of spiritual and worldly wealth to be gained in the East. When he decided to shake off his original commission and remain in America, he was joined by three others in his escape—and later we learn of others who had already given up their East India plans to remain in New Spain. By deciding to sail with the Spanish fleet in the first place, but even more, by deciding to follow his own path in America, Gage and his cohorts joined the group of cosmopolitan European travelers whom Alison Games has demonstrated

10. Gage, *English-American*, 12.
11. Gage, *English-American*, 12.
12. He details his deliberations; *English-American*, 82–83.

circulated worldwide, and whom she argues helped create a vision of the world for Europeans that was, for the first time, whole rather than fragmented.[13]

If the historical details of Gage's journal to America are not unique, the representation of his "travail" in print carries a great deal of particular symbolic weight. A sailor who aims at Asia but makes landfall in the Americas: Gage's story can be read—as I will argue here—as a latter-day version of Columbus's voyage west to reach the Great Kahn. There can be no question that Gage, unlike Columbus, was well aware of global geography. His work suggests that he stumbles into America not because of an accident of navigation as Columbus supposedly did, but because of a wavering of his will.[14] Nevertheless, the parallels between Gage's voyage and Columbus's are striking. J. H. Parry has argued that even in Columbus's time, the idea that by sailing west from Europe mariners would reach Asia relatively quickly, the "Asia in the West" thesis, was an argument that relied on ideology at least as much as on geography.[15] Likewise, a close look at Gage's descriptions of his voyage show that even with a firm understanding of America as its own place and in its own place, he had as much reason to seek Asia in the West in 1625 as Columbus did in 1492, an impulse that is elaborated in his appropriation of Columbus's voyage and "discovery" of a route to Asian riches. With this appropriation, Gage imagines England as the moral and even legal heir of Columbus and the lands claimed by Spain in the fifteenth and sixteenth centuries.[16]

To be sure, Gage is no Columbus. He is an obscure, reportedly not very pleasant Protestant convert with a thin opus. By making him the central subject of this chapter, I don't mean to argue that his was the text that launched a thousand ships. Nonetheless, in the two works in which he directly argued for English involvement in New Spain (the 1648 *English-American* and its second edition in 1655, as well as the letter to Oliver Cromwell of 1654), we have writings meant both to reflect and to drive English opinion and foreign policy. Gage's influence has been long recognized. Frank Strong suggests that "it is entirely possible that the connecting link between the Elizabethans and Cromwell was *The English-American, or A New Survey of the West Indies,*

13. Games, *Web of Empire.*

14. Or perhaps he always intended to hit America by setting sail for Asia. Early on in his account, he notes that "after a whole nights strife and inward debate...rose in my minde a firme and setled resolution to visit *America,* and there to abide till such time as Death should surprise my angry Father." But it is clear that his superiors believe that he is signing up for a stint as an Asian missionary (*English-American,* 13).

15. "No purely geographical consideration could account for its [the Asia-in-the-West thesis's] long persistence." J. H. Parry, "Asia-in-the-West," *Terra Incognitae* 8.1 (January 1976), 68.

16. Robert Markley suggests that English encounters with and imagination of Asia "became a catalyst for the recognition that the discourse of European empire was an ideological construct." *The Far East and the English Imagination, 1600–1730* (Cambridge: Cambridge University Press, 2009), 9.

by Thomas Gage, published in 1648."[17] At the turn of this century, J. N. Hilgarth, in *The Mirror of Spain*, sees a "direct contemporary source for Cromwell...in Thomas Gage's *The English-American*.[18] And the *Oxford Dictionary of National Biography* notes that the Venetian ambassador and Bishop Gilbert Burnet "report secret meetings" between Gage and Cromwell and "credit Gage with inspiring his 'Western Design.'"[19] Even if we do not admit such a direct influence, Gage's writings can at least be understood to illuminate midcentury English global ambitions that led to the invasion. In particular, Gage reimagines the past in order to shape the future. It is in this sense of an interconnected past, present, and future that I read the punning title of Gage's work *The English-American his Travail*. In this tract, he recounts both his travels in the Atlantic and New Spain and his travails giving birth to a new future for his reclaimed country, England. Of particular interest to me is the way his work channels a widespread idea in the seventeenth century—what Robert Appelbaum calls the "Columbus topos"—in which the feats of Columbus were invoked as an inspiration for English heroes.[20] Gage intensifies that topos, unfolding it within an overarching Protestant-Puritan view of millennial history.

That Gage, at least in hindsight, clearly sees his journey as ideological as much as geographical is laid out in the early chapters of his book. The book's full title doubly promises that it concerns American experiences: Gage terms himself an "English-American" and promises to provide a "New Survey of the West-India's [*sic*]," but the main text is awfully slow in attending to the western continents. The first chapter of his text instead is rather balanced, a description of "How Rome doth yearly visit the American and Asian Kingdoms."[21] The intelligence he presents in general throughout the early chapters is shot through with references to the missions in the Philippines, to descriptions of the ships, men, friars, and resources sent to and extracted from the West but also from the East Indies. The book's global ambitions are intensified on the title page of the second, 1655 edition (fig. 2.2). In this reissue, the title and the subtitle are switched, so the main title becomes *A New Survey of the West-India's*, perhaps to make the intelligence value of Gage's text clearer at a moment when the English fleet was about to set sail to Hispaniola. In addition, the second edition is "beautified with MAPS."

17. Frank Strong, "The Causes of Cromwell's West Indian Expedition," *American Historical Review* 4.2 (January 1899), 233.

18. J. N. Hilgrath, *The Mirror of Spain, 1500–1700: The Foundation of a Myth* (Ann Arbor: University of Michigan Press, 2000), 478.

19. Boyer, "Gage, Thomas." See also S. A. G. Taylor, *The Western Design: An Account of Cromwell's Expedition to the Caribbean*, 2nd ed. (London: Solstice Productions, 1969).

20. Robert Appelbaum, *Literature and Utopian Politics in Seventeenth-Century England* (Cambridge: Cambridge University Press, 2004), 27.

21. Gage, *English-American*, 1.

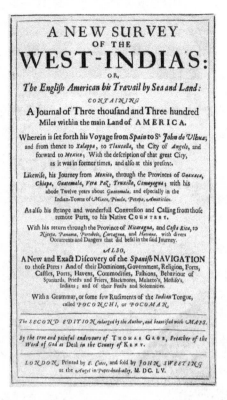

A NEW SURVEY
OF THE
WEST-INDIA'S:
OR,

The Englifh American his Travail by Sea and Land :

CONTAINING

A Journal of Three thoufand and Three hundred
Miles within the main Land of A M E R I C A.

Wherein is fet forth his Voyage from *Spain* to St *John de Ulhua*;
and from thence to *Xalappa*, to *Tlaxcalla*, the City of *Angels*, and
forward to *Mexico*; With the defcription of that great City,
as it was in former times, and alfo at this prefent.

Likewife, his Journey from *Mexico*, through the Provinces of *Guaxaca*,
Chiapa, *Guatemala*, *Vera Paz*, *Truxillo*, *Comayagua*; with his
abode Twelve years about *Guatemala*, and efpecially in the
Indian-Towns of *Mixco*, *Pinola*, *Petapa*, *Amatitlan*.

As alfo his ftrange and wonderfull Converfion and Calling from thofe
remote Parts, to his Native COUNTREY.

With his return through the Province of *Nicaragua*, and *Cofta Rica*, to
Nicoya, *Panama*, *Portobelo*, *Cartagena*, and *Havana*, with divers
Occurrents and Dangers that did befal in the faid Journey.

ALSO,

A New and Exact Difcovery of the *Spanifh* NAVIGATION
to thofe Parts : And of their Dominions, Government, Religion, Forts,
Caftles, Ports, Havens, Commodities, Fafhions, Behaviour of
Spaniards, Priefts and Friers, Blackmores, Mulatto's, Meftifo's,
Indians ; and of their Feafts and Solemnities.

With a Grammar, or fome few Rudiments of the *Indian* Tongue,
called *POCONCHI*, or *POCOMAN*.

The SECOND EDITION enlarged by the Author, and beautified with MAPS.

By the true and painful endevours of T H O M A S G A G E, *Preacher of the
Word of God as Deal in the County of* K E N T.

LONDON, Printed by *E. Cotes*, and fold by *JOHN SWEETING*
at the *Angel* in *Popes-head-alley*, M. DC. LV.

Figure 2.2. Title page, Thomas Gage, *A New Survey of the West-India's.* 1655. Photo Courtesy of The
Newberry Library, Chicago. Call # Graff 1471.

The frontispiece in particular sheds light on Gage's construction of the
Americas as England's stepping stone to the world (fig. 2.3). It is a copy of
Mercator's sixteenth-century projection, and the center of the map is nei-
ther America nor the Atlantic but the Pacific Ocean.

Thus, Gage begins his "travail" textually and figuratively in each of the
two editions of his book with representations of America at the intersection
of West and East and with a representation of Spain as an empire that encompasses the globe. As Gage explains quite early, "the Sunn never sets
upon their Dominions,"[22] an idea visually represented in the 1655 frontispiece map. Inasmuch as *The English-American* describes New Spain in order
to advise England on the feasibility of invasion, Gage thus promotes England
as the heir to this global empire.

America as the nexus of East and West is both insisted upon and natural-
ized, so much so that Gage expresses himself to be most fully transported to
America only when particular commercial markers of the Spanish global

22. Gage, *English-American*, A4r.

Figure 2.3. Frontispiece, Thomas Gage, *A New Survey of the West-India's*, 1655. Photo Courtesy of The Newberry Library, Chicago. Call # Graff 1471.

empire from East to West are brought together. Consider a scene from chapter 8 that comes after his fleet has spent six weeks crossing the Atlantic. It comes after they have landed on several Caribbean Islands, have eaten plantains, "those *Indian* fruites,"[23] have traded with Carib islanders, have fought against an armed attack by an Indian-maroon force, and have buried Friar John de la Cueva at sea, who was shot with a poisoned arrow. Despite all these experiences at sea and in traversing the West Indian archipelago, Gage reports that he does not feel that he is well and truly in America until he is settled on the mainland in the Vera Cruz cloister.

In this feeling, Gage seems to share the geopolitical gaze of some contemporary literary scholars whom Margaret Cohen describes as suffering from hydrophasia, a "disregard for global ocean travel even where it is a work's explicit subject matter."[24] That is, such scholars see ocean travel only as a means to a mainland text. Similarly for Gage, the maritime experience seems only a placeholder for the moment when the travelers are not just physically transported to America but spiritually become Americans. A closer look at what transforms Gage from European to American reveals that it is not just setting foot on the mainland; it is the access gained there to the commingled commodities of the West and East Indies, as collected and enjoyed by the prior of Vera Cruz at a dinner party held in the newly arrived travelers' honor.

Gage characterizes the sights and sounds of the intervening weeks between the moment the fleet lost sight of the Canaries until this dinner party— including those several stops in the Caribbean—as "the hideous noise of the Mariners hoisting up Sailes, when wee saw the deep and monsters of it, when we tasted the stinking water, when we smelt the Tarre and Pitch."[25] By contrast to such pollution of the senses, the travelers were treated to the prior's chambers, in which "our senses of hearing [were] delighted well with Musick, our sight with the objects of Cotton-Wool, Silke and Feather workes" and laid out before them were "all his store of dainties, such variety as might likewise relish well and delight our sense of tasting."[26] The result was an instantaneous, mystical transformation not just of their setting but of the travelers themselves: "Thus as wee were truely transported from *Europe* to *America,* so the World seemed truly to bee altered, our senses changed from what they were the night & day before."[27] Here Gage plays with the Christian concept of conversion—and remember, he is writing this account after his

23. Gage, *English-American,* C3r.
24. Margaret Cohen, "Literary Studies on the Terraqueous Globe," *PMLA* 125.3 (May 2010), 658.
25. Gage, *English-American,* 23.
26. Gage, *English-American,* 23.
27. Gage, *English-American,* 23.

own conversion to Protestantism. He suggests that the luxuries of the New World create the kind of "new creature" promised in 2 Corinthians 5:17.[28] Even sensory perceptions have changed.

It's a strange—and vaguely blasphemous—claim to link the pleasures of the flesh to spiritual renewal in this way, but we may gain some purchase on its political and theological import if we examine his treatment of the Atlantic passage, compare it to similar descriptions by contemporaries, and contrast it with his reported experiences in Vera Cruz. Compare his refusal to engage with his surroundings during his Atlantic passage (or at least his refusal to view the passage in any but negative terms) with the attitude of his contemporary Richard Ligon. Ligon spent time from 1647 to 1650 as manager of a new sugar plantation on Barbados. His *A Sure and Exact History of the Island of Barbadoes* (1657) recounts that experience; he lived on the island just as the sugar economy that would come to dominate the Caribbean was getting its start. He describes in great detail husbandry practices and the "ingenios" (machines) that enslaved workers used to extract juice from the cane and refine it into sugar. He prepared the text for print just after Cromwell's invasion of Hispaniola but likely before it was clear how thoroughly disastrous the attack had been.[29] We can understand this publication, like Gage's, as an attempt to participate in the great national plans and ambitions of Cromwell and his advisors (as well as an attempt to earn a little cash for the impoverished Ligon).[30] If Gage was offering intelligence on Spain's holdings and military strength, Ligon was offering a blueprint (a literal one in his drawings of the engines of sugar production) for successful English plantations.

While most of Ligon's text concerns his time on the island of Barbados proper, Susan Scott Parrish argues that we can find a key to the text's political meaning quite early, in Ligon's description of his voyage. She asserts that Ligon saw his trip as an exercise to be mined for political allegory, and she locates the key to that allegory in his Atlantic passage. Far from hydrophasic, far from finding the marine experience hideous, monstrous or stinking, Ligon reassures his readers that "there is no place so void and empty, where some lawfull pleasure is not to bee had for a man that hath a free heart and

28. "Therefore if any man be in Christ, he is a new creature: old things are passed away; behold, all things are become new."

29. Accounts of the debacle were coming out, but the results and meaning of the invasion were still under discussion and debate. According to Nicole Greenspan, news of the defeat reached England in July 1655. On 25 October Cromwell publicly justified the attack, and Spain declared war on England in March 1656. See "News and the Politics of Information in the Mid Seventeenth Century: The Western Design and the Conquest of Jamaica," *History Workshop Journal* 69.1 (Spring 2010): 1–26.

30. Karen Ordahl Kupperman has edited the most recent critical edition of Ligon's work, *A True and Exact History of the Island of Barbados* (Indianapolis: Hackett, 2011).

a good Conscience."[31] In particular, Parrish argues that Ligon elevates the tiny sea creature he calls the *Carvil* (Portuguese man-of-war; from Port. *caravel*) as an emblematic alternative to his contemporary Thomas Hobbes's leviathan and that he offers a model of social interrelation as the foundation of a right-working commonwealth. By doing so, he "sought to broaden and correct the English debates (and indeed warfare) of his day about the just enactment of power in society by forcing a consideration of the colonial sphere."[32] Parrish sees Ligon's reading of oceanic wonders, then, as helping to establish his text "as a work of serious political science in a revolutionary Atlantic world."[33]

If Ligon's *History of the Island of Barbados* is a work of political science, then Gage's is a work of political science fiction. Gage does not linger in the oceanic passages of his travels because from his perspective—unlike Ligon's—the future (or at least *his* future) lies not in inventing a British commonwealth to plant on islands in the Caribbean archipelago. Rather, as I will argue, he reimagines the past in order to secure a place for English polity on the mainland by overwriting established Spanish colonies with English rule. To return to the scene of the prior's sumptuous entertainment: as a good Protestant, Gage in 1648 must present the excess and luxury of this meal as suspect, but Gage sees himself as transformed by the experience. A discommoded and homeless English man beforehand, at this dinner he becomes the feted English-American. And the agents of the transformation are not American per se but an amalgamation of the products of European trade from the East as well as the West Indies, while Old World treasures are neglected. In the prior's study they "found not above a dozen old Bookes, standing in a corner covered with dust and Cobwebs." The chamber itself is upholstered in cotton and "coloured feathers of *Mechoacan*"—American goods—while his tables and cupboards sport East Indian commodities, such as silk carpets and "*China* Cups and Dishes."[34] Gage is aware that this wealth exists because of its extraordinarily cosmopolitan origins: "the great Trading from *Mexico*, & by Mexico from the *East-India's*, from *Spain*, from *Cuba*, *Sto Domingo*, *Jucatan*, *Portables*, and by *Portabello* from *Peru*, from *Cartegana*, and all the Islands lying upon the North Sea, and by the River Alvarado going up to *Zapetecas*, St. *Ildesonso*, and toward Guaxaca, and by the River Grijala, running up to *Tabasco*, *Los Zoques* and *Chiapa de Indios*, maketh this little Town very rich, and to abound with all the Commodities

31. Quoted in Susan Scott Parrish, "Richard Ligon and the Atlantic Science of Commonwealth," *William and Mary Quarterly* 67.2 (April 2010), 209.

32. Parrish, "Richard Ligon," 215.

33. Parrish, "Richard Ligon," 215.

34. Gage, *English-American*, 23.

of the Continent Land, and of all the East and *West-India's* Treasures."[35] America, it seems, is most itself when it most reflects Spain as a global power.

Clearly this baroque chamber seduces Gage's senses, even as he is careful to distance himself from its excesses and implications in his work, addressed as it is to an English Protestant (and Puritan-leaning) readership. The description of the dinner that precedes their retreat to the prior's rooms for entertainment, for instance, presents just this push-pull of attraction and revulsion: "a most stately Dinner both of Fish and Flesh; no Fowles were spared, many Capons, Turky Cocks, and Hens were prodigally lavished, to shew us the abundance and plenty of Provision of that Country."[36] The dinner is both "stately" and "prodigal." If the music "delighted" the senses, the fact that the tunes were love songs performed by the prior himself added "scandall to scandall."[37] With such contradictions, Gage was very much in tune with his audience. England desired America and the Indies— both East and West—but had to disavow that desire, or at least qualify it so that the rewards of goods and gold are understood as incidental rather than the goal of the efforts to claim and colonize these lands. From the midcentury mission writings emerging from New England to the republication of Sir Francis Drake's exploits, English writers described the accumulation of American wealth as a providential reward for more godly accomplishments: the conquest of the devil's territories by Christian heroes and the "harvest" of souls by English evangelists.

Take, for instance, the imagery employed by New England mission writers and their supporters, which directly invokes the language of economic conquest that English readers often associated with other countries, particularly with the Spanish and the Dutch. In his dedicatory epistle to the New England tract *A Late and Further Manifestation of the Gospel*, which describes efforts in the Massachusetts Bay Colony to convert coastal Algonquians to Christianity, Joseph Caryl praises his countrymen in New England for their missionary efforts and those in England for their support. He employs an elaborate economic metaphor: "This gaine of soules is a *Merchandize* worth the glorying in upon all the *Exchanges*, or rather in all the *Churches* throughout the world. This *Merchandize is the Holinesse to the Lord*: And of this the ensuing Discourse presents you with a Bill of many particulars, from your spirituall *Factory in New-England*."[38] In *Dry Bones and Indian Sermons*, I read such imagery as betraying the anxiety of New England writers about colonial competition, about their relative impoverishment compared to the

---

35. Gage, *English-American*, 24.
36. Gage, *English-American*, 23.
37. Gage, *English-American*, 23.
38. Joseph Caryl, "To the Reader," in John Eliot, *A Late and Further Manifestation of the Gospel* (London, 1655), n.p.

wealth of Caribbean and Chesapeake colonies.[39] Gage's assessment of English colonies suggests that these fears were well founded. In his letter to Cromwell advising on invasion tactics, dated December 1654, Gage encourages Cromwell to rely on established English plantations for troops but dismisses them—including New England—as already failed endeavors: "Virginia, and New England, and other plantations, which are even worne out, and have but drosse for that treasure, but copper for that gold, but dirt for those riches now ready to our hands, will flocke thither with speed, to further such a glorious worke." The future of English colonization, he urges, lies in a conquered New Spain, the invasion of which, he optimistically opines, "may bee a worke of one halfe yeare."[40]

While negative assessments of the established colonies would seem naturally to lead to provincial anxieties, David Shields suggests that such concern is also metropolitan rather than merely colonial. In his essay "Sons of the Dragon," Shields traces the extraordinary resurrection of Sir Francis Drake in reprints of tales of his exploits in midcentury (and beyond). Shields argues that English writers anchored the genre of the "imperial adventure tale" with heroic figures—especially Drake—who combined the best of noble qualities with the ability to generate wealth for the nation (not to mention for themselves). Unlike the corrupt and greedy Spaniard described in countless seventeenth-century works, these English heroes promised "to make grace and gold agree."[41] Following his analysis, we would do well to remember that the rather awkward metaphor making the New England missions into factories that produced wealth for the English stock exchange/churches was written not by colonists eager to make the case for their plantation but by the Reverend Caryl, a nonconformist preacher in London addressing English metropolitan readers.

Robert Markley would have us widen our gaze even more. He argues that such texts, so anxious about English standing in the world, and especially anxious about the trade imbalance between England and other European powers, should be considered from a global perspective. He asks "what might happen if we reread the classical texts of the colonization of the Americas...as compensatory narratives for the failures of the British to

---

39. Kristina Bross, *Dry Bones and Indian Sermons: Praying Indians in Colonial America* (Ithaca: Cornell University Press, 2004), 33.

40. Thomas Gage, "Some Brief and True Observations Concerning the West-Indies," December 1654 Memorial to Oliver Cromwell, in *A Collection of the State Papers of John Thurloe*, vol. 3, *December 1654–August 1655*, ed. Thomas Birch, originally published London: Fletcher Gyles, 1742, British History Online, http://www.british-history.ac.uk/, accessed 12 March 2015.

41. David Shields, "Sons of the Dragon, or The English Hero Revived," in *Creole Subjects in the Colonial Americas: Empires, Texts, Identities*, ed. Ralph Bauer and Jose Antonio Mazzotti (Durham: University of North Carolina Press, 2009), 102.

penetrate East Asian markets before 1740?"[42] My answer to his provocative question is that if we understand colonial texts as written against a background of the Indies, West *and* East, we can better understand the reasons why the claims of Gage, mission writers, and others who constructed national fantasies of England in America were so eagerly consumed, and more, we can better understand why Cromwell and others chose to act on these fantasies. Markley's question sheds new light on Caryl's promise of profit through New England's missions. The language of "factory," "merchandize," and "Exchange" was a lexicon that belonged to the East Indies rather than to America. "Factories" had been established in the Spice Islands. These were small settlements manned by temporary "factors," representatives of the Dutch and English East India Companies, and the Dutch factories were far more successful than the English ones. As shown in Gage's letter to Cromwell, written shortly before *A Late and Further Manifestation* was published, many in England understood that New England was no "factory" but at most a "plantation" of "drosse"—mere copper and dirt. Caryl is attempting to match New England spiritual with East Indian material success.

Gage's works should therefore be counted among the "compensatory narratives" that Markley identifies. In them, Gage issues a clear call to English action in the Americas, against a background of Spanish global success. His text argues that England will inherit an empire's worth of goods and power when it seizes control of the Americas. In his dedication to the 1648 edition of his *English-American* (included as well in the 1655 edition), Gage offers his work to Thomas Fairfax, commander of the New Model army, as evidence that the West Indies should "be the subject of your future pains, valour, and piety" and as a spur to the idea of an English conquest of Spanish America.

In that dedication, Gage bills his work as the first eyewitness description of the West Indies published in a hundred years and promises that his account differs from previous descriptions "as the picture of a person grown to mans estate, from that which was taken of him when he was but a Childe."[43] Gage's assertion of a grown-up perspective on the West Indies suggests an early Caribbean literary history with a definite telos: nearly 100 years earlier Bartolomé de Las Casas, like Gage a Dominican, had published his accounts of New Spain. In his works, Las Casas sought to reform Spanish colonial practices, especially abuses offered to the indigenous population. It's easy to see why Gage would invoke Las Casas to authorize his own work. By 1648, Las Casas's *Brevíssima Relación de la Destruyción de las Indias*

---

42. "Nothing Was Moribund, Nothing Was Dark: Time and Its Narratives in the Early Modern Period," *Eighteenth Century* 41.3 (Fall 2000), 182. Robert Markley lists *Oroonoko* and *Robinson Crusoe* here, but his question is productive for earlier and less well known texts. See also his broad analysis in *Far East,* which considers more than 200 texts concerned with Asia.

43. Gage, *English-American,* A3v.

had already been translated and printed in two separate English editions, which Robert Valdéon notes had been "widely used by the ideologues of Elizabeth I."[44] Las Casas was clearly on the minds of the Interregnum intelligentsia; John Phillips, nephew of John Milton, published an influential translation titled "Tears of the Indians" in 1656. Gage seems to have seen himself as daring to complete the journey—both physical and ideological—that Las Casas was understood by the English to have begun.

The appeal of Las Casas's text to an early modern English readership is clear. In it, he sharply criticizes his compatriots in New Spain for their abuses of indigenous people. The *Relación* is a report to the Crown, addressed to Prince Philip II, intended to remind him of his responsibilities to *all* his New World subjects, including Indians, whom Las Casas characterizes as suffering, innocent lambs in need of the Crown's protection against the depredations of Spanish conquistadores. Although Las Casas wrote as a loyal subject, it was easy for English translators to extend the condemnation to Spain's highest authorities and to see themselves as the true moral patrons of Las Casas's appeal for Christian mercy toward the Indians. In their appropriation of Las Casas for their own ends, English treatments of Las Casas denaturalized him, stripped him of his Spanish identity, and made him, in E. Shaskan Bumas's words, an "honorary Protestant."[45] This treatment of Las Casas constitutes an element of colonial fantasy that is quite provocative in the midcentury translations of Las Casas. By making themselves the authorities who would act on Las Casas's arguments, English writers such as Gage laid claim to the riches of New Spain while distancing the English from Spanish colonial and creole enormities. English writers and readers thus used Las Casas to construct the English colonial presence as benevolent, if not downright liberating.

One striking element of Las Casas's original is its lack of specific geography. Islands, provinces, and towns are named, of course, and sometimes their dimensions are cited, but specific details are usually omitted. A reader could not use *Brevíssima Relación* actually to navigate to the scenes of horror that Las Casas describes. To some extent that fuzziness is deliberate; Las Casas counts on overwhelming the reader with tragedy. He paints a picture of a generalized American landscape completely dipped in blood.[46] The

44. Robert Valdéon, "Tears of the Indies and the Power of Translation: John Phillips' Version of *Brevíssima Relation de la destrucción de las Indias, Bulletin of Spanish Studies* 89.6 (2012): 839–858. In this essay Valdéon discusses how English writers appropriated Las Casas throughout the early modern period and how the translation of Las Casas has figured in the construction of the Black Legend.

45. E. Shaskan Bumas, "The Cannibal Butcher Shop," *Early American Literature* 35.2 (2000), 108.

46. Scholars note this tactic in their assessments of Las Casas's calculation of indigenous victims of Spanish greed. Also rhetoric and general numbers: "Las Casas's figures... were not

flattening of West Indian geography and cartography may have also have been an aesthetic choice designed to frustrate—or at least contrast with— the expectations of those looking to profit from Spain's exploration and colonization of the Caribbean and the Americas. In contrast to Las Casas, Gage and his readers certainly knew about and made use of such geographic knowledge—after all, the second edition of *The English-American* is "Beautified with MAPS." But essentially his text hearkens back to older ways of representing territory in which something other than mercantilist desire is at stake.

It's difficult to parse the various layers of representation at work in the English translations of *Brevíssima Relación*. On the one hand we have Las Casas's own encounters with of America and its residents. He describes all Native people as innocent and noble victims. His formulations yield most information when we analyze them for fantasy in the sense usually applied to colonial texts. He does not construct counterfactual, alternative histories but erases nuance in his representation of Indians—they are all gentle souls in need of redemption—in order to suit his desires for them as objects of Spanish colonization.[47] Midcentury English reprints and translations of his work add a layer of complexity. They have Las Casas's colonial fantasies embedded within them, but they are overlaid by the English writers' and readers' own ideologies and formal experimentation.

For instance, to return to the issue of mapping within the text, if the lack of geographic precision in Las Casas's account reflects an older mode of representing imperial territory, the wholesale adoption of his geographic imaginary by seventeenth-century English translators and by Gage in his work carries a particularly ideological charge. At a moment when other writers of the colonial landscape were providing their readers (investors) with detailed maps, lists of supplies, budgets, and so on, the anti-Spanish tracts of Gage and the anglicized Las Casas returned readers to representations of imperial claims in a broad sense rather than offering specific plans for English factories and settlements.

So Gage improvises on Las Casas in *The English-American*, and the text is marked throughout by uses and allusions to his predecessor. Gage's own identity as a Dominican observer of Spanish colonization would have invited the comparison by a well-educated English reader, but Gage does Las Casas one better. If Las Casas had become an "honorary Protestant" by

---

offered as a factual record" but were meant "to impress upon the reader the literal magnitude of the event." Anthony Pagden, introduction to Bartolomé de las Casas, *A Short Account of the Destruction of the Indies* (London: Penguin, 1992), xxxiii.

47. This is not to say that Las Casas was not a knowing manipulator of images, but only that reading between and against the lines of his texts can teach us something more about the colonial discourse he helped to create.

midcentury, Gage claimed to be a Protestant in truth. And by doing so, he situated his work within a century-long literary history as well as an imperial context.

Gage is ambitious. In general, he doesn't hesitate to compare himself to explorers and adventurers who have gone before him, nor do his closest supporters. In the dedicatory poem of *The English-American*, written by Thomas Chaloner (a member of the commission that would try to execute Charles I), Chaloner suggests that Gage's work supplants generations of European writing on the Americas:

> ...he the state which of these Parts would know,
> Need not hereafter search the plenteous store
> Of Hackluit, Purchas and Ramusio,
> Or learn'd Acosta's writings to look o're;
> Or what Herera hath us told before.⁴⁸

Gage's readers could disregard the writings of his predecessors because he took care to search their "plenteous store" for them. Indeed, a late nineteenth-century historian of Cromwell's Western Design suggested that Gage knew (and directly copied passages from) the accounts of Thomas Nicholas's translation of Gomara on Mexico, and argued that he likely read (and maybe cadged from) Purchas, Hakluyt, and Raleigh as well as Las Casas.⁴⁹

Some of the borrowing may have been pragmatic—his is a long description of New Spain, after all, and arguably, Gage would have seemed more credible to his readers if he echoed authorities they knew and trusted. But one set of allusions—if not outright borrowing—supports the text's argument in particular for English imperial legitimacy, both in moral and legal terms. These are the moments when Gage occupies the role of Columbus as "discoverer" of America, moments that I find particularly interesting both because of the implicit argument they make for English imperial legitimacy and because of their flirtation with alternative history as a mode of colonial fantasy.

Gage's 1654 memorial to Oliver Cromwell, "Some brief and true observations concerning the West-Indies," summarizes the main points of *The English-American*; in it Gage suggests that he is claiming Columbus's legacy, both personally and on behalf of the nation, directly likening his writings to Columbus's petition for support to King Henry VII, which—unlike Gage's efforts—failed to win the approval of English authorities. As Gage argues in his letter to Cromwell, "God would not make [King Henry] such an instrument

48. Gage, *English-American*, A5r.
49. Strong, "Causes of Cromwell's West Indian Expedition," 234.

for the advancing of his glory, as hee hath made your highnesse."[50] Indeed, in *The English-American* the one-two punch of Gage's dedicatory epistle to Lord Fairfax and Chaloner's prefatory poem make Gage's mission clear: to give England a second chance to say yes to Columbus and so claim the Americas. "*To your Excellency,*" Gage writes to Fairfax, "*I offer a* New-World."[51] And in his prefatory poem, Chaloner directly echoes him: "behold presented to thine eye, / What us *Columbus* off'red long agoe, / Of the *New-World* a new discoverie."[52] The language they use is slippery—a "discovery" of the New World can, of course, be just a description of it, but Gage is doing more: the text urges England's leaders to follow his advice and "direct your Noble thoughts" to the conquest of America.[53] He is offering England a chance to roll back the clock and rewrite history. The time is ripe for England to claim what was passed over in King Henry's time.

Gage's invocation of Columbus is key to his text's significance as both a representative and an exemplary text from the midcentury. Appelbaum describes the "Columbus topos" throughout the seventeenth century as an "adjustable and portable" idea "founded...in incontrovertible fact...that a single obscure individual...had ended up changing the world."[54] Such a figure was necessary for the national imaginary, and Columbus was not the only inspiration for heroic English manhood in the 1640s and 1650s. As David Shields points out, Sir Francis Drake was another such hero. As Shields sees it, he was *the* hero: "All of the English adventurers were really one adventurer, Sir Francis Drake."[55] And unlike Columbus, Drake was a homegrown hero to boot. As Gage expands on the topos in *The English-American*, he hales Drake and others into his story, pairing his legacy with theirs and presenting Drake as an early forerunner to his own travels, which he argues affords him an in-depth eyewitness experience of New Spain. Indeed, Chaloner in the prefatory poem places Drake in a hierarchy, with Gage at the top. Chaloner argues that Gage supersedes the likes of superficial explorers such as Raleigh or even Drake, who took stock of America merely as passing observers, "wherein they might as well / Talk of a Nut, and onely show the shell."[56] Thus Gage and his supporters inserted him squarely into the ongoing conversations that his countrymen were having about the past and the future, making himself and his arguments about America legible to readers eager for news of England's place in the world.

50. Gage, "Some brief and true observations."
51. Gage, *English-American*, A3v.
52. Gage, *English-American*, A5r.
53. Gage, *English-American*, A3v.
54. Appelbaum, *Literature and Utopian Politics*, 27.
55. Shields, "Sons of the Dragon," 102.
56. Gage, *English-American*, A5v.

But it seems to me that Gage is doing more than simply laying claim to the legacy of earlier explorers. Unlike those who invoked Columbus as heroic similitude, by putting himself in Columbus's place and casting Cromwell in the role of King Henry, Gage is creating what we might call a uchronic narrative. "Uchronia" is a term associated with contemporary science fiction. Parallel to the term "utopia," it is a variant on time rather than utopia's imagining of an ideal place. "Utopia," of course, properly belongs to the seventeenth century, having been coined by Sir Thomas More in 1516. "Uchronia" is a later variant, first used by Charles Renouvier in 1857 to identify a "utopia of past time."[57] Although it can be conflated with the term "alternate history," Amy J. Ransom has distinguished it from alternate history, arguing that "if taken literally the term *uchronie*, an obvious calque upon More's word-play *utopia*... embraces *any* alternate timeline." In other words, alternate history narratives only describe the past-that-might-have-been, whereas the uchronia may "rewrite the past, explore the future or lie parallel to the reader's present."[58] It is in this broader sense that I find the term helpful in unpacking Gage's use of Columbus in his midcentury English writings. His rewriting of the Columbian past in order to point the way to a Nova Anglian future depends on his professed belief in biblical prophecy. The millennial context of Gage's address invokes (and appropriates) long-standing speculation on the cosmic significance of Columbus's "discovery." For instance, in his wildly popular compilation of travel narratives published earlier in the century, Samuel Purchas called Columbus "worthy to be named unto the Worlds end," a man of *"Dove-like* simplicitie" who, "with more then [*sic*] Giant-like force and fortitude," carried Christ's banner to a new world.[59] In other words, because his sense of time is millennial, Gage can imagine a past that is not "alternate" in the sense of "counterfactual," as we sometimes term alternative historical fiction today. It is alternative in the sense that it leads to the true—prophesied—future.

Uchronic narratives—and alternate history narratives in general for that matter—depend on a point (or points) of departure from received historical narratives. In Gage's uchronic fantasy, Columbus approaching King Henry VII is the point of departure. However important other, subsequent English heroes were, they would have all been unnecessary if Henry had accepted Columbus's offer.[60] If he had done so—because he should have done so— then New Spain would not be New Spain but truly New England. The invasion

---

57. Paul K. Alkon, *Origins of Futuristic Fiction* (Athens: University of Georgia Press, 1987), 115.

58. Amy J. Ransom, "Warping Time: Alternate History, Historical Fantasy, and the Postmodern *Uchronie Québécoise*," *Extrapolation* 51.2 (Summer 2010), 259.

59. Samuel Purchas, *Purchas His Pilgrimage* (London, 1626), 802.

60. Purchas says Henry *did* accept the offer, proffered through Christopher's brother Bartholomew. But accident (pirates!) prevented him from a timely solicitation of Henry's favor.

plans Gage draws up for Cromwell, then, describe not invasions of another sovereign European nation's lands or colonies but an emigration to colonies that the English should have (would have already) possessed. Thus, by inhabiting the role of Columbus to Cromwell's Henry, the alternate idea or timeline Gage presents purports to set history aright, to put events (back) on the paths they were meant to take. Early modern uchronia thus meshes with millennial time. Uchronia simply writes a narrative of the past that follows the same progressive linear history of the millennium but gets there faster: when Cromwell as Henry invades America, he will in effect fix a mistake of the past and in so doing will fulfill prophecy. By accepting the offering of America—a "new-found world"—from Gage he will create the history that was always meant to be.

COLUMBUS IN MINIATURE

We can see this vision of past, present, and future illustrated in the tract's chapter 6, which is a presentation in brief of the work's whole argument. In it, Gage suggests that the legal and historical consequences of Columbus's discovery of the Americas are provisional, that England can claim Columbus's legacy, and that the Spanish hold on these territories is shaky at best, needing only the right force—England's—in league with the Native peoples, blacks, and Spanish creoles who desire to shake off the yoke of Spanish rule. The chapter recounts the first landfall of Gage's fleet in the Caribbean. What we find is a retelling of Columbus's voyages in search of Asia in the West, recast in a new register, by turns comic and tragic, but always with an eye to the advantage that the English can gain from Spanish mismanagement of their colonial holdings, if only Fairfax and others in charge have the wisdom to take his advice.

The chapter opens with a recapitulation in miniature of Columbus's voyage. It's even titled "of our discovery of some islands," and although I acknowledge the broad scope of that word "discovery," descriptions of other places are not so described elsewhere in the tract. Like Columbus's fleet (like all Spanish fleets), Gage's stops over in the Canary Islands before sailing across the Atlantic. Like Columbus's fleet on the first voyage, Gage's compatriots become worried that they are off course, that they should have already sighted land. But unlike accounts of nervous and angry sailors' challenges to Columbus's authority, Gage paints the scene as comic rather than fraught. In Purchas's account of Columbus's first voyage, "the Spaniards, after three

---

In the meantime, Columbus had secured the backing of the Spanish Court. See Purchas, *Purchas His Pilgrimage*, 801–802.

and thirtie days sayling, desperate of success, mutinied, and threatned to cast *Columbus* into the Sea."⁶¹ In Gage's voyage, the pilots of the various ships are summoned before the admiral to give their best estimates of the fleet's location while passengers look on. The atmosphere is light—no one's going to be thrown overboard this time. Rather, the disparity in the pilots' testimony "was cause of laughter enough"; unlike their predecessors, the men of Gage's fleet are sure of making land, even guided by bumbling sailors. And sure enough, the cry goes up the very next day: "by Sun-rising wee plainly discovered an Island."⁶²

Despite what seem like considerably lower stakes, Gage makes his fleet's voyage resonate with Columbus's in 1492 by repeatedly drawing parallels between his own and his predecessor's experiences. The island his fleet discovers at sunrise is *Desseada*, the "first Land the *Spaniards* found," he explains, "at the first discovery of the *India's*." Actually, contemporary readers knew this to be, as Purchas reported, an island encountered in Columbus's second voyage, not the first. But it is important that Gage's mission fleet be read as recapitulating Columbus's voyage of initial discovery. Gage goes so far as to equate his relief at seeing an end to cabin fever with the desperation felt by those who sailed on that first voyage in 1492: he notes that Columbus's crew named the island "*Desseada*... or the desired Land... being then as desirous to find some Land after many dayes sailing as wee were."⁶³ The discovery by Europeans of Indian lands, it seems, is an iterative process.

Up to this point, Gage repeats the oceangoing experiences of the "giant-like" Columbus. Their experiences diverge, however, as Gage encounters the inhabitants of the island. Although he affects a neutral tone in his descriptions, they add up to an indictment of Spanish control over these lands, whether he remarks on similarities or changes between Columbus's time and his own. Purchas, for instance, describes the Columbian encounter between European sailors and "naked Natives" who "knew not the use of Iron, or Weapons, but layd their hands on the edge of the Sword." They were "well formed" and painted, with "Rings of Gold in their Nosethrils."⁶⁴ In the 140 years since this first encounter, little in the material conditions of the native inhabitants has changed—despite the lip service paid by Spanish colonists and Crown to evangelism and "civilization." Gage and his fellows are greeted by "naked Barbarians." He even comments on the "plates hanging at their Noses," though (perhaps because they are not gold?) he compares them to "Hog-rings." There is only one significant shift from the

61. Purchas, *Purchas His Pilgrimage*, 802.
62. Gage, *English-American*, 17.
63. Gage, *English-American*, 17.
64. Samuel Purchas, *Purchas His Pilgrimes in Five Books* (London, 1625), 11.

earlier account—these people know well the value of iron and weapons, seeking them out in trade in service to interisland conflicts.

The changes in the experience of landfall are also instructive. For instance, whereas according to Purchas the islanders thought that the ships "were living Creatures,"[65] in Gage's time, he reports, they eagerly know and anticipate the arrival of the Spanish fleet. Most significantly, he suggests that no one country controls the trade—"Before our Anchors was [sic] cast, out came the *Indians* to meet us in their Canoa's, round like Troughes, some wereof had beene painted by our *English*, some by the *Hollanders*, some by the *French*, as might appear by their severall Armes, it being a common Rode and harbor to all Nations that saile to *America*."[66] The detail is important, because as Gage knew firsthand, after Columbus claimed these islands for the Spanish Crown, Spain denied entrance to its national competitors. Nonetheless, as this international display demonstrates, in practice the West Indies are open to "our English," and Gage even goes so far as to argue that Spanish claims are trumped by Native rights. In the preface addressed to Fairfax, he takes up the thorny issue of Spanish precedence:

> to me it seems as little reason, that the sailing of a Spanish Ship upon the coast of India, should intitle the King of Spain to that Countrey, as the sayling of an Indian or English Ship upon the coast of Spain, should intitle either the Indians or English unto the Dominion thereof. No question but the just right or title to those Countries appertains to the Natives themselves; who, if they shall willingly and freely invite the English to their protection, what title soever they have in them, no doubt but they may legally transferr it or communicate it to others.[67]

Whatever Spain may claim, title to the islands belongs to the "Natives," Gage argues, and he is sure that they will invite the English to rule in place of the Spanish.

While the English can look forward to such friendly dealings, the Spanish do not enjoy the support of indigenous peoples, as is illustrated by Gage's account of the fleet's experience on Guadeloupe, where they are met by an armed uprising that drives the fleet from its shores. A summary of events: Gage and others disembark to the island to wash themselves and their dirty laundry in fresh water, wander about, meet the islanders, and taste new foods, in short, to get their land legs back after weeks at sea. During his rambles, Gage comes across a small group of Jesuits in close conversation with a man who is dressed like the Indians but turns out to be an escaped slave, a "mulatto" as Gage terms him, a man named Lewis. The Jesuits urge him to come back to the Spanish fold, promising freedom for him and for

---

65. Purchas, *Purchas His Pilgrimes in Five Books*, 11.
66. Gage, *English-American*, 17.
67. Gage, *English-American*, A4r.

his family and reminding him of his eternal damnation should he die a heathen. He agrees to meet them the next morning to board their ship and leave the island with them. However, in the morning, the party finds that "the Barbarians were mutinied."[68] They are attacked with a shower of arrows from the trees; several are killed outright, and more are wounded.

What I find especially notable in this anecdote is the response of the Spanish military and religious forces. Although the Jesuits have assured Lewis that they will protect him with their "Souldiers, Guns and Ordnance," and although the "mutiny" is quelled when "our Admirall shot off two or three Peeces of Ordnance and sent a Company of Souldiers to shore to guard it and our people with their Muskets" (and here I note that there was no definitive victory; rather the "*Indians* soon dispersed"), the Spanish weigh anchor and leave the island the next day. Gage makes it clear that the Spanish were routed, despite their seeming military superiority. Just the day before, most of the friars, Gage tells us, having been charmed by the island and its hospitable inhabitants and faced with another leg of the tedious journey, were pushing to stay and create a mission there. When confronted with the difficulties, they boasted that they would risk death, "saying the worst that could happen to them could bee but to be butchered, sacrificed and eaten up; and that for such a purpose they had come out of *Spain* to be crowned with the Crowne of Martyrdome."[69] After the attack, "their zeale was coole, and they desired no more to stay with such a Barbarous kind of People."[70] The change of heart is ridiculed by others on the ship, whose taunts Gage happily repeats.

The significance Gage attaches to this defeat at the hands of those the Spanish profess to rule can better be understood by contrasting it with other moments when "mulattos" or "blackamoors" play a significant role. Gage details elsewhere the threat that escaped slaves pose to the Spanish: "some two or three hundred *Black-mores; Simarrones*, who for too much hard usage, have fled away from *Guatemala* and other parts from their Masters unto these woods...so that all the power of *Guatemala*, nay all the Countrey about (having often attempted it) is not able to bring them under subjection."[71] Gage suggests such allies would make English invasion relatively easy. Although the Spanish cannot conquer them by force, the maroons "have often said that the chiefe cause of their flying to those mountaines is to be in a readinesse to joyne with the *English* or *Hollanders*, if ever they land in that Golfe."[72] Given the danger that one such man—Lewis— posed to the mission fleet in Guadeloupe, the argument seems persuasive.

68. Gage, *English-American*, 19.
69. Gage, *English-American*, 19.
70. Gage, *English-American*, 19.
71. Gage, *English-American*, 130.
72. Gage, *English-American*, 130.

The grand claim of prospective insurgent support is borne out later in the narrative by Gage's description of his relationship with a powerful figure, Miguel Dalva, whom Gage describes as a "blackamoor" (even "my blackamoor"). Dalva comes on the scene as a personal bodyguard for Gage in Guatemala, when Gage raises the ire of Spanish colonists and Indians alike. He provokes the former by preaching, à la Las Casas, against abuses offered to Indians. He provokes the latter by publicly burning an idol. Dalva, "a very stout and lusty fellow" stands between Gage and the wrath of other colonial actors.[73] For a time Dalva sleeps in Gage's house, fighting off night-time attackers, and his very presence is enough to discourage roadside attacks by Spanish enemies. When Gage finally makes the decision to leave New Spain and return to England, setting in motion the events that will lead to the publication of *The English-American*, he turns to Dalva again to aid him in what is, basically, an escape from ecclesiastical authority. He knows "by long experience" that Dalva is "true and trusty" and moreover believes that they have sentimental ties: "I would not tell him that I intended *England*, lest the good old *Black-more* should grieve thinking never more to see me."[74] Whatever the truth of Gage's suppositions regarding Dalva's motivation and sentiments, the results seem to speak for themselves; Gage escapes to England with Dalva's help.

By comparison, in Guadeloupe the Jesuits completely misread and underestimate Lewis, with fatal results. In order to represent that misreading, Gage gives us, in essence, an embedded slave narrative. It is difficult to disentangle the several voices: Gage's remembered point of view as Dominican friar, his current anti-Jesuitical sensibilities, and Lewis's own perspective as the historical actor setting events in motion. Gage first takes care to explain the presence of Lewis on an island otherwise inhabited entirely by Native people, and we get a glimpse of Lewis's extraordinary journey. It seems he is a twice-escaped slave, having run away from two masters because of abuse. Born a slave in Seville, some twelve years earlier he came up with a plan to escape a cruel master he describes as a "rich Merchant." Did Lewis learn about trading and mission voyages, about the logistics of his escape while in service to this master? He put himself in the service of a man bound for America. Upon reaching Guadeloupe, he considered that as long as he was under Spanish control, he could not be safe: "remembering the many stripes which hee had suffered from his first cruell Master ... and also jealous of his second Master (whose blowes hee had begun to suffer)."[75] So he jumped ship, hiding in the mountains, taking with him Spanish trade goods to ease

73. Gage, *English-American*, 167.
74. Gage, *English-American*, 181.
75. Gage, *English-American*, 18.

his entry into Carib society. The Indians "liking him and hee them," he married within their community and had three children.

Enter the missionaries. For twelve years, Lewis has hid himself when the Spanish made port, but for some reason this time he is spotted. The conversation that follows can be construed a couple of ways. Because of Gage's double vision (his desire to reflect the credulity of the missionaries in the moment versus his later more cynical perspective) we get a tricky little passage in the text when we can see Lewis's masterful performance to save his life and preserve his freedom. Gage remembers: "Poore soule, though hee had lived twelve yeares without hearing a word of the true God, worshipping stockes and stones with the other Heathens, yet when he heard again of Christ, hee began to weep, assuring us that hee would goe with us, were it not for his Wife and Children."[76]

When this expression of patriarchal sentiment fails—the missionaries would be delighted, delighted! to welcome his entire family on board— Lewis abruptly changes roles to that of a "poore and timourous *Mulatto*" who fears the Indians will kill him—and the missionaries—if he tries to leave. The Jesuits hatch a plan whereby he will trick his family into accompanying him to the beach, where the Spanish will be waiting for him with a boat to convey them all to the ship. Lewis specifically asks for the Jesuits to meet him—"whom hee said he should know by their Black Coates"—a request the Jesuits celebrate since it means they will get the credit for five quick conversions. But in the morning, Gage remembers, "Our *Mulatto Lewis* came not according to his word; but in his stead a suddaine Army of Treacherous *Indians*." Moreover, "most of their Arrowes was directed to the black Markes [that is, the Jesuits' black coats], and so five of them [the Jesuits] in a little above a quarter of an houre slaine and wounded."[77]

Despite the evidence of Lewis's betrayal—he had, after all, specifically asked the Jesuits to meet him on the beach, knowing that their black clothes would make them excellent targets—Gage is still unsure what has happened. In the end it's clear that he understands Lewis as having crossed them, but nevertheless he takes a moment to speculate about his motivation: either Lewis had betrayed them to his fellows or else they "had made him confesse it." It seems Lewis's performance of allegiance to Christianity and his European "rescuers" was persuasive enough at least to open up the possibility that he had betrayed them against his will. Like Gage, we cannot know with certainty anything about Lewis's motives in this encounter; his absence from the archival record is profound. We will never know anything concrete about his experiences in Seville, whether he was seasick on the Atlantic

76. Gage, *English-American*, 18.
77. Gage, *English-American*, 19.

passage, how long it took the Caribs to accept him, the names of his wife and children—or even what he called himself on Guadeloupe. We don't know when he was born or how he died. Nevertheless, this fleeting appearance in Gage's text inscribes the shape of a quick-witted survivalist into the print record and sketches the outline of an early Atlantic slave narrative.

But of course, Lewis's story is incidental to Gage's purpose, which is to hammer home the idea to his English readers that Spain's tenure in America is at an end and that England, not Spain, is the rightful heir of Columbus's discoveries. The gap between the Jesuits' hopes and the dire reality of ambush is, Gage believes, prophetic—such scenes will be repeated throughout the West Indies if England offers encouragement and support to the Lewises of the Caribbean and New Spain. He may never have known that England's own hopes would be thoroughly crushed. He was chaplain on the ill-fated expedition to conquer Hispaniola (a move he had promised would meet with success) but died shortly thereafter of disease. His death, like the fate of the Western Design itself, proves that however powerful a piece of alternate history, as prophetic writing his colonial fantasies were miserable failures.

Coda: "A Query"

Myra Jehlen calls it "history before the fact": allowing early American accounts to speak to us from their own moment, before empire, before nation. Among the domestic correspondence of Charles I is a document that demands that a contemporary researcher take Jehlen's advice to "open the historical scene to other possibilities."[78] Sometime in 1628, a few years after Gage first arrived in New Spain, someone folded up a memorandum into a tidy packet and on its flip side neatly inked a note about the contents: "A Query whether The East or West Indies be the most advantage to England." Here we may be encountering what Jehlen describes as a narrative moment "in which several histories can be and are being written (told)," a hint at the existence of "alternate histories" of the sort that Gage stages in *The English-American*. Or if we turn to the lexicon of genre fiction, perhaps we can understand this as the uchronic moment of departure from which multiple universes are spawned. Such moments are, as Jehlen asserts "the very stuff of historical process."[79] This little text and its surrounding archival apparatus can be read as a test case in history before—and after—the fact of English global empire.

This document is held in the British National Archives in Kew and has been collected in the domestic correspondence of Charles I, where it is sandwiched between a document detailing problems with wool manufacturing in England and an argument for collecting saltpeter from "the almost unpeopled islands belonging to the king"; as a consequence one might read it as simply another entry in the mercantile history of England.[80] And so it must surely be, but its existence is also a salutary reminder that in 1628, the first decade of moderately successful American colonization and Asian trade, the question of where England should direct its efforts was open. And if we look carefully at how the document is described by the Victorian historians who had its charge, we can see how this document, which when it was written spoke more to the uncertainties of England's overseas ventures, was made to fit into grand historical narratives after the fact.

Because of its global scope this document is—rather unusually—described in three series of the *Calendar of State Papers*. It appears in volume 3 of the domestic calendar, edited by John Bruce, which was published in 1859. It appears twice in the colonial series, in volume 1, *America and West Indies*, published in 1660, and in volume 6, *East Indies, China and Persia*,

---

78. Myra Jehlen, "History before the Fact: John Smith's Unfinished Symphony," *Critical Inquiry* 19.4 (Summer 1993), 685.

79. Jehlen, "History before the Fact," 688.

80. *Calendar of State Papers Domestic Series, Charles I, 1628–1629* (1859), (reprint, Nendeln, Liechtenstein: Kraus Reprint 1967), 436.

printed in 1884. Both of the colonial calendars were edited by W. Noel Sainsbury. The differences among the three summaries are suggestive. Not surprisingly, the document's appearances in the domestic calendar and *America and West Indies*, which were published just a year apart, are similar. Given the gob-smacking amount of work that surveying and summarizing the state papers required, any short cut to the labor must have been welcome. And in his preface to *America and West Indies*, Sainsbury thanks Bruce, who preceded him in the work: "I cannot conclude without acknowledging, in the most public manner, the kind assistance that I have received throughout my labours from my valued friend, John Bruce, Esq."[81] Yet Sainsbury didn't do the Victorian version of cut and paste. His entry is in a clipped style, more of a note, whereas Bruce's version smooths the clauses out into full sentences.[82] My point is that on the one hand Sainsbury consulted Bruce's earlier work; on the other he didn't just copy the domestic calendar's summary into his own volume. He edited it, however lightly. So when we turn to the entry in *East Indies, China and Persia*, published some twenty-four years later, we may take its considerably different content as a conscious deviation by Sainsbury from the earlier versions.[83]

All three calendars make clear that the question of East versus West is answered in favor of America. But in the domestic calendar and in *America and West Indies*, the decision is fairly straightforward. The question is simply "answered in favour of the West Indies." And as a consequence, an appeal is made to the king "to give encouragement to a company to be formed for working the mines there of gold and silver." But in *East Indies, China and Persia*, this appeal is not summarized. Rather, the entry goes through the several reasons why ultimately "the arguments are in favour of the trade with the West Indies" and notes the reassurance that "it is not meant suddenly to forsake that trade" in the East Indies. As for the mines of gold and

81. Preface to *Calendar of State Papers Colonial, America and West Indies*, vol. 1, 1574–1660, ed. W. Noel Sainsbury (London, 1860), vii–xxxii, British History Online, http://www.british-history.ac.uk/cal-state-papers/colonial/america-west-indies/vol1/vii-xxxii, accessed 12 September 2016.

82. Bruce's version: "Considerations upon the question, whether trade with the East or West Indies would be most beneficial to England, which is answered in favour of the West Indies, and an appeal made to the King to give encouragement to a company to be formed for working the mines therein of gold and silver." "Undated, 1628," in *Calendar of State Papers Domestic Series*, 436. Sainsbury's version is shorter by five words: "Considerations upon the question, whether trade with the East or West Indies would be most beneficial to England; answered in favour of the West Indies. Appeal to the King to give encouragement to a company to be formed for working the mines there of gold and silver."

83. I'm aware, even as I write this sentence, that I am glibly assuming Sainsbury's total recall of his decades of work, in an age of manuscript scholarship and before text searching. It's entirely possible that he hadn't remembered that he'd previously indexed the document. However, considering his years of experience, it's hard to imagine him not working with volumes of previous calendars lying open on his desk, available for constant cross-checking.

silver, if the metals are to be mined in America, they are wasted if shipped to the East: "The East Indies are so remote that our mariners shipping and victual are consumed, and will admit of no trade unless with good store of gold and silver, and albeit the commodities are bought cheap enough the length of the voyage makes them over dear."[84]

The way that the document has been calendared helps to create its historical meaning. If you are researching the East, used to looking in *East Indies, China and Persia*, then you will find summarized a document that asks the question whether England should invest in the East or the West Indies, and you will find that the West has won out. But despite the verdict, the summary suggests that the debate was meaningful, the outcome not clear-cut. Moreover, the entry in *East Indies, China and Persia* notes that the original record advises against suddenly forsaking Eastern trade. But if you encounter the record through *America and West Indies*, the question seems to have been easily settled, and there's no mention of the continued East Indian trade. Rather, the document is described as advising England to double down on English investments in the West. It makes sense, perhaps, that different audiences would get different summaries, but it does make it more difficult to use the *Calendar of State Papers* to think globally—what does it mean for the researcher of East or West to see that the original record notes *both* the necessity of gold and silver for Eastern trade *and* the desire to increase mining of gold and silver in America? To be asked to reckon with the global circulation of goods, capital, and people as we write our more parochial accounts?

The calendars, far from being a straightforward representation of the contents of the state papers, were, as their original editors and readers understood very well, a product resulting from the sifting of those contents through the particular sieves of individual editors' minds, though the works aimed to be impartial reflections of the history they indexed.[85] In her study

---

84. "East Indies: December 1628," in *Calendar of State Papers Colonial, East Indies, China and Persia*, vol. 6, *1625–1629*, ed. W. Noel Sainsbury (London, 1884), 579–601, British History Online, http://www.british-history.ac.uk/cal-state-papers/colonial/east-indies-china-japan/vol6/pp579-601, accessed 13 September 2016. The original document has three paragraphs: the first presents the case for and against the East Indies, the second does so for the West Indies, and the third takes up the legal and diplomatic ramifications of pursuing the West Indies—especially in frustrating the Dutch there. The original record is held by the British National Archives, Domestic Correspondence, Charles I, Vo. CXXVI. SP 16/126, no. 53 (p. 436).

85. Contemporary reviews of various calendars praised them primarily as resources for historians and only obliquely as histories in and of themselves. The *Calcutta Review*, while decrying the neglect of the history of British rule in India ("it seems odd, and hardly in accordance with the dignity of the Indian Government, that our Indian Records should be treated merely as a subdivision of the British Colonial archives; but the fact is only another illustration of the sublime indifference about the preservation of the memorials of its reign"), suggests that Sainsbury's East Indies calendar for 1617–1621 "must ultimately revolutionise the history of that rule." "*Calendar*

of Mary Anne Everett Green, who edited calendars from 1855 to 1895, Christine Krueger argues that Green and the other editors of the calendars were understood as standing apart from their product, and she argues that professional historians were defined in part by their distinction from para-scholarly work such as that performed by the index-compilers of the Public Records Offices. Histories were understood to be written by particular his-torians with individual perspectives, whereas the calendars were polyvocal and so could be claimed by the English nation as a sui generis product of abstract authorship, the "progeny of English History itself." The calendars were, as T. D. Hardy wrote in 1870, "a species of historical literature pecu-liar to this country—exclusively of English birth and growth."[86] Especially as compared to traditional narrative histories, they are "remarkably decentered, particularistic, and context sensitive," as Krueger puts it.[87] Despite these char-acteristics, it is not difficult to identify an individual editor's stamp on the material. For instance, Krueger traces Green's care to document the individ-ual in the state papers, resulting in, she argues, "a form of history writing that bears the marks of social history and anecdotal history *avant le* [*sic*] *lettre*."[88]

Green had enormous influence on the ways the calendars were con-structed after she was appointed in 1854, and Sainsbury seems to have ac-commodated himself to the anecdotal approach, though he also admired, as I will show, a sweeping historical narrative. The three-way calendaring of the 1628 "Query" document gives us a hint of the kind of history Sainsbury was writing: atomized, bounded by colonial or national borders. And, I will argue, he joined the seventeenth-century writer of this memorandum in judging America as the better investment.

---

of State Papers, Colonial Series; East Indies, China, and Japan, 1617–1621," Calcutta Review 53.106 (October 1871), 47. The review in the *Athenaeum* believes that Sainsbury "deserves the thanks of the literary world for the able manner in which he has discovered, arranged and calendared all available papers bearing on a very interesting subject." "*Calendar of State Papers. Colonial Series. East Indies, China and Japan, 1513–1616," Athenaeum* 1849, 4 April 1863, 453–455. And the twenty-nine-page review of three volumes of Sainsbury's calendars published in the *Edinburgh Review* praises Sainsbury for "possess[ing] all the gifts so necessary in an editor—an independent knowledge of the subject on which he treats, a happy knack in seizing the salient points of the papers before him, great care in the collating of manuscripts, and an evident inter-est in the duties entrusted to him, which renders him jealous of error and confusion." "*Calendar of State Papers, Colonial Series, East Indies, China, and Japan...," Edinburgh Review* 152.312 (October 1880), 407. Nevertheless, the review subordinates Sainsbury's work to that of histori-ans: "What the Calendar of Mr. Brewer is to Mr. Froude's history of the Reformation, what the Calendar of Mr. Hamilton is to Mr. Rawson Gardiner's history of the Stuarts, this Calendar of Mr. Sainsbury will be to the future historian of our Asiatic empire" (380).

86. Christine Krueger, "Mary Anne Everett Green and the Calendars of State Papers as a Genre of History Writing," *Clio* 36.1 (Fall 2006), 2; T. D. Hardy to Welby, quoted in Krueger, "Mary Anne Everett Green," 2.

87. Christine Krueger, "Why She Lived at the PRO: Mary Anne Everett Green and the Profession of History," *Journal of British Studies* 42.1 (January 2003), 84.

88. Krueger, "Mary Anne Everett Green," 15.

It is perhaps easier to see Sainsbury's perspective as a historian in the calendars by contextualizing his work there with his other activities. He was a regular correspondent with researchers, especially in the United States, historians who turned to him for help locating and transcribing documents in the Public Records Offices. Just a few years before his death he recalled that aspect of his career, remembering how more than forty years earlier "I had the honor of being introduced to the Honorable George Bancroft," who "was making researches among our State Papers for his History of America."[89] Bancroft was working on his monumental and influential history of the United States and began publishing volumes of it in the 1850s. Sainsbury attributes to Bancroft his own "special interest in our Colonial State Papers."[90] As a consequence of this interest, over the years Sainsbury became a corresponding member of the historical societies of most if not all of the states that had been England's colonies. In all these works and activities, he displayed a keen appreciation for the United States, which he calls the "Great Republic," and at times we can see him inscribing a teleological view of the United States on the papers he has read and indexed from the former colonies. In his view, these are the founding documents of the United States. Though a British clerk in the Public Records Office, Sainsbury participated in the project—embraced by historians, politicians, and laypeople alike—of constructing an exceptionalist, triumphalist idea of the United States.

It may seem that with Sainsbury I've moved far afield from the prophetic impulses and assurances of men like William Lilly and Thomas Gage. But as Dorothy Ross argues in her "Historical Consciousness in Nineteenth-Century America," if "Reformation prophecy allowed the millennium to be seen as a progressive historical period into which the reformed world was about to enter . . . when independence was won, fervent Protestants identified the American republic with the advent of that millennial period."[91] Decades later, when historians began assessing the history of the United States, such ideas were formative. In Bancroft's work, as Ross argues, "providence" is still understood as "an active, shaping force in history." It is a concept he retains from "early modern modes of historical perception."[92]

In Sainsbury's work, we can most clearly see how he brings such sentiments to bear on the anecdotal impulse in his one published narrative,

---

89. "Sainsbury, W. Noel, 1825–1895," in *The British Public Record Office and the Materials In it for Early American History* (Worcester, MA, 1893), 379.

90. "Sainsbury, W. Noel, 1825–1895," 379.

91. Dorothy Ross, "Historical Consciousness in Nineteenth-Century America," *American Historical Review* 89.4 (October 1984), 912.

92. Ross, "Historical Consciousness," 915.

Hearts of Oak: Stories of Early English Adventure, published in 1871.[93] The book seems a natural fit for Sainsbury's talents and experiences, a children's gift book that draws on his immersion in the archives of English exploration and trade to relate the stories of English adventurers in America, the West Indies, and Asia. Gilt-edged, with an embossed cover and spine, the book has chapters that alternate between stories of the West Indies and the East. In this sense, the book seems a balanced account of England's seventeenth-century global interests and indeed of Sainsbury's own decades of work sorting through and summarizing the records of America and of Asia.

Hearts of Oak has eight chapters, recounting stories from early American explorations, the Virginia colony, Bermuda, India, Barbados, Japan, Jamaica, and "the Cannibal Islands" in the Caribbean. Like Sainsbury's work in the Public Records Offices up to the time he published *Hearts of Oak*, the book switches its attention between the West and East Indies. By 1871, Sainsbury had published *Calendar of State Papers Colonial, America and West Indies*, volume 1, *1574–1660*, and *Calendar of State Papers Colonial, East Indies, China and Japan*, volumes 2 and 3, covering 1513–1516 and 1617–1621. He must have been at work on volume 4, *1622–1624*, as he was writing *Hearts of Oak* and preparing it for publication. So perhaps it is not surprising given the longer sweep of American history that he'd already summarized that on balance he seems inclined in *Hearts of Oak* to celebrate America's colonial legacy and downplay Asia's importance to English national pride.

To be clear, Sainsbury claims both East and West as sources of England's pride and asserts: "It was owing to [English] love of adventure, and to our national indomitable perseverance, that we first came to have colonies in America and possessions in India."[94] But it is equally clear that whereas the fate of the English in the East is still unfolding, he sees America as having fulfilled its destiny: "by America we mean those colonies which have since combined into a mighty Republic, whose power and influence extend throughout the civilized world."[95] Sainsbury thus participates in the "exceptionalist" impulse of U.S. history that Ross has argued "weakened the strands of historicism" in the work of U.S. historians, because a belief in the United States as the fulfillment of providence disallows attention to uncertain, contingent possibilities.[96] In other words, Sainsbury seems to read the

---

93. Sainsbury published several other works, the letters of Rubens, and guides to the holdings of the Public Records Offices, but *Hearts of Oak: Stories of Early English Adventure* (London: Bradbury, Evans, & Co, 1871) is his only work of "stories."

94. *Hearts of Oak*, x. Note also his assertion that England was always ahead of France.

95. Sainsbury, *Hearts of Oak*, 3.

96. Dorothy Ross, "A New Look at Nineteenth-Century Historical Consciousness from the Modern/Postmodern Divide," *Modern Intellectual History* 9.2 (2012), 455.

"future history" of the United States as present and predicted in the words and actions of bold Sir Walter Raleigh or "manly" John Smith.[97] He couches even setbacks to English colonists in terms of the future United States. After chronicling Ralph Lane's trials in Virginia at the end of the sixteenth century and describing his decision to abandon Roanoke, Sainsbury quotes the received wisdom on Lane: "it has been truly said 'he had one chance for immortality.'"[98] He quotes here Edward E. Hale's "Life of Sir Ralph Lane" and goes on to plagiarize outright the rest of the paragraph in which Hale describes Lane's failure of vision, echoing Hale's assessment that Lane threw away the chance to found the United States: "He might have been the founder of the United States of America. That chance, without any reasons of weight, he threw away. His colony was at the time he deserted it amply supplied by Drake with all that a truly resolute man would have demanded. Failing that chance, he never had another."[99] The passage is nearly word for word Hale's assessment.[100] They diverge, and Sainsbury goes his own way, however, where Hale continues to excoriate Lane. Hale claims that "history has passed him by as he deserved, till the children of the American nation which he did not plant have explored the almost worthless records he left behind him, to try to find what man he was, to whom, by misfortune, Raleigh intrusted the infant fortunes of Virginia." Sainsbury replaces this severe criticism with a more prosaic assessment: Lane "has however left behind him a monument to his fame—he introduced tobacco into England."[101] It is possible to read this passage as light wit, a contrast of Lane's heroic ambition with the bathetic results. But I prefer to think that Sainsbury is simply gentler here than Hale—his broader interests and perspectives perhaps make him more forgiving, and after all, Sainsbury's life work is taken up with just such "worthless records" as Hale dismisses.

Sainsbury, then, perhaps sees Lane not just as a failed founder of the United States but also as a historical actor in an uncertain time. But if this moment suggests some nuance as a historian, Sainsbury nonetheless shares the assumption that the United States is unique and worth celebrating. The chapter "Our First Colony," in which Lane's sad story is related, ends on a crescendo. Sainsbury recounts how the Jamestown colony was on the brink of failure when a new governor, Lord De La Warr, arrived with supplies just in

---

97. *Hearts of Oak*, 76.
98. Sainsbury, *Hearts of Oak*, 24.
99. Sainsbury, *Hearts of Oak*, 24.
100. The only difference is an extra phrase in Hale's original: "He might have been the founder, on this continent, of the United States of America." Edward E. Hale, "Appendix: Life of Sir Ralph Lane," *Archaeologica Americana; American Antiquarian Society Transactions and Collections* 4 (1860), 343.
101. Sainsbury, *Hearts of Oak*, 24.

the nick of time "and thus laid the foundation of the greatest Republic of modern times—The United States of America."[102] No other chapter ends on such a high note. Of England's incursion into India, after the first few years that he chronicles, he hints at the "subsequent fortunes of the East India Company, the "glorious successes of our arms in India" as well as "the dreadful tragedies that have been enacted there, and the political and critical position of the country at different times," but gives over telling those stories himself, referring readers to previously "written pages in our history."[103] Similarly he cedes the story of England in Japan to "the interesting volumes of our late Ambassador to the Japanese court, Sir Rutherford Alcock."[104] At least in these chapters he suggests that there are English national stories to tell. He ends the chapters on Bermuda, Barbados, and Jamaica by offering, respectively, Bermuda's dimensions, a catalog of hurricanes that have hit Barbados, and an account of the great earthquake that hit Jamaica in 1692. The closest he gets to a truly heroic account that is not set in a colony that became part of the United States is in his account of Thomas Warner, explorer of St. Kitts and other Caribbean islands. Even there, he compares Warner to a colonial founding father of the United States: "He was the father of the Caribbee Islands in the same way as the celebrated John Smith was the father of Virginia."[105]

Hearts of Oak is aimed at children—its reviewers obviously saw it as entertaining but wholesome, its appealing style masking serious historical effort. Both the *Saturday Review of Politics, Literature, Science and Art* and the *Athenaeum* reviewed it on 24 December 1870. The two reviews term Sainsbury's book "unpretending" even as they note its erudition. The *Athenaeum* notes its "gay binding," and my own copy of the book suggests that its packaging held up over time; it is inscribed as a "garden prize" given to Jessie Roberts of Eversley in 1886. But despite its gilt edging, the *Athenaeum* assures potential readers, the book "contains the result of much research, and affords information that does not lie in the way of everyone to obtain." (And even for those who do have access to Hakluyt and Purchas, the reviewer suggests that Sainsbury's interpretations are needed. The originals are "too long and too quaint for the impatient readers of the present generation.")[106] The *Saturday Review* notes Sainsbury's specific qualifications, noting his role as the editor of the colonial calendars: by virtue of his special access, he is privy to stories of English adventure that "will be new to old readers as well as young."[107]

102. Sainsbury, *Hearts of Oak*, 77.
103. Sainsbury, *Hearts of Oak*, 160, 161.
104. Sainsbury, *Hearts of Oak*, 236.
105. Sainsbury, *Hearts of Oak*, 329–330.
106. "A Batch of Children's Books," *Athenaeum*, 24 December 1870, 841.
107. "Christmas Books," *Saturday Review of Politics, Literature, Science and Art*, 24 December 1870, 814.

As I've shown, despite the reviewer's expectations given Sainsbury's access to the archives, much of the book repeats received history, even to extensive, direct (and unattributed) quotation of earlier historians.[108] Yet there are some details that are less well known, and he emphasizes some elements of the stories that others might pass over more quickly. Perhaps he included such details because he was not writing a sweeping history but collecting "stories" that he "relates," as the title page indicates. A close look at one such detail, the story of an enslaved girl in Asia, especially as compared to the much better known story of Pocahontas in America, exemplifies the historiographical filters that Sainsbury brought to bear on the state papers.

Sainsbury's recital of Pocahontas's story is nothing new, a succinct account of details already well known.[109] Working a middle-ground register, he includes both pragmatic detail drawn from the sources and his own editorializing: "her history is both romantic and sad."[110] He inserts her story in the middle of John Smith's, detailing her first encounter with Smith and recounting the well-known tale of how at age ten she saved him from her father's sentence of death, and describes how she was "kidnapped" by the English, converted and married at age nineteen, traveled to London, and died at Gravesend.[111] She is significant to Sainsbury's account of English heroism and America's founding, of course, but her life story is a diversion from the main thrust of this chapter—"Our First Colony"—and he soon wraps it up in order to return to Smith.

Pocahontas had to be included—her story was too well known and celebrated, on both sides of the Atlantic to be ignored—and his treatment of it does little to give us a sense of Sainsbury as historiographer. But he includes a smaller account of another young indigenous girl that is much more telling. The fact that he includes this second story at all in *Hearts of Oak* is significant. In his chapter "Japan and the Japanese," he includes this brief story of an enslaved girl as part of his discussion of criminality and the Japanese legal system. He repeats his source's assessment of Japan that "in all civil matters a land could not be better governed" but goes on to note that

---

108. I haven't even attempted to track Hakluyt and Purchas through Sainsbury's work, but it's clear that their versions of colonial America runs through his treatment.

109. See, for instance, Sarah Josepha Buell Hale, *Woman's Record, or Sketches of All Distinguished Women, from the Creation to AD 1868*, 3rd ed. rev. (New York, 1870), Sabin Americana, accessed 23 September 2016. Hale describes Pocahontas: "She was like a guardian angel to the white strangers who had come to the land of the red men.... thus proving the unity of the human family through the spiritual nature of the woman" (475). Or John L. Denison, ed., *An Illustrated History of the New World* (Norwich, CT, 1870), which describes the motivation of Pocahontas for saving John Smith: "the youthful and favourite daughter of this savage chief, was seized with those tender emotions which form the ornament of her sex" (216). Sainsbury is considerably less florid in his account.

110. Sainsbury, *Hearts of Oak*, 61.

111. Sainsbury, *Hearts of Oak*, 60–66.

despite this good government, the Japanese tolerated slavery.[112] The example he gives, however, is not of Japanese practices but of an Englishman's purchase of a slave. Sainsbury has obvious distaste for the story: "The English factor bought a wench for three taels, about fifteen shillings sterling. She was forced to serve five years and then repay the three taels, or else remain a perpetual captive. At the time of her purchase the poor child was only twelve years old."[113]

If we look at the original letter—and Sainsbury's summary of it in the *Calendar of State Papers*, we can see that he has expurgated the tale for the audience of *Hearts of Oak*. The girl was purchased as a sex slave by Richard Cocks, the head of a Japanese factory. He mentions the purchase in a letter dated 9 March 1614 that otherwise concerns matters of Company trade. Sainsbury gives quite a bit of space to the story of this girl's purchase in his small entry in the *Calendar of State Papers* concerning this letter, even including a direct quotation about the girl: "she is but 12 years old, and over small yet for trade; but you would little think that I have an other forthcoming that is more 'lapedable;' yet it is true, and I think a gentlewoman of your acquaintance; you must be no blab of your tongue."[114] Note that Sainsbury (as does Cocks) sets the word "lapedable" apart. As Samuli Kaislaniemi explains, in the early seventeenth century, this word described a woman who was mature enough for sex, and the term belonged "to the broad genre of erotic, obscene, pornographic and bawdy literature."[115] Even if Sainsbury did not know the connotation, it's clear from the context that Cocks isn't picking up the twelve-year-old as a housemaid; even though he judges another woman more suitable for his purposes, there's no doubt he places the girl on the same crude scale of sexual availability. As for why Sainsbury summarized this anecdote in his calendar, much less why he included it

112. Sainsbury, *Hearts of Oak*, 215.

113. Sainsbury, *Hearts of Oak*, 215.

114. "East Indies: March 1614," in *Calendar of State Papers Colonial, East Indies, China and Japan*, vol. 2, *1513–1616*, ed. W. Noel Sainsbury (London: Her Majesty's Stationery Office, 1864), 279–289, British History Online, http://www.british-history.ac.uk/cal-state-papers/colonial/east-indies-china-japan/vol2/pp279-289, accessed 28 August 2016. Compare Sainsbury's summary to the original: "I bought a wench yisterday, cost me 3 taies, for w'ch she must serve 5 yeares & then repay back the three taies, or som frendes for her, or else remeane a p'petuall captive. She is but 12 yeares ould, over small yet for trade, but yow wold littell thynke that I have another forthcominge that is mor *lapedable*, yet it is true, & I think a gentelwoman of your accoyntance. Yow must be no blab of your tonge, yet I make no dowbte but Sturton & yow eather are, or else will be, p'vided shortly." Anthony Farrington, ed., *The English Factory in Japan, 1613–1623*, vol. 1 (London: British Library, 1991), 140. Also quoted in Samuli Kaislaniumi, "Early East India Company Merchants and a Rare Word for Sex," in *Words in Dictionaries and History: Essays in Honour of R. W. McConchie*, ed. Tanja Säily and Olga Timofeeva (Amsterdam: John Benjamins, 2011), 170.

115. Kaislaniumi, "Early East India Company Merchants and a Rare Word for Sex," 178. Kaislaniemi traces the etymology of "lapedable" to the English slang word "stone" (testicle).

in his children's book *Hearts of Oak*, it might be worth remembering that he had eight daughters.[116] Perhaps he was so appalled by the story that he could not let it go. Whatever the reason, it sounds a discordant note in his stories of heroic English adventure.

But Pocahontas, though acknowledged to be a victim of kidnapping, is never presented as a "poor child." In the end, despite his modest entry into historical literature, Sainsbury is primarily a calendar-indexer, not a narrator. And as he prepared *Hearts of Oak* for publication, he had dealt with a much wider swath of colonial American than colonial Asian state papers and had been working with—or at least for—George Bancroft for a quarter century. Small wonder then that his book, though ostensibly telling the story of English adventure throughout the world, lingers on American stories. Like Thomas Gage, once Sainsbury arrives in America, he desires to stay. For him, it seems, America's colonial history had fulfilled its promise. Whatever "advantage" for England the West Indies had turned out to be, in terms of the kinds of universalist history Sainsbury constructs, firmly in the vein of Bancroft and other nineteenth-century historians of the United States, the question was always already decided in favor of the West.

Yet Sainsbury's admiration for the United States and for Bancroft do not tell the whole story of his encounter with the English colonial and overseas archives. In small anecdotes, Sainsbury affords us a glimpse of the possibilities of history-before-the-fact that he must have encountered time and time again in the state papers he puzzled out and catalogued for almost half a century. And a handful of these anecdotes, such as the little girl forced to buy her freedom or serve as a sex slave, would surely need to be excluded from celebratory grand histories of nation. Its inclusion suggests that for Sainsbury, and for those of us who still rely on his work to access England's state papers, what the past "will have meant," in Derrida's formulation, is not always certain.[117]

116. C. A. Harris, "Sainsbury, William Noel (1825–1895)," rev. G. Martin Murphy, in *Oxford Dictionary of National Biography* (Oxford: Oxford University Press, 2004), http://www.oxforddnb.com/view/article/24474, accessed 14 March 2017. His daughter, Ethel Sainsbury, assisted him in his indexing work at the end of his life.

117. Jacques Derrida, *Archive Fever: A Freudian Impression*, trans. Eric Prenowitz (Chicago: University of Chicago Press, 1995), 36.

CHAPTER 3

"These Shall Come from Far"

Global Networks of Faith

I f we search for cosmopolitans in early modern English literature, for "global citizens" as well as "global fantasies," some figures are easy to identify: Pocahontas, certainly, or as I have argued, Thomas Gage. But consider a broadside—an advertisement—published in 1660 by James Gough, enticing residents of Oxford to come to his shop to taste the new and exotic comestibles chocolate and coffee. Consider those patrons, quaffing cups of chocolate confected from ingredients imported from East Indian Spice Islands and West Indian plantations. Their lives were likely circumscribed by local identities, by parochial landscapes, or by limited communication networks. Certainly many of Oxford's citizens, not to mention the residents of English colonial settlements such as Boston or Nonantum, New England's first "praying Indian" town, or the "Mardiker"—that is, freedmen and -women in England's clove-producing factory on the island of Amboyna—were focused in the mid-1650s on hearth, home, or simply survival. Yet chocolate: threaded through their lives were new knowledges and tastes culled from others' far-flung experiences. In this chapter, I turn to writings that synthesized information brought to England by world travelers such as Gage into at-a-distance fantasies of England as a leader of a worldwide Protestant empire.

The first edition of Thomas Gage's *English-American* hit the bookstands in 1648. Two years later, Hannah Allen, a busy radical sectarian bookseller, displayed a new work on her shelves that also described and celebrated England's presence in the Americas and explored Protestant evangelism in both the West and the East Indies. This chapter closely examines that work, *Of the Conversion of Five Thousand Nine Hundred Indians on the Isle of Formosa*, which was edited by the nonconformist minister Henry Jessey.

I take this tract as key to the exploration of personal and professional associations, intertextual influences, and discourses that linked England to the East and West Indies in the mid-seventeenth century. The text in and of itself demonstrates a global sensibility that was just coming into its own among seventeenth-century English men and women. But more, by considering the real and discursive connections among the individuals who produced this text, we can better understand how that new global sensibility was activated within a particular network that included not only adventurous men, such as Thomas Gage, who could set sail expecting to see the world, but also less privileged individuals, especially women, who perhaps traversed a narrow geographical circuit but whose influences, interests, and imaginations were exceedingly wide-ranging.

A BALANCE OF EAST AND WEST

At first glance, *Of the Conversion* seems unlikely to shed much light on the English imagination of the world. It is one of innumerable Interregnum-era texts produced by busy London printers. The main text is a simple sketch of Dutch mission work in Taiwan containing little concrete detail. A postscript promises information about evangelism in New England, but rather than offering new facts and stories, it summarizes previous publications about English colonial missions—the first three of the so-called Eliot tracts, which hit London booksellers beginning in the late 1640s and described English efforts to introduce Christianity to Algonquian peoples.

Indeed, *Of the Conversion of Five Thousand and Nine Hundred East-Indians* has attracted very little critical attention. A closer look, however, reveals the tract as a valuable part of the seventeenth-century global Archive in English. It was written by an Independent minister seeking to affirm his place in the chaotic religious and political landscape of England in the 1650s, and it was published by a woman whose catalog placed her at the center of contentious religious debates. It offered a concrete response to Cromwell's Western Design, and it is representative of the Americana produced in the wake of the English Civil Wars. It provides an intriguing example of the ways New England was understood by metropolitans, and it suggests England's connection to the East through its Protestant kinship with Holland, which had an enviable track record at midcentury of successful Asian factories, trading partnerships, and missions. *Of the Conversion*, though a slender work, has much to reveal about the global currents that linked East and West in the English imagination.

The pamphlet's title announces that it is primarily concerned with Formosa (present-day Taiwan) and with Dutch missionary efforts there.

Indeed, Jessey was a hopeful millennialist, interested in global Christendom, and so had good reason to take note of his Protestant brethren's work in the Eastern missionary fields.[1] His concern with the Dutch presence in Asia would have been met by many other English readers. Interest in the Netherlands was high in the early 1650s. English observers closely followed the struggle of the Low Countries to cast off Spain's rule, charted rising Dutch republicanism, and agitated for a Dutch declaration of support—on either side—in the English Civil Wars. Further, just two years after the tract's publication, rivalry between England and the Netherlands would erupt into the First Anglo-Dutch War. Nevertheless, despite the seemingly clear tilt of the title toward the Dutch and the East Indies, it is clear that Jessey's main interest is in the England colonial missions and his concern with the "West Indies" balances if not outweighs his account of East Indian action. While the discussion of America is ostensibly confined to a "Post-script," the bulk of the publication concerns New England. The report on New England is a robust twenty-six pages, compared to the paltry eighteen of the "main" text, and the context in which Jessey places his discussion pertains specifically to England's national and religious concerns.

The title page of the tract is a key to its concerns. A close look at its many elements—typical of seventeenth-century pamphlets—reveals how Jessey maps American concerns onto what is ostensibly a timely account of Dutch work in the East. As befits the titular subject, most of the page is devoted to describing the tract's treatment of the Formosan mission. Nonetheless, the font size of "East-Indians" matches that of "West-Indians," giving the tract a visual balance on the page. The "proof text" of the title, that is, the scripture

1. In one of the only recent analyses of this tract, Laura Stevens argues that it presents Dutch and English missions "as parallel projects, moving in opposite directions around the earth to fulfill a shared goal." See *The Poor Indians: British Missionaries, Native Americans, and Colonial Sensibility* (Philadelphia: University of Pennsylvania Press, 2004), 76. While it is true that Jessey was personally and professionally connected to Dutch theologians and presents a clear ecumenical vision here, one that linked all Protestants everywhere in a common task of global evangelism, his readers may not have matched his hopeful view of the Dutch, and the tract suggests that even Jessey saw England as first among Protestant equals. For Jessey's biographical details, see Stephen Wright, "Jessey, Henry (1601–1663)," in *Oxford Dictionary of National Biography* (Oxford: Oxford University Press, 2004), http://www.oxforddnb.com/view/article/14804, accessed 6 November 2015. See also David Katz, "Philo-Semitism in the Radical Tradition: Henry Jessey, Morgan Llwyd, and Jacob Boehme," in *Jewish-Christian Relations in the Seventeenth Century: Studies and Documents*, ed. Johannes van den Berg and E. G van der Wall (Dordrecht: Kluwer Academic, 1988); and David Katz, "Henry Jessey and Conservative Millenarianism in Seventeenth-Century England and Holland," in *Dutch Jewish History: Proceedings of the Fourth Symposium on the History of the Jews in the Netherlands*, ed. Joseph Michman (Jerusalem: Grf-Chen Press, 1987), 75–93. On Jessey's contributions to Eliot's mission in New England, see Richard Cogley, *John Eliot's Mission to the Indians before King Philip's War* (Cambridge, MA: Harvard University Press, 1999), 213. Jessey also kept up close relations with a variety of pro–New England men. See Francis Bremer, *Congregational Communion* (Boston: Northeastern University Press, 1994), 102, 190.

offered as the divine prophecy or description of the human evangelism being reported, is Isaiah 49:12, "*Behold, these shall come from farre; and loe, these from the* NORTH, *and these from the* WEST; *and these from the Land of* SINIM.*"* The East/West balance on the title page, along with the use of this particular verse, signals the author-editor's belief in an imminent millennial crisis: both elements suggest the worldwide conversion that biblical scholars linked to the Second Coming.[2] After all, Jessey was publishing in the auspicious year 1650. Thomas Brightman, "the most famous contemporary commentator on the Book of Revelation," whose most important innovation was to map the prophecies of Revelation onto human history, projected that the fall of the antichrist (Rome) would occur in 1650, after which widespread conversion to Christianity would begin.[3] Jessey presents proof in this tract that these prophecies are being realized worldwide— from the East to the West. Once we dip into the text itself, we immediately find additional millennialist proof texts. Jessey dedicates the pamphlet to "his Christian Friends…that pray of *the Coming in of the fullnesse of the* Gentiles, *that so all* Israel *may be saved*," a clear reference to the millennial belief that first gentiles and then Jews would convert as worldwide Christianity manifested itself.[4] The three verses then cited in the opening of this dedicatory letter are all passages understood to foretell global Christianity. For instance, Jessey quotes Malachi 1:11 ("From the rising of the sun even unto the going down of the same my name shall be great among the Gentiles"), a verse I have traced as foundational to New England evangelism in this period.[5] The title page iconographically illustrates these prophecies, presenting the calling of unbelievers from the East—the rising of the sun—to New England in the West—the going down (fig. 3.1).

All of this coding might seem so much esoteric speculation, but the East-West mapping in this tract is more than theological wish fulfillment. The balance of East and West on the title page—seemingly a straightforward representation of Christian prophecy—also points to specific political views. In particular, the title's claim to discuss "West-Indians, in *New-England*" strikes a discordant note. At this time the West Indies could refer to all of the Americas, but it was most often used to refer to the islands in

2. Note that Jessey feels it necessary to gloss "Sinim," suggesting that he expected his readers would know the geographic location of "North" and "West"—England and America, perhaps?

3. Avihu Zakai, "Thomas Brightman and the English Apocalyptic Tradition," in *Menasseh ben Israel and His World*, ed. Yusef Kaplan, Henry Méchoulan, and Richard H. Popkin (Leiden: Brill, 1989), 35. See also David S. Katz, *Philo-Semitism*, 92.

4. Henry Jessey, *Of the Conversion of Five-Thousand Nine-Hundred East Indians* (London, 1650), A2r.

5. Kristina Bross, *Dry Bones and Indian Sermons: Praying Indians in Colonial America* (Ithaca: Cornell University Press, 2004), 61–80.

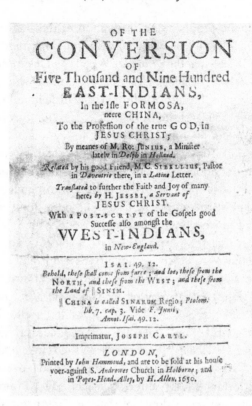

OF THE
CONVERSION
OF
Five Thoufand and Nine Hundred
EAST-INDIANS,
In the Ifle FORMOSA,
neere CHINA,
To the Profeffion of the true GOD, in
JESUS CHRIST;
By meanes of M. Ro: JUNIUS, a Minifter
latelv in *Delph* in *Holland.*

Related by his good Friend, M. C. SIBELLIUS, Paftor
in *Daventrie* there, in a *Latine* Letter.

Tranflated to further the Faith and Joy of many
here, *by* H. JESSEI, *a Servant of*
JESUS CHRIST.

With a POST-SCRIPT of the Gofpels good
Succeffe alfo amongft the
WEST-INDIANS,
in *New-England.*

ISAI. 49. 12.
Behold, thefe fhall come from farre ; and loe, thefe from the
NORTH, *and thefe from the* WEST *; and thefe from*
the Land of ‖ SINIM.

‖ CHINA *is called* SINARUM Regio; *Ptolom.*
lib. 7. *cap.* 3. Vide *F. Junii,*
Annot.Ifai. 49. 12.

Imprimatur, JOSEPH CARYL.

LONDON,
Printed by *Iohn Hammond*, and are to be fold at his houfe
voer-againft S. *Andrewes* Church in *Holborne* ; and
in *Popes-Head-Alley,* by *H.Allen.* 1650.

Figure 3.1. Title page, Henry Jessey, *Of the Conversion of Five Thousand and Nine Hundred East-Indians*, 1650. The Huntington Library, San Marino, California, Rare Books 8872.

the Caribbean, or sometimes to Spanish holdings more generally.[6] One need only consider Abraham Cowley's description of his mistress's body to realize that impoverished New England did not fit: "Mine too her rich *West-Indies* were below, / Where *Mines* of gold and endless treasures grow."[7] If Jessey had described New England as part of the West Indies in his title alone the phrase would not be worth remarking, but he insists on the description throughout the tract, including in the postscript, which reprises these earlier mission tracts: *Day-Breaking, if not the Sun-Rising of the Gospel* (1647), *Clear Sun-shine of the Gospell* (1648), and *Glorious Progress of the Gospel* (1649). Jessey edits and condenses elements of these pamphlets to fit his publication. At times he simply rewrites the originals so that they

6. Histories of the world in this period lumped New England, Virginia, Florida, and the Caribbean under the term "West Indies." So does Edward Philips's dictionary, *The New World of English Words* (London, 1658), but publications specific to New England or to the English cause in the Americas make a distinction between New England and the West Indies—and the New England colonists themselves insisted in the division.

7. Abraham Cowley, "Leaving Me and Then Loving Many," in *Poems Written by A. Cowley* (London, 1656), lines 15–16.

suggest that the term "West Indian" is claimed by New Englanders themselves. He inserts it twice into the title of the New England tract *Glorious
Progress of the Gospel,* once on the introductory page to his postscript, and
once on the title page reproduced in the body of the postscript. Whereas
the original main title is "The Glorious Progress of the Gospel, Amongst
the Indians in New England," Jessey renders the title as "The Glorious
Progresse of the Gospell, amongst the (West-) Indians in New-England."
He also changes the original tract's discussion of the progress of Christianity
in New England so that it appears that colonists see themselves as working
in a "West Indian" mission field. In the original, Eliot contrasts "Southern
Indians" on Martha's Vineyard with "our Western Indians" on the mainland,
whom he presents as more pious. Jessey cuts the reference to "Southern"
Indians so that Eliot's reference to "Western Indians" feels more like naming
and less like geographic relativism. And throughout passages written in his
own voice, Jessey consistently names Indians in New England "western."[8]

This forced symmetry matching New England's "West Indians" to
Formosa's "East Indians" might seem just a rhetorical tic. But the historical
context of Jessey's tract suggests something more is at stake. In 1650, the
date of publication, Cromwell was considering whether to seek expansion
of English rule beyond the British Isles—including Ireland, which he had
invaded and conquered in 1649. In the late 1640s and early 1650s Cromwell
was encouraged to launch a parallel invasion and conquest of New Spain. I
see the repeated westering of New England Indians in Jessey's tract as a
tactic that associates New England's settler-colonial evangelism (which
Jessey supported spiritually, politically, and financially) with the increasing
interest at midcentury in expanding England's power into New Spain. In
this way Jessey, a friend to New England both personally and theologically,
articulates a strategy for judging New England's continued relevance in the
tumultuous years of the 1650s.[9]

If Jessey made note of the potential marginalization of New England by
Cromwell's foreign policies, New England could not avoid responding to
these developments, at its doorstep as it were. Although John Winthrop
had preached in his 1630 sermon "A Modell of Christian Charitie" that the
eyes of the world were upon the colonists, in the 1640s during the Civil
Wars England's attention had been on events at home. Now that the king
was dead and the Commonwealth established, attention could once again
be paid to "foreign" as well as "domestic" concerns. As events played out,

8. Jessey, *Of the Conversion,* B4v, 14, 13, 34.
9. On Cromwellian era foreign policy see Carla Pestana, *The English Atlantic in an Age of
Revolution, 1640–1661* (Cambridge, MA: Harvard University Press, 2007), and Steven Pincus,
Protestantism and Patriotism: Ideologies and the Making of English Foreign Policy, 1650–1668
(Cambridge: Cambridge University Press, 1996).

the Bay Colony was increasingly positioned as peripheral to more important concerns.[10] Thomas Gage counseled Cromwell that New England was
no going concern but mere colonial "drosse." In 1656, Cromwell even commissioned an agent, Daniel Gookin, to encourage New Englanders to consider moving to Jamaica to shore up English control there. The commission
empowered Gookin to offer ships, land, farm animals, and military protection to any who would remove forthwith to Jamaica, "it being his Highness
Pleasure that the work of Transporting should be begun before the end of
September next."[11]

Given this context, Jessey's tract ingeniously and disingenuously promotes New England's mission as already having established a foothold in
the West Indies: there will be no need to divert populace or money from
New England. His tract suggests that colonists there are already competing
with Catholic Spain for colonial control of West Indian bodies and souls,
and they're winning. In the appendix to the original edition of *Glorious
progress,* John Dury also hints at this understanding. Like Jessey, he makes
praying Indians "Western": "the Gospel in its advancement amongst these
Western Indians, appears to be *not in word only* (as it was by the *Spaniards*
among their Indians) *but also in power, and in the Holy Ghost, and in much
assurance.*"[12] Later mission tracts produced by colonists similarly take this
tack and position New England as already accomplishing Cromwell's goals,
successfully countering Spain's influence on the Natives of the West Indies.
Jessey's is an extended use of such rhetoric.[13]

This reasoning can help us understand the element of Jessey's title that
seems most risible today, the inflated-sounding number of Dutch conversions in Formosa, at once hyperbolic and specific—some 5,900 souls saved.

10. Many in New England agreed with this assessment—or fought against it. See Andrew
Delbanco, *The Puritan Ordeal* (Cambridge, MA: Harvard University Press, 1989), and
Theodore Bozeman, *To Live Ancient Lives: The Primitivist Dimension in Puritanism* (Chapel Hill:
University of North Carolina Press, 1988) on colonial self-perception in the 1630s and 1640s
as well as the crisis of identity experienced during the English Civil Wars. In *Dry Bones and
Indian Sermons,* I argue that the New England mission effort was in part an attempt to find a new
purpose for the Bay Colony in midcentury concerns.

11. Oliver Cromwell, *To All Persons Whom These May Concern, in the Several Townes, and
Plantations of the United Colonies in New-England* (London, 1656). On Cromwell's recruitment
of New Englanders, see Karen Kupperman, *Providence Island, 1630–1641: The Other Puritan
Colony* (Cambridge: Cambridge University Press, 1995). In the end, Gookin's mission to encourage emigration from New England to Jamaica failed, and he remained in the Bay Colony,
eventually becoming superintendent of the Algonquian Christians whose conversion the "Eliot
tracts" documented.

12. Edward Winslow, *The Glorious Progress of the Gospel Amongst the Indians in New England*
(London, 1649), 25. Although Jessey does not summarize Dury's appendix, he does recommend it to his readers.

13. On New England's response to the Western Design in mission tracts see Bross, *Dry
Bones and Indian Sermons,* 1–27.

Indeed, the tract later claims that some 17,000 are "affected." The numbers are similar to reports circulating in England of Spanish claims to mass conversions, and national competition was ratcheted up in 1648 with the publication of *The English-American* by Thomas Gage. The claim to mass Protestant conversions in Jessey's tract thus has contradictory overtones— the huge numbers claimed by Catholics were widely discredited by English writers but remained impressive and worrying nonetheless. Jessey tries to have it both ways in his tract. New England's converts appear to be well-informed and pious, though colonial writers could only report modest success. Worldwide, however, the mission efforts of Protestant churches were doing well, as is evidenced by the large numbers of converts in the East. In this way the main text, though given over to a report on Dutch evangelical success, doesn't celebrate a Dutch so much as a more generally Protestant response to the overwhelming Jesuit presence in the East Indies, even as the postscript serves as a pointed attempt to insert New England into England's anti-Catholic, anti-Spanish policies in the West Indies.

NETWORKS

One other element of the title page is significant to the tangle of beliefs and people I am teasing out in this chapter: it is studded with names that suggest that the text's power comes from its production within a network of radical— or at least heterodox—believers. Robert Junius, a Dutch-Scots missionary working in the Formosan mission field, Junius's "good friend" Casper Sibelius, who relates his success in a Latin letter, and Henry Jessey, who translates that letter and publishes the good news to English readers are all prominently mentioned, of course. But the title page also lists other individuals directly involved in the production of the tract: moderate Independent Joseph Caryl, who licensed the tract, publisher John Hammond and—most intriguing, as I will discuss—bookseller Hannah Allen. Of course, it is not unusual for seventeenth-century title pages to list publisher, bookseller, or licenser, but in this instance, these more formulaic citations add to the sense that this work belongs within and to an extensive Independent religious community.

Within the text itself we soon encounter more name dropping. Jessey describes himself as bowled over by the good news from Formosa, rushing about to find confirming witnesses. As Laura Stevens argues, we cannot understand this strange little tract without "understanding Jessey's position with Interregnum religious networks and beliefs."[14] Indeed, *Of the*

14. Stevens, *Poor Indians*, 73.

Conversion is remarkable in the degree to which networks—religious, political, and commercial—are registered both on the title page and within the
text. Through them, the tract constructs a global network of believers that
links Algonquian goodwives and reformed Formosan "enchantresses" to
Christians in the reformed religious communities of London.

Of the Conversion follows the pattern of other newsy mission tracts
emerging from the London presses at midcentury. The English mission
tracts were written ostensibly for a general audience and are a pastiche of
letters, narratives, and editorial statements, a polyvocality designed to overwhelm the reader with expertise and evidence. *Of the Conversion* contains
varied paratextual elements, multiple letters, and summaries of previous
publications. The tract is attributed to Casper Sibelius and to Jessey, but it is
clear that Jessey's hope for global Christianity is the controlling vision of
the work. Jessey was a nonconformist minister. Though a moderate—he
advocated open communion throughout his life—he was active in politics
and often came under official scrutiny. He was arrested several times for his
beliefs. He supported moves to readmit Jews to England because he believed that such a step would facilitate their conversion to Christianity—
prophesied to take place in conjunction with the millennium. Indeed,
he was an ardent millennialist, and his views are on full display in *Of the
Conversion*, which is of a piece with other of his writings, such as his extremely popular account of Sarah Wight's prophecies, *Exceeding Riches of
Grace*,[15] and the many calendars and almanacs that he published nearly
annually from the late 1640s until the early 1660s. Almost all of these
calendars and almanacs included an icon of Daniel's prophecy of the four
kingdoms that were to precede the establishment of the fifth monarchy,
Christ's own.

However certain Jessey is of his millennialist interpretation of events, in
Of the Conversion he recognizes the need to muster a cloud of witnesses to
testify to the accuracy of Dutch reports—and the witnesses are linked together by their connection to Jessey himself; there are few character-only
testimonials. Rather, as Stevens argues, "almost no one appears in the text
without connections drawn from him or her to Jessey and to other well-
known people."[16] Upon hearing reports of Robert Junius's mission success,
he excitedly bustles off to confirm the rumors: "I delayed not therefore to
goe to *Chelsey*," where Edward Cresset, formerly an ex-pat Englishman in

---

15. Jessey's account of Wight's speeches galvanized believers throughout the seventeenth
century. *Exceeding Riches* was immensely popular, going through seven editions before 1670
and reappearing in abridged editions in the late 1700s. See Carola Scott-Luckens, "Propaganda
or Marks of Grace? The Impact of the Reported Ordeals of Sarah Wight in Revolutionary
London, 1647–52," *Women's Writing* 9.2 (2002): 215–232.

16. Stevens, *Poor Indians*, 76.

Holland, resided. Finding his friend "providentially" away, Jessey records Mrs. Cresset's confirmation of the account: she "certified me as followeth; which I write downe."[17] In later correspondence with Edward Cresset, Jessey receives confirmation from an additional witness—Mr. Halhoad, who knew Junius in Delft. Halhoad contacts Junius on behalf of Cresset and Jessey and obtains from him a "Booke in *Latine*" describing the Formosan mission efforts, which Cresset then deposits with Lady Mayerne, also residing in Chelsea, to pass on to Jessey. There are more witnesses involved, and the requisite statement of apologies for publication: "It seems this M. *Junius* was willing that this so Glorious a Worke, that the Lord had done by him among these East-*Indians*, should rather be published by his good Friend."[18] Thus Jessey describes himself as following a labyrinthine path of information, witnessing, and reporting in order to determine the truth of the news that thousands of East Indians had been turned to the faith by Dutch efforts in Formosa. His descriptions of his research serve both to offer proofs to skeptical readers and—intentionally or not—to place him at the center of a personal and religious network of evangelism stretching around the world. That network included the linked group of Dutch, English, and expatriots who knew something first- or secondhand about Junius's work in Taiwan.

That the networks represented in the tract are not entirely religious, or rather, that in midcentury London the religious and the political are inextricable, is underscored by the appearance of Lady Mayerne, the woman to whom Junius's Latin missive is sent to pass on to Jessey. If we consider her appearance in the tract in light of the Independent religious context that most of the text is concerned with, she seems, as Stevens suggests, a "trivial" reference.[19] Indeed, it is hard to understand her appearance—surely the means by which Jessey received Junius's book has little to do with the main points of his work. On its face, Lady Mayerne's appearance in *Of the Conversion* seems a minor bit of name dropping. Lady Mayerne is Isabella Mayerne, the second wife of Theodore Mayerne, also named by Jessey, a well-connected French Huguenot physician.[20] He served as King James's doctor, and by the late 1640s and 1650s had thrown his lot in with Parliament.

But Isabella is significant to Jessey because she is Dutch. Born Isabella Joachini, she was the daughter of Albert Joachini, the Netherlands'

17. Jessey, *Of the Conversion*, A2v.

18. Jessey, *Of the Conversion*, A4r.

19. Stevens, *Poor Indians*, 76.

20. For details of the couples' life, see Hugh Trevor-Roper, "Mayerne, Sir Theodore Turquet de (1573–1655)," in *Oxford Dictionary of National Biography* (Oxford: Oxford University Press, 2004), http://www.oxforddnb.com/view/article/18430, accessed 6 November 2015.

ambassador to England. Theodore and Isabella would have been a well-known couple, certainly known to the well-connected readers Jessey most hoped to attract. When we consider Jessey's careful inclusion of so many details, so many names of supporters and means of verifying his arguments, we can see clearly that the pamphlet, far from being only a derivative work of mission ephemera, is a carefully constructed piece promoting England's place in the world. Its layers, epistolary, personal, theological, or other, are complex, but they add up to a cohesive argument. A complicated divine pattern is coming into focus. The conversion of the gentiles has truly begun, and prophecies of the end-times are being realized. At the same time the tract creates a coherent ethos for its editor-author, that of a figure with extensive global ties to the movers and shakers of God's divine plan.

The social network in which Henry Jessey is embedded is only one that we might use to make sense of the text; it is perhaps the easiest network to recognize, since literary historians are more accustomed to analyzing the author's biography as context for his publication. But *Of the Conversion* has no singular author. The pamphlet is catalogued under Jessey's name at times and at times Sibelius's, and even a cursory reading suggests the work's polyvocality, drawing as it does on previous publications and accounts from many sources. Jessey thematizes his personal network, so that network is a ready place to begin analyzing the work.

However, *Of the Conversion* can also be usefully read within the network of its bookseller, Hannah Allen. Allen comes into archival focus with the death of her husband in 1646. As a widow, Allen assumed control of the business and began printing and selling books under her own name. We can follow her as a printer and bookseller until 1650, when she freed her apprentice Livewell Chapman and married him. As male head of the business, his name appeared on subsequent imprints.

But during the time when Allen published under her own name, as Maureen Bell argues, the business took a discernibly radical religious turn.[21] She published a reprint of Thomas Brightman's millennial prophecies in 1647 and in 1650 printed Menasseh ben Israel's influential treatise *The Hope of Israel*. Moreover, whatever Henry Jessey's ties to New England, Allen's interest in the colonies is also tangible through her business decisions. Under her first husband's name, the Allen business published the *Capital Laws of Massachusetts* (1642) and the *Laws of New Haven Colony* (1656), and in 1653 the Allens held the initial copyright to the *Cambridge Platform of*

---

21. Maureen Bell provides the best treatment of Allen's work. See "Hannah Allen and the Development of a Puritan Publishing Business, 1646–51," *Publishing History* 26 (1989): 5–66.

Church Discipline.[22] Her list suggests close ties to New England. In 1647 she published both John Cotton's *Bloudy Tenent,* his reply to Roger Williams on issues of religious tolerance, and Cotton's *Singing of Psalms.* Certainly the Allens had reason to be sympathetic to the colonists' point of view. Benjamin Allen fled Laudian persecution and lived in Leiden from 1638 to 1641, and Hannah Allen's own booklist reveals her to be committed in her own right to the reformed religious cause, as well as to Parliamentarian politics and to millennial and Independent beliefs.[23] Perhaps these earlier publications led Edward Winslow to seek her out as publisher of the original 1649 mission tract *The Glorious Progress of the Gospel,* which Jessey summarizes in *Of the Conversion.* Indeed, it is not a stretch to imagine that Jessey first encountered *Glorious Progress* while browsing her shelves—checking on the sales of the second edition of *Exceeding Riches of Grace,* perhaps. It seems possible that she first introduced him to John Eliot and to the Algonquian Christians he describes in his letters. It seems quite possible that the mission tract fired his imagination and helped shape his fantasy of a worldwide Christian empire stretching from New England in the West to Formosa in the East.

Allen and Jessey ran in overlapping circles—their religious and professional lives had multiple points of contact. Consider the celebrated case of Sarah Wight. Wight was a young woman swept up in the religious fervor and foment of the 1640s. In 1647, she experienced a profound spiritual shock, one that left her completely paralyzed for a time and launched her as a prophet. Henry Jessey ministered to her, wrote down her words, and published an account of her trials in 1647: the wildly successful *Exceeding Riches of Grace Advanced by the Spirit of Grace, in an empty nothing creature.* Hannah Allen published that account and sold it in her bookshop. But Allen's involvement was not merely professional. She is listed among those who paid a visit to Sarah Wight's bedside (as did Lady Mayerne). Strictly speaking, the mutual interest of Allen and Jessey in Wight's prophecies does not belong to an analysis of *Of the Conversion.* But if we consider that *Exceeding Grace* and *Of the Conversion* are at the intersection of the overlapping spheres of the minister and the bookseller, we may be prompted to give more significance to the influence and significance of women in our reading of the midcentury mission report. The significance of Sarah Wight to both Jessey's and Allen's careers can shift our attention from a network of (primarily) influential men who executed and published the Indian

22. Hugh Amory, "British Books Abroad: The American Colonies," in *The Cambridge History of the Book in Britain,* vol. 4, *1557–1695,* ed. John Barnard and D. F. McKenzie (Cambridge: Cambridge University Press, 2002), 746.

23. Amory, "British Books Abroad," 746. Benjamin and Hannah Allen married in 1632, but I have not been able to determine whether she accompanied her husband to Leiden in 1638.

mission and to a consideration of the women who also participated in colonial evangelism.[24] Such a shift in perspective can bring Henry Jessey's careful attention in his narrative to Mrs. Cresset and Lady Mayerne into sharper
focus. *Exceeding Riches* is an early and prominent example of Jessey's ecumenical willingness to understand voices coming from unlikely sources—
including women—as prophetic, as harbingers of cosmic events. Indeed,
near the end of *Exceeding Riches*, he advises those who have not yet felt as
moved by the spirit as Sarah Wight to "pray for more pourings out of his
Spirit upon his sons and daughters, as he hath promised to do in the last
dayes," a reference to Acts 2:17.[25]

A "GOOD DEATH"

One such daughter, coexisting with Sarah Wight at the intersection of
Jessey's and Allen's spheres of interest and influence, is an Algonquian
woman who goes unnamed in the print archive. First introduced to English
readers in the original tract *Glorious Progress of the Gospel* in 1649, she becomes an important subject of Henry Jessey's revision of that tract, an
anchor to his fantasy of global conversion.

Sometime before 1647 in the Massachusetts Bay Colony, this woman
and her husband decided to join a New England community of recent converts to Christianity. Some of them had begun living together in the town of
Nonantum, and this couple found reason to move there also: perhaps they
had lost kinfolk in the several plagues that swept through Native communities since the English had come; perhaps the members of their families who
had survived the plagues had become "praying Indians," and this couple
wished to remain with them. Perhaps they had lost land to English settlers,
or felt that they soon would, and hoped to make land claims based on new
Christian identities. Perhaps they wished to enter the colonial economy
and knew that praying Indians were being given new tools and being taught
new skills. The latter possibility is likely at least a part of the reason they
joined the praying Indian movement; after her move, the woman supported
herself with traditional skills—she made and sold baskets—and with new
ones: she was given a spinning wheel and learned to use it. Then again,
perhaps the couple had heard the missionary John Eliot (known to his

24. I have discussed the women who made Indian evangelism possible, including the
unnamed Algonquian women I consider here, in "The Women of the New England Mission,"
paper presented at conference "London and the Americas 1492–1812," Society of Early
Americanists, Kingston University, London, 17–20 July 2014.
25. Henry Jessey, *Exceeding Riches of Grace Advanced by the Spirit of Grace in an Empty
Nothing Creature* (London, 1647), 158.

contemporaries and to subsequent generations of New Englanders as the "apostle to the Indians") or one of the new converts preaching and had simply felt their spirits incline to join the movement.

In any case, sometime before 1647, an Algonquian woman and her husband moved their belongings to the praying Indian town of Nonantum: "they fetched all the corne they spent, sixteen miles on their backs from the place of their planting."[26] And then, sometime in 1648 this woman, middle-aged, with several grown children, died from an infection contracted during the birth of another child. According to English mission literature, she made a proper deathbed speech—proper in that it adhered to the genre as it was being worked out by Puritans in old and new England—and then, away from the minister's gaze, she also called her adult children to her and admonished them to stay with the praying Indian community rather than returning to live with non-Christian relatives after her death.[27]

Something about her story was compelling to the English missionaries and their supporters who were busy exchanging their views across the Atlantic about Indian missions, English national identity, and God's cosmic plan for English and Native peoples alike.[28] John Eliot devoted considerable space to the woman's story in his letter to a well-wisher in England—so much so that he worried he was "too tedious in this Story."[29] John Dury, minister, millennialist, and agitator for religious toleration, found her story inspiring enough to single out in his commentary on New England's mission work, included as an appendix to *Glorious Progress*, in which Eliot's

---

26. Winslow, *Glorious Progress*, B3v.

27. For discussions of the deathbed confession genre, see Erik R. Seeman, *Pious Persuasions: Laity and Clergy in Eighteenth-Century New England* (Baltimore: Johns Hopkins University Press, 1999), and Bross, "Dying Saints, Vanishing Savages," chapter 7 in *Dry Bones and Indian Sermons*.

28. She goes unnamed in the mission literature, but Eliot tells us that she is the wife of Wampooas, whose life receives somewhat more attention in Eliot's writings. See Thomas Shepard, *Clear Sun-shine of the Gospel* (London, 1648), 6–7. See Linda Gregerson, "Commonwealth of the Word: New England, Old England, and the Praying Indian," in *Empires of God: Religious Encounters in the Early Modern Atlantic* (Philadelphia: University of Pennsylvania Press: 2010), 70–83, for an account of the connections the Indian mission made between Old and New England. A very short list of studies of the seventeenth-century New England mission includes Elise Brenner, "To Pray or to Be Prey: That Is the Question: Strategies for Cultural Autonomy of Massachusetts Praying Town Indians," *Ethnohistory* 27.2 (1980): 135–152; Cogley, *John Eliot's Mission to the Indians*; Dane Morrison, *A Praying People: Massachusett Acculturation and the Failure of the Puritan Mission, 1600–1690* (New York: Peter Lang, 1995); Kenneth M. Morrison, "'That Art of Coyning Christians': John Eliot and the Praying Indians of Massachusetts," *Ethnohistory* 21.1 (1974): 77–92; Robert James Naeher, "Dialogue in the Wilderness: John Eliot and the Indian Exploration of Puritanism as a Source of Meaning, Comfort, and Ethnic Survival," *New England Quarterly* 62.3 (1989): 346–368; Neal Salisbury, "Red Puritans," *William and Mary Quarterly*, 3rd ser., 31 (January 1974): 27–54; and David J. Silverman, *Faith and Boundaries: Colonists, Christianity, and Community among the Wampanoag Indians of Martha's Vineyard, 1600–1871* (New York: Cambridge University Press, 2005).

29. *Glorious Progress*, B4r.

letter first appeared. And Henry Jessey in turn found her story significant, worth retaining and even expanding in *Of the Conversion*. The colonial print archive thus contains several views of this Algonquian woman's life and death. Her story survives because, whatever her personal sorrows, hopes, and achievements, Englishmen understood it to be useful, confirmation of various, even competing, theological beliefs, millennial hopes, and political designs. The record of her "pious life and good death" affords us an unusual opportunity to trace the influence of one individual on the global fantasies of English evangelical literature.

A NEW ENGLAND THEME

John Eliot and Edward Winslow, both New England colonists, brought the woman's story to England in 1649, and the account recorded in his letter reprinted in *The Glorious Progress of the Gospel* establishes a colonial theme for metropolitan variations. John Eliot was minister to an English congregation at Roxbury, Massachusetts, but spent much of his life ministering as well to the praying Indians, whom he worked to settle in towns set aside for them throughout the Massachusetts Bay Colony.[30] Edward Winslow, a Plymouth Colony divine, was appointed New England's agent and came to London in 1646 to solicit support for the colonies. As part of this campaign, he published *The Glorious Progress of the Gospel*. Their combined gloss on the Algonquian woman's life and death demonstrates the pragmatic value the mission had for the colonies. In *Glorious Progress*, as in other New England mission tracts, Christian Indians are offered as evidence of the importance of colonization. They were meant to persuade English men and women to open their hearts and purses to support the colonies, and both writers contextualized their accounts of the woman's life and death with discussions of what observers in England should do to support the cause.

In his letter, dated 12 November 1648, Eliot writes that he has decided to report on the Algonquian woman's death because she "was the first of ripe yeares that hath dyed since I taught them the way of salvation" and "of the dead I may freely speak." He reports on her deathbed scene in brief: "*She told me she still loved God, though he made her sick, and was resolved to pray unto him so long as she lived, and to refuse powwawing. She said also, that she beleeved* [sic]*God would pardon all her sins, because she believed that Iesus*

---

30. For accounts of the New England mission and Eliot's role, see Bross, *Dry Bones and Indian Sermons*; Cogley, *John Eliot's Mission to the Indians*, and William Kellaway, *The New England Company, 1649–1776* (New York: Barnes & Noble, 1962).

*Christ dyed for her; and that God was well pleased in him, and that she was will-
ing to dye, and beleeved to goe to Heaven, and live happy with God and Christ
there."*[31] The reader, by evaluating her deathbed speech for orthodox beliefs,
had confirmation that Eliot's catechism was taking hold of those he taught.
In addition to her professions of belief about the saving power of Christ and
about God's mercy, a key component of her statement is the repudiation of
"powwowing," that is, of traditional healing practices, an element particular
to the deathbed confessions of Indian converts. Reports of the "good
deaths" of Indian converts regularly included this assertion that Christian
Indians would rather die than resort to "heathen" medicine, however effective.[32] That the woman eschews traditional medicine confirms Eliot's assertion, published in a previous tract, that "they have utterly forsaken all their
Powwaws, and given over that diabolicall exercise, being convicted that it is
quite contrary to praying to God."[33]

Here, Eliot paraphrases the woman's deathbed confession, but in the
next paragraph, he allows her to speak in her own words. She offers a "deathbed charge" to her children, another element that I have elsewhere identified as conventional for Indian dying speeches:

> When I am dead your Grand-Father and Grand-Mother and Unckles, &c. will send for you to
> come live amongst them, and promise you great matters, and tell you what pleasant living it is
> amongst them; But doe not beleeve them, and I charge you never hearken unto them, nor live
> among them; for they pray not to God, keep not the Sabbath, commit all manner of sinnes and
> are not punished for it: but I charge you live here, for here they pray unto God, the Word of God
> is taught, sins are suppressed, and punished by Lawes; And therefore I charge you live here all
> your dayes.[34]

His account does not describe her motivation in giving these instructions.
He claims that he learned of them only when her prophecy came to pass,
when the extended family, as expected, reached out to the young women,
and their stepfather brought the case to Eliot for counsel. Whatever her reasons, Eliot is careful to assure his readers that her instruction to her children
was her own idea. The shift in point of view is significant. By paraphrasing

31. Winslow, *Glorious Progress*, B3v.
32. In the same tract, Thomas Mayhew, ministering on Martha's Vineyard, tells a counter-
story of a "bad death" brought about because of traditional medicine. A man he calls Saul, who
when taken sick first consulted with Mayhew, seemed to be persuaded by his prayers, but later
"sought againe unto Witches." Mayhew sent word to Saul that because of his backsliding he
would follow the example of Ahaziah, "who because he had the knowledge of the great God,
and sought unto an inferiour God; God was angry with him, and killed him . . . and so it shortly
came to passe." Winslow, *Glorious Progress*, B2v.
33. Shepard, *Clear Sun-shine of the Gospel*, 18.
34. Winslow, *Glorious Progress*, B4r.

her deathbed confession, he implies that he is present in her final moments, actively ministering to her, and we can attribute her sound theology to him. By switching to the first person for the charge to her family and making it clear that he is not present at that scene, he implies that her desire for the family to continue in Nonantum is independent of her English minister. Thus, she supports Eliot's efforts to resettle Christian Indians in lands set aside for their use and to isolate them from "wild" Indians, a project Eliot describes in detail in the succeeding pages. The change in narrative style assures readers in England that praying Indians both are good Christians under the influence of sound ministers and are voluntarily choosing a "civilized life."

Eliot goes on to capitalize on the woman's "good death" by making it clear that if well-wishers in England approve of the mission and its results, as illustrated by what he calls the "exemplary" life of this woman, they must reach deep into their pockets to support efforts to evangelize and civilize.[35] In another letter included in *Glorious Progress*, Eliot writes to a "*Gentleman* of New-England" explaining that if the mission is to succeed, "it [is] absolutely necessary to carry on civility with Religion: and that maketh me have many thoughts that the way to doe it to the purpose, is to live among them in a place distant from the *English*, for many reasons; and bring them to cohabitation, Government, Arts, and trades: but this is yet too costly an enterprize for *New-England*, that hath expended itself so far in laying the foundation of a Common-weale in this wildernesse."[36] It is a canny presentation of his argument. Because this plan is addressed to a fellow colonist, readers are eavesdropping, as it were, on a discussion among colonial insiders.[37] The notion of New England exhausting itself in "laying the foundation of a Common-weale" makes the colonists' endeavor parallel to that of Parliamentarians charting the course of the rising Commonwealth, but because Eliot does not make a request for metropolitan funds, his words seems a simple self-description rather than a complaint. Eliot's role is that of eyewitness. It is up to Winslow, New England's agent in London, to make the direct appeal.

---

35. Winslow, *Glorious Progress*, B3r.

36. Winslow, *Glorious Progress*, 16.

37. Eliot also describes the project in another letter included in *Glorious Progress*, addressed to a recipient in London (likely Winslow himself). Although he mentions the expense in that letter as well, he leaves out any mention of New England establishing a "Common-weal": "a place must be found … some what remote from the English, where they must have the word constantly taught, and government constantly exercised, meanes of good subsistence provided, incouragements for the industrious, meanes of instructing them in Letters, Trades, and Labours, as building, fishing, Flax and Hemp dressing, planting Orchards, &c. Such a project in a fit place would draw many that are well minded together: but I feare it will be too chargeable" (B4r).

Indeed, Winslow, acting as the missionary's editor and the colonies' agent, is quick to follow Eliot's lead. His preface wastes little time in getting to the point. On the first page of *Glorious Progress*, he rehearses the legislative action that was sparked by the publication of the mission tract *Cleare Sun-shine of the Gospel* a year earlier: Parliament had taken note of the good work among the Indians in New England and had referred the matter to the Committee on Foreign Plantations. Parliament now had an act before it "for the Promoting and Propagating the Gospel of Jesus Christ in New England." The act would establish a corporation charged with raising and dispersing funds in support of New England's evangelism efforts.[38] Winslow uses *Glorious Progress* to urge its ratification. Like Eliot in his letter to his friend in New England, Winslow also suggests that there are parallels between the great work of Parliament and the more humble work of the colonies: "As God hath set a signall marke of his presence upon your Assembly, in strengthning your hands to redeem and preserve the civill Rights of the Common-weale: so doubtlesse may it be a comfortable support to your Honours in any future difficulties, to contemplate, that as the Lord offered you (in his designe) an happy opportunity to enlarge and advance the Territories of his Sonnes Kingdom: So he hath not denied you ... an heart to improve the same."[39] This is a remarkable passage, the references to current events subtle, yet clear. Political and theological concerns are completely imbricated. It even includes a veiled, threatening prophecy. The year of publication was 1649. Charles I had been executed in January that year. Winslow was in London, well aware of recent events and the anxious mood of even the most committed regicide. He begins with encouragement: God had strengthened Parliamentarians to "preserve the civill rights of the Common-weal"; the House of Commons had followed the king's execution with acts to ensure that there would be no royal successor and that a representative government would be the ultimate authority in England.[40] In an echo of Eliot's letter to his fellow colonist, Winslow parallels these political

---

38. For a discussion of the New England mission's links to the metropole and especially of Parliament's support of the mission, see Gregerson, "Commonwealth of the Word."

39. Winslow, *Glorious Progress*, A4v.

40. The House of Commons passed in short order an act making it treasonous to declare a successor to King Charles (30 January 1649), an act establishing a counsel of state for the Commonwealth (13 February 1649) and an act abolishing the "Kingly office" in March, stating that "it is and hath been found by experience, that the Office of a King in this Nation and Ireland, and to have the power thereof in any single person, is unnecessary, burthensom and dangerous to the liberty, safety and publique interest of the people." The act to support New England's missions was passed 27 July 1649. These acts are collected in C.H. Firth and R. S. Rait, eds., *Acts and Ordinances of the Interregnum, 1642–1660* (1911), British History Online, University of London and History of Parliament Trust, 2009, http://www.british-history.ac.uk/Default.aspx, accessed 16 July 2009.

actions with mission work in New England—as Parliamentarians are establishing Christ's kingdom (as opposed to the corrupt kingdom of Charles I) in England, so too are New Englanders expanding Christ's territories into the colonies.

The most surprising moment in this passage, however, has to do with potential failure rather than celebration. If Parliament's more worldly ends are frustrated, if England encounters "future difficulties," Winslow suggests, they will always be able to draw comfort from their support for the propagation of the Gospel in New England, an apolitical, enduring, divinely inspired effort. While the phrase "future difficulties" is appealingly vague and low-key, its import could not have been lost on readers. Winslow is addressing avowed regicides: their "future difficulties," should the political wheel turn again, would include imprisonment, arrest, and execution as traitors.[41] It is perhaps a stretch to see Winslow here as offering actual refuge in New England should the Commonwealth fail, but several of the men who passed judgment on Charles I would indeed fly to the colonies for safety after the Restoration.[42] Whether or not Winslow foresaw such events, this passage demonstrates that as a colonial agent, he wished to be cautious, and to anchor the colonial mission effort in cosmic rather than temporal events, even as he appealed for concrete, worldly support.

METROPOLITAN VARIATIONS

Winslow was a savvy observer of events and ideas in London, and he touches on the more enthusiastic discussions of Native Americans then circulating among metropolitan observers: "There are two great questions…which have troubled ancient and modern writers….what became of the ten Tribes of Israel… [and] what Family, Tribe, Kindred or people it was that first planted, and afterward filled that vast and long unknown Countrey of America?"[43] Winslow's two questions frame a theological debate about the identity of Native Americans and the role they were to

41. Of course, several of the men who presided over the trial and execution of Charles I were hung, drawn, and quartered as traitors.

42. On the regicides in New England, see Mark Sargent, "Thomas Hutchinson, Ezra Stiles, and the Legend of the Regicides," *William and Mary Quarterly* 49.3 (1992): 431–448, and Lemuel Welles, *The History of the Regicides in New England* (New York: Grafton Press, 1927).

43. Winslow, *Glorious Progress*, A3r. Eliot would go on to become an ardent millennialist and subscribe to the theory that Indians were members of the lost tribes of Israel, but, as I argue in *Dry Bones and Indian Sermons*, his fellow colonists were not as eager to embrace these theories. His most aggressive print articulation of his views, which included clear antimonarchical sentiments, was published in 1659, just before the Restoration. He recanted his views at that point, and the book was burned.

play in the end-times. The debate turned on whether Indians were gentiles or Jews. If gentiles, their conversion was laudable, just as the saving of any English soul was to be desired. If Jews, however, their conversion was potentially earth shattering. Millenarians read scripture as prophesying a general, worldwide conversion, but more specifically, they believed that the conversion of Jews would accompany the particular historic moment of the Second Coming, which many believed would occur at midcentury. Monumental events such as the execution of Charles I and the establishment of the Commonwealth seemed to confirm that the end-times were imminent. If it could be proven that "Jews in America" (as one tract was titled) were becoming Christians, it would be an important sign that Brightman was right.[44] Winslow, of course, was familiar with these predictions and speculations, and although he himself offered further evidence that such theories might be correct, noting especially the "juncture of time" between Indian conversions and calculations about the date for the end-times conversion of the Jews, he hedged: "I confesse questions are sooner asked than resolved."[45]

Compare his measured enthusiasm with that of another contributor to *Glorious Progress*, the ecumenical theologian John Dury, who wrote a rather breathless appendix to the tract. Dury began by stating his agreement with those divines who were convinced that Brightman's prophecy of imminent end-times events was being fulfilled: "The palpable and present acts of providence, doe more then [*sic*] hint the approach of Jesus Christ: and the Generall consent of many judicious, and godly Divines, doth induce *considering minds* to beleeve, that the conversion of the Jewes is at hand."[46] Next, he wrote that he was convinced that Indians were Jews: "the serious consideration of the preceding Letters, induceth me to think, that there may be at least a remnant of the *Generation of Jacob* in *America* (peradventure some of the 10. Tribes dispersions)."[47] Their conversion in New England thus supported millenarian speculation. The logic of the proof was straightforward:

44. Thomas Thorowgood, *Iewes in America* (London, 1649).
45. Winslow, *Glorious Progress*, A4r, A3v. On millennial beliefs in this period, see Katz, *Philo-Semitism*; Bernd Engler, Joerg O. Fichte, and Oliver Scheiding, "Transformations of Millennial Thought in America," introduction to *Millennial Thought in American: Historical and Intellectual Contexts, 1630–1860*, ed. Bernd Engler, Joerg O. Fichte, and Oliver Scheiding (Trier: Wissenschaftlicher Verglad Trier, 2002), 9–37; and J. F. Maclear, "New England and the Fifth Monarchy: The Quest for the Millennium in Early American Puritanism," *William and Mary Quarterly*, 3rd ser., 32.2 (April 1975): 223–260.
46. Winslow, *Glorious Progress*, D3v. Dury had met with Manasseh ben Israel in 1644. See Tudor Parfitt, *The Lost Tribes of Israel: The History of a Myth* (London: Phoenix, 2002), 74–77. See also Kenneth Gibson, "John Dury's Apocalyptic Thought," *Journal of Ecclesiastical History* 61.2 (April 2010): 299–313.
47. Winslow, *Glorious Progress*, D3v.

the Bible tells us that Christ's return will be accompanied by the conversion
of Jews. All the signs indicate that Indians are Jews, and lo, here is proof of
their conversion. Ergo, the Second Coming is upon us!

Although Dury says that he himself is convinced that the end-times are
nigh, he recognizes that such beliefs are controversial. Nonetheless, he asserts, the reports from New England should be received with gladness by
even the most skeptical Christian reader, who can agree simply that "*the
work of God among the Indians in America, is glorious.*"[48] At this point in the
appendix, he turns away from high-flying theological speculation to a more
immediate understanding of the praying Indians' significance. Here we get
a hint of the reasons for his own interest in the Algonquian woman and her
dying speech. He too is lobbying Parliament for ratification of the act to
support New England evangelism, and he notes that "as Ministers, so
Statists do finde personall examples, the most powerfull motives to practick
doctrines."[49] He seems to be offering both a description of his rhetorical
practice and advice for ministers and "statists" who will subsequently join
him in advocating for the New England mission: find a real convert who can
drive your point home.

Dury may have understood himself to be using Christian Indians as
"personal examples" to achieve practical ends, but a closer look at his appendix suggests that the Algonquian woman has a more important place in
his remarks. For several pages, he lists, in good plain style, the many pieces
of evidence regarding praying Indians' divine role that he has derived from
the colonial letters included in the main body of the tract. When he turns at
last to the woman's dying speech, he spends nearly as much time on it as on
all the preceding anecdotes, presenting a five-point explication of her testimony. He then goes on to apply the example of godly Indians, most especially the unnamed woman, to English readers, castigating them for hypoc-
risy and lukewarm faith. In essence, she becomes the text of a sermon that
he delivers. He notes her speech, "opens" it with his five points, just as a
sermon opens scripture, and then suggests its uses for his readers. (A marginal note usefully identifies this section as the "application," as in countless
printed sermons.) Among the applications for Dury's readers is his direction to the "*heads of our Tribes in Old England*" to pass the "Act for the
Promoting and Propagating the Gospel of Jesus Christ in New England."
Thus the woman's story has been altered from a simple anecdote of Indian
godliness, attested to by colonial eyewitnesses, to a sermon text made to
provide lessons not for Native colonial subjects in New England but for

---

48. Winslow, *Glorious Progress*, D4v.
49. Winslow, *Glorious Progress*, E2r.

Parliamentarians and for (other) "apostate," but still important, English readers in London and throughout the Commonwealth.[50]

I have been reading Dury's version of the Algonquian woman's story as "metropolitan" rather than "colonial," but perhaps, like Winslow's, Dury's interpretation is better classified as in-between. After all, he was recruited by colonial agents to write his appendix, and it is clear that he read the reports from New England carefully and followed them closely as he prepared his gloss on colonial experiences. For a more purely metropolitan viewpoint, we must return to the version produced by Henry Jessey and published in the 1650 tract *Of the Conversion of Five Thousand and Nine Hundred East*. In this version, Jessey extends and intensifies the metropolitan trend toward radical theological interpretation that we see in Dury's treatment.

Although I term his point of view "metropolitan," Jessey had close ties to New England. He was a friend of Massachusetts governor John Winthrop. He seriously considered emigrating himself and made monetary donations to the Massachusetts mission. In *Of the Conversion*, he clearly sought to forward his friends' efforts, offering them, as Richard Cogley puts it, "free publicity."[51] He was also a Cromwellian, working to establish "respectable nonconformity" during the Interregnum.[52] Despite these credentials, fairly orthodox for the Interregnum, Jessey was also a Baptist, a millennialist, and a philo-Semite.[53] His diverse interests mark this publication, and as a consequence it also rereads and re-presents New England mission writings in ways that may not have made their original authors or their colonial allies entirely comfortable. The New England minister Thomas Shepard, for instance, was willing to allow mission reports to feed the religious fantasies of metropolitan supporters; important supporters such as Jessey could greatly further New England's cause. But his own contributions to mission literature were skeptical on the point of the Jewish origins of Indians. Dury's and especially Jessey's excitement about the possibility are in marked contrast to many colonial writings.[54]

The tract's most significant break with previous mission publications lies in its treatment of the Algonquian woman whom John Eliot first introduced to English readers in 1649, in a treatment in line with Jessey's early publications. In *Of the Conversion* Jessey rewrites the spiritual example of the

---

50. Winslow, *Glorious Progress*, E2r.

51. Cogley, *John Eliot's Mission to the Indians*, 207.

52. The phrase is Murray Tolmie's, quoted in David S. Katz, "Menasseh Ben Israel's Christian Connection: Henry Jessey and the Jews," in Kaplan et al., *Menasseh ben Israel and His World*, 117–138.

53. See Katz, "Menasseh ben Israel's Christian Connection."

54. For a discussion of Shepard's skepticism (especially as compared to Eliot's beliefs), see Bross, *Dry Bones and Indian Sermons*, 13, 31–32.

unnamed Indian woman as conveyed to him by his colonial sources into a first-person account that offers readers a pattern for their own faith and a confirmation of the millennial expectations suggested by his title page and choice of scriptural proof text. Jessey's alterations to Eliot's original suggest that he sees her testimony as of a piece with the experiences of Sarah Wight and other radical believers to whom he ministered in London.

As I have shown, when Eliot presented the unnamed woman's experiences, he did so initially by paraphrasing her: *"She told me she still loved God, though he made her sick, and was resolved to pray unto him so long as she lived, and to refuse powwawing."* Compare his version to the same moment in Jessey's rendition: *"she said, I still love God, though he made me sick. I resolve to pray to him, whilst I live: and no Pawaw.—I beleeve [sic] God will pardon all my sins, because Iesus Christ died for me: and God is well pleased in him. I am willing to die, I shall goe to Heaven, and live happily with God and Christ there."*[55] Whereas Eliot's version emphasized his mediating role, Jessey renders this moment as an example of the women's religious agency. She speaks for herself, the repeated, insistent "I" making her voice especially strong. The changes Jessey has made in his account of the woman seem intentional and unusual. In contrast to this instance of clear editorial interference, Jessey leaves most of the speeches that Eliot reports elsewhere as they originally appeared, changing third to first person in just a couple of instances. By changing her testimony to first person, Jessey drops Eliot's construction of it as confirmation of his own influence. Instead, the woman is presented as speaking in her own voice and testifying to her own faith just as any good Protestant experiencing an "easy death" should do.

As noted, Eliot describes her deathbed charge to her children as focused on keeping her family within the bounds of English authority. He reports that acting on her own she warns her daughters against the blandishments of their relatives and charges them to remain in Nonantum. By contrast, in Jessey's version the emphasis is on her personal beliefs and experiences: "Before her *Death*, she called her up-growne Daughters, with her other Children, and said to them; *I shall now die; Then your Grand-father, and Grand-mother, and Unckles,—will send for you, to come back to live there, and promise you much.—But I charge you, never goe; for they pray not to God, nor keep Sabbath: sinne, and not punished, etc."*[56] Here, whereas Eliot's version puts the most weight on the protoreservations of the praying Indian towns (in Eliot's version she says *"here* they pray unto God"), all emphasis is on the sinfulness of her extended family. The effect is a focus on the dying woman— she prays, keeps the Sabbath, subjects herself to church discipline—rather

55. Winslow, *Glorious Progress*, 27.
56. Winslow, *Glorious Progress*,

than on Eliot's work, with an immediacy not fully realized in the original publication, an immediacy that may have appealed especially to the readers who had made Jessey's earlier account of a prophetic woman so popular.

It is important to recognize this context because it points to the ways the description of Algonquians in colonial writings produced a flexible discursive figure who would be put to use by Englishmen with varied goals.[57] In Eliot's original version, he takes pains to demonstrate that the Algonquian woman's behavior was strictly according to English gender norms. As Eliot would have it, she was eager from the first to inhabit a proper gender role, willingly silencing herself in public. In addition to her deathbed scene, he offers one other anecdote from her Christian life. At a meeting, she joins a number of converts posing "spiritual questions" to Eliot. Although she stands out—she was "the first woman that asked a question," her behavior is unexceptional: she finds a way to stay silent in public; the question was "by another man propounded for her." Both the method of questioning and the content of the question reveal her willingness to subject herself to male authority: *"When my Husband prayeth in his house, my heart thinketh what he prayeth; whether is this praying to God aright or no?"* Eliot approves: "I thought it a fit question for a woman."[58] Jessey cuts this detail, and his treatment of her, unlike the pictures of a quiet, safely orthodox women that Eliot paints, makes her something else—someone Eliot would not have recognized, nor perhaps even the woman herself. By giving the Algonquian woman a strong, even unique voice in the New England mission, Jessey offers his readers more evidence of the "powerings out of his Spirit upon his sons and daughters" that they had encountered in his *Exceeding Riches*. If this American daughter is not exactly prophesying, she is certainly speaking publicly and forcefully of Christ and salvation. And by including her voice—directly quoted—Jessey extends his fantasy of a global network of faith to the "West Indians" whose Christian profession is, he believes, a concrete sign of an imminent Christian global empire.

57. I argue elsewhere that the treatment of praying Indian women generally in the original New England mission tracts was meant to assure English readers that Native women proselytized by New Englanders were safely orthodox. *Dry Bones and Indian Sermons,* 107–109; 135–137.
58. Winslow, *Glorious Progress,* B3v.

Coda: A Nonantum Life

Consideration of English uses of the Algonquian woman's story shows how important Native figures could be to debates over the most significant events of the time, from regicide to imperialism, to millennialism, and even to individual ministries. Yet, however valuable these accounts are to our understanding of the transatlantic English community, they offer no direct reflection of their subject's own experiences. The problem, of course, is to recover any sense of those experiences through such heavily mediated accounts. Indeed, on the face of it, there seems little more to glean from the printed accounts of this woman's testimony than the facts of her move to Nonantum and her death in 1648.

Yet the print Archive that encodes various English interpretations of her life bears the traces of at least one other key version of her story. The publication of the story of her life and death, although produced and preserved by the Englishmen whom it served, nevertheless mediated the story she herself crafted. At most we can but speculate about that version of her experiences, but if we broaden our definition of the colonial Archive to include material as well as print culture, there are clues to suggest that even as she was afforded a significant place in the English religious world as it was described in the mission tracts, the woman saw her praying life and deathbed speech as a sign of the persistence of her local community and of the emergence of praying Indian towns as "Indian places" in that world.[59] Eliot's accounts give us one more important detail of her life: she makes and sells baskets. This fact suggests that if we are to know anything—or even just to speculate about—the woman's own sense of her conversion and removal to Nonantum, we need to go beyond the print Archive for clues.

We know that Indian women used their traditional skills as basket makers as part of their bid to become members of the colonial economic system, adapting their technologies to new markets.[60] In 1671, Daniel Gookin notes the basket making practices among praying Indians: "Some of their baskets are made of rushes; some of bents, others of maize husks; others of a kind of silk grass; others, of a kind of wild hemp; and some of barks of trees; many of them, very neat and artificial, with the portraiture of

59. I borrow the phrase "Indian place" from Jean O'Brien's study of the praying Indian town of Natick, *Dispossession by Degrees: Indian Land and Identity in Natick, Massachusetts, 1650–1790* (Lincoln: University of Nebraska Press, 2003).

60. For accounts of basket making in this period see Ann McMullen and Russell G. Handsman, eds., *A Key into the Language of Woodsplint Baskets* (Washington, CT: American Indian Archaeological Institute, 1987); and Laurel Thatcher Ulrich, *The Age of Homespun: Objects and Stories in the Creation of an American Myth* (New York: Knopf, 2001).

birds, beasts, fishes, and flowers, upon them in colours."[61] His description is tantalizing; what might the "artificial"—"artful"—decoration of such baskets have communicated to their makers, to others in the community, to their purchasers? The meaning of such basketry design is, in Native American studies scholar Stephanie Fitzgerald's words, "imbued with cultural and spiritual power."[62] We can even see in the print Archive the recognition by colonists of that power, albeit only in a limited way. John Eliot recounts an attempt to "read" a basket within a Christian missionary context, despite the fact that he is functionally illiterate when it comes to traditional signification practices. In response to a question about whether God could understand converts who prayed in their native language, Eliot reports, "wee bid them looke upon that *Indian* Basket that was before them, there was black and white strawes, and many other things they made it of, now though others did not know what those things were who made not the Basket, yet hee that made it must needs tell all things in it."[63] Importantly, this basket and its design are understood as *Indian,* and a uniquely *Indian* meaning is assumed by Eliot, but this meaning is elided as he "translates" the text of the basket into a parable for potential converts.

We cannot examine a basket of this woman's design or manufacture. Just a few Algonquian baskets have survived since the seventeenth century. Nevertheless, the fact that this woman made and sold baskets has the potential to tell us something new about her, the potential to alter our understanding of her deathbed confession and her participation in the transatlantic discourse I have been tracing. Even though none of her work survives, we know that she created texts with meanings that could not be fully contained by Eliot or the colonial print Archive. Not that colonial writers didn't try: Eliot mentions the woman's basket making ability—along with her willingness to spin—because it makes clear her membership in the colonial labor economy. In the tracts, he regularly touts his converts' ability to do hard, English-style work, contrasting them with "lazy" traditionalists. But basket making, like beading and wampum making, has an important cultural as well as practical meaning, and has been an important signing practice for Native woman. Even if we cannot make positive statements about the meaning encoded in her particular basket designs, the fact that she made them, coupled with the provocative arguments offered by recent scholars of

61. Daniel Gookin, *Historical Collections of the Indians in New England* (Boston: Apollo Press, 1792), Nineteenth Century Collections Online, accessed 22 March 2017, 11.

62. Stephanie Fitzgerald, "The Cultural Work of a Mohegan Painted Basket," in *Early Native Literacies in New England,* ed. Kristina Bross and Hilary Wyss (Amherst: University of Massachusetts Press, 2008), 84.

63. *Day-breaking, if not the sun-rising of the Gospell with the Indians in New-England* (London, 1647), 5.

Native material culture in the colonial period, allows us to reconsider the print Archive in which she appears.

We know that other baskets from the colonial period encoded references to colonialism, traditional spirituality, tribal histories, and politics. For instance, Ann MacMullen and Stephanie Fitzgerald analyze space and place in Mohegan basket designs of the early nineteenth century.[64] Although their conclusions differ, they agree that these baskets often represent the Peoples' migration—originary, cyclical, or forced. Could this woman, though she created her baskets decades earlier than the Mohegan women MacMullen and Fitzgerald consider, likewise have represented her own or her community's recent history, particularly their move to Nonantum? Christian converts were most readily drawn from badly splintered tribes and displaced families. Praying Indian towns were attractive because they could consolidate remnant families and help survivors form new connections.[65] A few years after the woman's death, men in Natick registered in their Christian confessions their attachment to that praying Indian town—indeed, quite often they explained that their decision to convert to Christianity was initially driven by their love of the place where they lived and their hope that conversion would allow them to remain.

Eliot tells us that when this woman and her family moved to Nonantum, they traveled sixteen miles with their goods and provisions on their backs. Given the effort she spent to get to Nonantum and her interest in and willingness to commit herself to the praying life, it should come as no surprise that she enjoined her children to respect her decision and remain with the praying Indian community. But it is perhaps too easy to read this as colonial ventriloquism on the part of the missionaries, as a statement about her dependence on or belief in Eliot and his message. Rather than only focusing on her concern with God's law, our recognition that the designs she created for her baskets may have included representations of Native lands, spaces, and movement can direct our attention to the repetition of her directions to her children: "*I charge you live here…I charge you live here all your dayes.*" While Eliot interprets her emphasis on Nonantum as an example of her thoroughgoing conversion to English mores and Christian rule, it may be that her deathbed charge to her daughters—her grown daughters by a first husband, a charge delivered out of the hearing of the English missionary—

64. As I read the significance of the woman's basket making, I'm extending arguments made about later Mohegan baskets to a woman in an earlier time and different place, but I think such speculation is possible because praying Indian town residents were drawn from several tribes, and their baskets likely did not have a unique style, at least not as the movement came together. See Fitzgerald, "Cultural Work of a Mohegan Painted Basket," Ulrich, *Age of Homespun*, and McMullen and Handsman, *Key into the Language of Woodsplint Baskets*, especially the essay by Ann McMullen, "Looking for People in Woodsplint Basketry Decoration."

65. See Morrison, *Praying People*.

has to do with her interest in Nonantum as a new Indian place.[66] As much as Eliot wants to see her life and death as adhering to conventional English norms, her desire for her daughters to remain in Nonantum (and her husband's desire to see her dying wish fulfilled) may not have been the expressions of piety that Eliot imagined them to be. We would do well to remember that among coastal Algonquian peoples women could traditionally hold positions of both political and religious authority.[67] Perhaps the woman's desire that her children remain in Nonantum reflects her establishment of a new matrilineal social structure, one that was not as well understood by her English missionary interpreters as it would have been by her neighbors in Nonantum's pan-Indian community, drawing as they would have on various traditions of women sachems and female agricultural practices that knit women to the land in particular ways.[68]

The few baskets that survive from the seventeenth century seem to point to women's spaces in the colonial world, though the archival evidence is apocryphal. A basket at the Rhode Island Historical Society was donated in 1842, along with a label explaining that it had been made by a "squaw, a native of the forest," to give to Dinah Fenner in exchange for milk. The basket was passed down, mother to daughter, until it came to the Historical Society.[69] The Connecticut Historical Society holds another small basket. Its eMuseum catalog description of object number 1842.4.1, "Yohicake Bag," identifies it as Mohegan, c. 1650, and includes a story from the donor parallel to that of the Rhode Island basket: "The donor purchased it in the 1840s from Mohegans living in the Norwich area, and supplied the following story: 'Yohcake Basket—A bag or basket so termed by the Mohegans— received from Cynthia, now 60 or 70 & daughter of Lucy Tecunwass the first member of the Mohegan Church.'"[70]

---

66. Eliot's emphasis on the "here" of Nonantum, I'm suggesting, was also her emphasis. Though they had different reasons, both colonial actors (Eliot and the woman) were interested in establishing Nonantum as a place of significance.

67. See Kathleen Bragdon, *Indians of Southern New England, 1500–1650* (Norman: University of Oklahoma Press, 1996), chapters 3 and 6; and chapter 3 in her later book with a similar title, *Indians of Southern New England, 1650–1775* (Norman: University of Oklahoma Press, 2009).

68. See Bragdon, *Indians of Southern New England, 1500–1650*, chapter 2. In the charge to her daughters that Eliot records, the woman worries that her daughters will be importuned by their grandmother in addition to their grandfather and uncles. Moreover, the woman must have understood by this time that the English would allow only men as authorities among the praying Indians, and so she emphasizes their imagined responses to her death. My speculation is not meant to establish some kind of utopian, early feminist consciousness on her part but to suggest alternatives to Eliot's interpretation of her speech.

69. The label is quoted in Ulrich, *Age of Homespun*, 42.

70. "Yohicake Bag," Connecticut Historical Society, http://emuseum.chs.org/emuseum/ view/objects/asitem/search$0040/0/title-ask?t:state:flow=d71b107e-95ba-4e9e-900f-04af- bb5eeed3, accessed 14 March 2017.

Archival documents stress just how rare and significant these baskets are. The Connecticut Historical Society describes its "extremely important woven bag," identifying it (mistakenly) as the "sole surviving example of seventeenth-century native textiles, other than fragments found in graves."[71] A poster advertising an exhibit at the Rhode Island Historical Society teases: "Two native Algonkian baskets from the 17th century exist in the world. Encounter one of them for just one evening."[72] And the accession for a third basket, held by the Heritage Museums and Gardens in Sandwich, Massachusetts, includes Sarah Peabody Turnbaugh's note that their basket "truly is very scarce and valuable."[73] Laurel Thatcher Ulrich argues that twining techniques used in the baskets' construction "link all . . . to ancient American textiles." And the incorporation of wool fibers in the decoration show the baskets to be embedded in the colonial economy within which the makers subsisted. The materiality of these baskets, she argues, "transforms an apocryphal story" of their archival documentation "into a powerful lens for understanding exchange relations in the first century of English settlement."[74] Similarly, contextualizing the story of the unnamed woman in the print archives of the New England mission with her work as a basket maker (rather than the other way around) allows us to speculate on an alternative description of her experiences to those fantasized by Eliot, Winslow, Dury, and Jessey.

The fact that the woman made baskets may suggest one reason why she felt Nonantum was a good place to live. Ulrich notes that the Rhode Island basket was made from bark, stripped and soaked, from husks, perhaps gathered from "abandoned field," and from "fragments of red and blue wool."[75] Nonantum was situated near the Charles River, where she would have been able to find materials and a ready supply of water. Eliot and other colonial authorities encouraged members of the praying Indian towns to practice English-style agriculture, so fields would have surrounded the settlement. And of course, Eliot regularly distributed English clothing in his bid to "civilize" those who became Christian—one wonders what were his thoughts if he witnessed this woman receiving his gifts of clothing, some of them

---

71. "Yohicake Bag."

72. "A Brief Encounter: The Narragansett Basket," website of the Rhode Island Historical Society, http://www.rihs.org/events/event/a-brief-encounter-the-narragansett-basket/, 30 July 2013, accessed 23 September 2016.

73. "Basket," Heritage Museums and Gardens, accession no. 1982.5, August 1987. For a description of the basket, see Ellen Rasmussen, "Rare Narragansett Basket Highlights Heritage Plantation Collection," *Northeast Basketmakers Guild Newsletter*, Fall 1992, 1–2. Ulrich considers all three of these baskets and another, held privately, in *Age of Homespun*, chapter 1, "An Indian Basket," 41–50.

74. Ulrich, *Age of Homespun*, 50, 44.

75. Ulrich, *Age of Homespun*, 43.

at least, only to unravel them for their materials. But perhaps she took care to dismantle them only when he was back in Roxbury. We learn from the Rhode Island and Connecticut archives that women—Narragansett, Mohegan, and English alike—passed on to one another the technologies and the baskets themselves. Did her daughters, whom she enjoined to stay in Nonantum, learn to make baskets from her? What of the baby whose birth led to the illness that caused her death? If a girl, did she learn to weave herself, or did her mother's death mean that no one was able to teach her?

My questions are even more distantly removed from this woman's experience than Ulrich's provocative speculation about the woman who made the basket for Dinah Fenner, since at least Ulrich can ask her litany of questions about a woman understood to be the particular maker of this basket, whereas I'm using the mere fact of these baskets to prompt my thinking about an individual who made baskets that may have resembled them. The chain of information is tenuous at best: the missionary print record leads to archives, leads to the objects themselves, and then to absence. But that absence need not be thought of as absolute. As Carolyn Steedman argues, in the archives "an absence is not *nothing*, but is rather the space left by what has gone ... the emptiness indicates how once it was filled and animated."[76] The effort to imagine that animation is worthwhile because at the very least it reminds us that an individual Algonquian woman had an encounter with the English missionary that sparked a wide-ranging exchange among colonial and metropolitan writers. Such speculation should also remind us that for England, the seventeenth-century religious world included places with names such as Nonantum and Natick no less than Boston and London. It should remind us that disruption, fears, fantasies, and hopes were characteristic of all reaches of that world. Religious, political, and personal upheavals prompted Eliot to immigrate to New England, moved Edward Winslow to return to London to represent the colonies, prompted Reverend Henry Jessey to search out millennial meaning in colonial reports, and persuaded Hannah Allen to sell those accounts in her London shop. These upheavals also led an Algonquian woman to walk some sixteen miles with all her possessions on her back to join with a new and untested religious community and create a place for her family—for her daughters.

76. Carolyn Steedman, *Dust: The Archive and Cultural History* (New Brunswick: Rutgers University Press, 2002), 11.

CHAPTER 4

"Why should you be so furious?"

Global Fantasies of Violence

The story begins half a world away from America, some thirty years before it lands on colonial New England shores. Reports and rumors began circulating in London and the Netherlands during the summer of 1624. The English and Dutch merchants on the lucrative spice island of Amboyna had clashed, fatally. Ten Englishmen had been executed for treason. Harman van Speult, the Dutch governor of the island, had charged that despite the formal alliances between their home governments, these men had been conspiring with Japanese mercenaries and the captain of slaves (identified in reports as Portuguese) to seize control of the Dutch factory in Amboyna. The men were rounded up, questioned under torture, and beheaded. The Dutch merchants no doubt felt they had good reason to act precipitously. They were distant from even their regional authorities, headquartered in Batavia (later Jakarta), and months away by ship from their supervisors in the Staten-Generaal in the Netherlands. Moreover, although the numbers of English and Japanese were small, Anglo-Dutch rivalry in the region had a recent, tumultuous history of national double-dealing and violence that suggested how even small forces could produce large effects, a situation one historian calls "all-out war."[1] In 1621, when the Dutch carried out punitive raids against natives of the Banda Island group, they were opposed, clandestinely, by the English, despite a treaty that specified English support

---

1. Vincent Loth, "Armed Incidents and Unpaid Bills: Anglo-Dutch Rivalry in the Banda Islands in the Seventeenth Century," *Modern Asian Studies* 29.4 (October 1995), 717. For broader discussions of Anglo-Dutch relations in the region, see Marjorie Rubright, *Doppelgänger Dilemmas: Anglo-Dutch Relations in Early Modern English Literature and Culture* (Philadelphia: Pennsylvania University Press, 2014), especially chapter 6; and Robert Markley, *The Far East and the English Imagination, 1600–1730* (Cambridge: Cambridge University Press, 2006), especially chapter 4.

for such Dutch efforts. Although the Dutch overwhelmed the Bandanese—
in just a few weeks, some 13,000 Native islanders were killed, driven into a
precarious existence in the mountains, or forcibly removed and enslaved—
the Dutch were incensed by the English opposition.[2] Small wonder then,
that two years later, when a report reached van Speult at the Dutch "castle"
on Amboyna that the English were plotting to overthrow Dutch rule, he
moved swiftly and decisively. When news of the events reached Europe, it
touched off a furious cycle of public condemnation, printed attacks, and
legal wrangling that persisted for decades.

All of this is quite grim, though because the annals of European colonialism are so often a register of suspicion, greed, and atrocity, we might ask
whether the deaths of a relatively small number of English and Japanese
men merits either the attention it received at the time or close analysis now.
But if the incident at Amboyna seems rather a minor moment in colonial
history, its publication history looms large. Accounts and images of the
"Amboyna massacre" are threads in what Alison Games terms the "web of
empire" that extended from the East Indies to London, to The Hague, even
eventually to Boston in New England. The bloody events of the East Indies
in the 1620s were resurrected within this network in the 1650s and used to
create a united colonial map of protoimperial England, a "spatial fantasy" in
which the nation's enemies threatened England and Englishmen wherever
in the world they were to be found—from the factories in the Spice Islands
to the colonies of North America—and in which an attack on English colonists on one small island was understood synecdochically as threatening all
of the English diaspora.[3] The Amboyna incident and its print representation, then, can be used as a case study of what we might call early modern
globalization.

Although English sources reported on the events at Amboyna to their authorities in mid- to late 1623, the public learned of the events nearly a year
later when the first accounts of the bloody "business of Amboyna" were

2. A tract giving the Dutch point of view on this action was printed in London in 1622: *The
Hollanders Declaration of the affaires of the East Indies. Or a True Relation of that which passed in
the Ilands of Banda, in the East Indies.* Several other tracts provided the English take: *A Courante
of Newes from the East India* (1622); Bartholomew Churchman, *An Answere to the Hollanders
Declaration* (1622). In her keynote address, "Anglo-Dutch Relations in the East Indies and the
'Massacre' at Amboyna, 1623," at the Symposium on Anglo-Dutch Relations in the Early
Modern World, Newberry Library, 19 October 2012, Alison Games explored the wider context
of the so-called Amboyna massacre. In her talk, she argued that although English historians
have long held that an English conspiracy on Amboyna was unlikely (with the notion verging
on the ludicrous given the imbalance in numbers), a more even-handed consideration of both
the events and relations in the East Indies in the first decades of the seventeenth century suggests how precarious was the Dutch hold on power.

3. The term "spatial fantasy" is Matt Cohen's, *The Networked Wilderness: Communicating in
Early New England* (Minneapolis: University of Minnesota Press, 2009), 155.

circulated in manuscript and then printed in a tract. In England, anti-Dutch sentiments were whipped up by the detailed descriptions of the torture. They struck me forcibly when I first encountered them. The central account is worth quoting at length here:

> First they hoised [sic] him up by the hands with a cord on a large dore, where they made him fast upon two Staples of Iron fixt on both sides at the top of the dore posts, haling his hands, one from the other as wide as they could stretch.... Then they bound a cloth about his necke and face so close, that little or no water could go by. That done, they poured the water softly upon his head until the cloth was full, up to the mouth and nostrils, and somewhat higher; so that he could not draw breath, but he must withall suck-in the water: which being still continued to bee poured in softly, forced all his inward parts, came out of his nose, eares, and eyes; and often as it were stifling and choking him, at length took away his breath & brought him to a swoune or fainting. Then they tooke him quickly downe, and made him vomit up the water. Being a little recovered, they triced him up againe and poured in the water as before.... In this maner they handled him three or foure severall times.[4]

Clearly, in today's parlance, the men were waterboarded. Several of them confessed to plotting against the Dutch—though they later recanted—and were put to death. Once loosed to the English public, reports of the terrible events took many forms. Soon, in addition to the pamphlet describing the torture, a play appeared containing the English version of the events, a sermon decrying Dutch perfidy, a ballad, and a large painting of the scene of torture. The "true relation" from which the above description comes appears in several editions of the tract, most accompanied by a woodcut illustrating the abuse (fig.4.1). To seventeenth-century English readers and viewers, the significance of these representations was self-evident: Dutchmen had martyred Englishmen. The central figure in the woodcut, included in a 1624 issue of the tract and again in 1651, even approximates a crucifixion.[5] The actions of the Dutch had been, the English argued implicitly and explicitly, at once illegal and damnable.

In the seventeenth century, the cultural currency of this image of torture was akin to that of the photographs Susan Sontag discusses in *Regarding the Pain of Others*. Early on in the book, even as she acknowledges the power of such images, she argues that the "pity and disgust that pictures [of war and atrocity] inspire should not distract you from asking what pictures, whose

---

4. *A True Relation of the Unjust, Cruell, and Barbarous Proceedings Against the English at Amboyna in the East-Indies* (London, 1624): 10–11.
5. Several editions of *A True Relation* were published between 1624 and 1651, and these included a couple of variations on the image of torture.

Figure 4.1. Frontispiece, *True Relation*, 1651. Photo Courtesy of the Newberry Library, Chicago. Case F682.24.

cruelties, whose deaths are *not* being shown."[6] Unlike assumptions we sometimes make about photographs (that they merely record reality, that the medium is transparent) the early modern images "documenting" the Dutch torture of Englishmen are obvious mimetic constructs. Nevertheless, as I will discuss, seventeenth-century writers relied on these images to shore up their truth claims. They served, as Sontag argues for photographs, as "both a faithful copy or transcription of an actual moment of reality," or so they were assumed to be by viewers, "and an interpretation of that reality."[7] Sontag's analysis of photography as a powerful and potentially deceptive medium affords a purchase on the politics of pain that is encoded—and elided—in these early modern paintings, engravings, and woodcuts.

These images of violence were taken as concrete evidence of Dutch crimes against English nationals. Wildly popular and widely circulated at the time, they have received little critical reading since. Perhaps because historians

6. Susan Sontag, *Regarding the Pain of Others* (New York: Farrar, Straus and Giroux, 2003), 13.

7. Sontag, *Regarding the Pain of Others*, 26.

have primarily used the written texts to understand the events on Amboyna, because literary historians have been most interested in John Dryden's late-century dramatization of them in his play *Amboyna*, and because art historians seem not to have found the engravings of much formal interest, we have not carefully considered their relations to the texts in which they are embedded, and we have allowed the images to speak for themselves.[8] We have not applied Sontag's concern with those whose pain is "not being shown"—a concern that should surely be a given for scholars today, informed by recent postcolonial and archival theories—to this representation of violence at the margins of empire. But if we consider the figure of violence presented by English propagandists in the context of global networks of trade and colonialism extending from the East to the West Indies, which at that time was understood to include North America; if we read this image of waterboarding against other colonial images of violence; if we consider the circulation of these images and their supporting texts throughout the seventeenth century and not just at the moment of their creation, we can trace a history of torture in which atrocities are justified by recalculating victim-aggressor hierarchies.

In what follows, I examine two parallel instances of colonial violence: the Amboyna incident in 1623 and the Mystic Fort attack in Connecticut in 1636. In one, the English are subject to violence; in the other, they are instigators of extreme violence. In the aftermath of both, however, the English see themselves as victims, despite differences in the patterns of colonialism, exploitation, and settlement in the East Indies and in New England, and despite profound differences in their relationships to the other, non-European peoples who were also involved. The two events can be traced in texts published near the time they occurred, of course. More surprisingly, in the 1650s, when the Amboyna event was resurrected in print, the Mystic Fort attack, though not invoked directly, nonetheless haunts New England's attempt to use the Amboyna incident to write American colonies into the

8. Among the many historical studies, the most helpful to my argument include D. K. Bassett, "The Amboyna Massacre of 1623," *Journal of Southeast Asian History* 1.2 (1960): 1–19; Karen Chancey, "The Amboyna Massacre in English Politics, 1624–1632," *Albion* 30.4 (1998): 583–598; Adam Clulow, "Unjust, Cruel and Barbarous Proceedings: Japanese Mercenaries and the Amboyna Incident of 1623," *Itinerario* 31.1 (2007): 15–34; Shankar Raman, *Framing "India": The Colonial Imaginary in Early Modern Culture* (Stanford: Stanford University Press, 2002); and Alison Games, "Violence on the Fringes: The Virginia (1622) and Amboyna (1623) Massacres in Comparative Perspective," *History* 99.336 (2014): 505–529. For studies of Dryden's play, see Markley, *Far East and the English Imagination*; Candy Schille, "'With Honour Quit the Fort': Ambivalent Colonialism in Dryden's *Amboyna*," *Early Modern Literary Studies* 12.1 (May 2006): 1–30; Ayanna Thompson, *Performing Race and Torture on the Early Modern Stage* (New York: Routledge, 2008): 99–120; Elizabeth Maddock Dillon, "London," chapter 2 in *New World Drama: The Performative Commons in the Atlantic World, 1649–1849* (Durham: Duke University Press, 2014), 60–96; Rubright, *Doppelgänger Dilemmas*.

broader English diaspora. Read intertextually, the midcentury republication of the Amboyna incident allows us to discern how such representations create the colonial fantasies that made—and make—real atrocities possible.

AMBOYNA IN AMERICA

That the descriptions and images of torture and execution circulated widely in the 1620s is no surprise. Interest among the English in the Amboyna events was immediate and pragmatic. Survivors and the victims' families sought reparations—or revenge. The Dutch and British East India Companies sought to consolidate or regain their control over the clove trade on the island of Amboyna and the spice trade more generally. The governments of King James I and the Staten-Generaal of the Netherlands actively debated the best response to the incident while trying to head off repercussions in other areas of their domestic and foreign policies. Moreover, there was a sizeable Dutch community living in England who found themselves the objects of suspicion. In fact, Dutch nationals and their English supporters feared that the violence in the East Indies would spill over on them in London. In the early spring of 1625, at the approach of Shrovetide—a festival that was often accompanied by street riots—authorities were moved to suppress a large and vivid oil painting of the tortures and a play based on the Amboyna events.[9] Some 800 extra guards patrolled the streets. In the midst of these responses to the incident—political, corporate, popular—multiple publications hit the booksellers' stands in the 1620s to recount or memorialize the "cruell and bloody usage of our English Merchants."[10]

Pro-Dutch propaganda circulated in England as well. One such account was translated and folded into *A True Relation* (1624) as a means to rebut the Dutch defense. The anonymous Dutch author begins: "it is given out in *England*, that in the examination of the Conspirators there was an ex-cesse...in the point of *Torture*." Although he doubts the veracity of the reports, he nonetheless considers them hypothetically, arguing that "this torture of ours (if any in *Amboyna* were so tortured) is to bee judged farre lesse than that pressing"—a legal practice in England in which heavy weights were piled on top of a prisoner in order to force a plea. Note that he's not arguing that no torture was used but that the torture used was not excessive or unusual. It was "ordinary torture." What's more, the official reports tell him, this

---

9. See Jeffrey L. Singman, *Daily Life in Elizabethan England* (Westport: Greenwood Press, 1995), 62.

10. The phrase comes from the title of the printed ballad *Newes out of East India of the Cruell and Bloody Usage of our English Merchants and Others at Amboyna* (London, 1624).

"ordinary" treatment of prisoners was effective. Englishmen, *"some of them, before any torture; others, after a little (or rather a touch) of it, confessed."*[11] To these denials and prevarications by the Dutch, supposed Protestant brethren to the English, the editor of *A True Relation* responds in frustration: "Parricides are more easily committed than defended."[12]

However fraught the tensions, however politically significant the events in the immediate aftermath and throughout the 1620s, what is especially striking is the staying power of the incident as an object of curiosity or of propaganda decades after it occurred. As Alison Games suggests, "Amboyna developed as a metaphor to encapsulate English ideas about Dutch betrayal."[13] In the decades after the English traders were put to death, whenever tensions between England and Holland ratcheted up, we find English publishers trotting out the descriptions and images of Amboyna from earlier in the century. In the 1650s, 1660s, 1670s, and beyond, authors enjoined readers once again to decry the bloody murder of Europeans by other Europeans, treating the events on Amboyna as if they were fresh outrages. Of particular interest to me is the recurrence of the incident in the British imagination at midcentury, as the First Anglo-Dutch War broke out. It was at this moment, some thirty years after the original events took place, that Amboyna went global. In the 1650s, the incident was rebroadcast in the London press, and English writers in America took notice and used the accounts of the Dutch treatment of English factors to argue that their colony was twinned in interest and significance with the longer-standing (and at this point more lucrative) East Indian colonial efforts.

English writers felt they had reason to dredge up the old events even decades after the fact. Charles I was dead. Oliver Cromwell was in power and was prosecuting an aggressive foreign policy of conquest as he tried to consolidate a global English empire.[14] In such a political climate, authors

---

11. *True Relation* (1624), 18. Of course the use of torture was widespread even as it was debated in England. For a discussion of that debate and the epistemological valence of torture in seventeenth-century England, see Elizabeth Hanson, "Torture and Truth in Renaissance England," *Representations* 34 (Spring 1991): 53–84.

12. *True Relation* (1624), 34.

13. Alison Games, "Anglo-Dutch Connections and Overseas Enterprises: A Global Perspective on Lion Gardiner's World," *Early American Studies* 9.2 (Spring 2011): 460.

14. That the Amboyna incident was associated with Cromwell's ambitious foreign policy—indeed was understood by some as an important part of Cromwell's reputation—is illustrated by one of Cromwell's elegists in an epitaph appended to Samuel Slater's *A Rhetorical Rapture as Composed into a Funeral Oration* (London, 1658). See line 7 here:

Stay, *Pilgrim,* Stay; Tread gently; Mourn a while
O're that rests under, Th'Honour of this Isle:
Englands PROTECTOR, Victorious OLIVER:
Europe's Arbitrator: The World's Wonder:
The *Nine Worthies* grace-chymickt Quintessence:

presumably hoped to find a more receptive audience than they had received officially in the 1620s or at least hoped that changing political circumstances would prompt a reconsideration of the case against the Dutch. The early 1650s saw several whole-cloth reprints of 1620s propaganda as if it were fresh news.[15] It is the slimmest of these publications that perhaps can unlock the fuller significance of the incident in the English imagination at midcentury: *The Second Part of the Tragedy of Amboyna: or, A True Relation of a Most Bloody, Treacherous, and Cruel Design of the Dutch in the New-Netherlands in America, for the Total Ruining and Murthering of the English Colonies in New England.* In this tract, a five-page pamphlet written by anonymous New England merchants and published in London in 1653, the business of Amboyna is domesticated via the curious appropriation of East Indian violence for West Indian purposes. The tract's colonial writers, riding the wave of anti-Dutch feeling and the resurrection of Amboyna's tragedy in the press, argue that the abuses of the Dutch against the few in Amboyna in 1623 threaten to lead to violence that will hurt England's interests in America in 1653. Benjamin Schmidt, one of the only scholars to deal with this publication, notes that it employs savvy rhetoric for its moment, linking it to the "topos of 'Dutch tyranny in America,'" which he argues became "fairly well established in English propaganda."[16] New England's merchant-authors remind England in this tract that its "national" boundaries extend across the Atlantic and warn their brethren in London that the enemy's arm has a long reach.

Key to the tract's rhetoric is the conflation of economic harm with bodily injury. The authors clearly imagine their audience to include both corporate

---

Diamond of Saints: Darling of Providence:
Amboyna's Blood-shed's Cure: A Pearl I'th'Eye
Of *Romes, Spaines,* Universal Monarchie:
Who broke the *Irish*-Harp: The *Welch* new-strung:
Refin'd Parliaments: did old *Scots* new-dung:
Was wise Servant: a religious Master:
Provident Parent: Bounteous Lord: no Waster:
Captives Ransomer: poor *Pilgrims* Patrone:
Champion 'gainst Gods Foes, Chaplain to his owne,
Hast, *Pilgrim,* Hast; Trip nimbly hence, Be gone:
Lest free in Tears Thou freeze into a Stone.

15. See for instance, James Ramsey, *Bloudy newes from the East-Indies* (1651); *A true relation of the unjust, cruel, and barbarous proceedings against the English, at Amboyna in the East-Indies,* attributed to John Skinner (1651); another variant of the pamphlet was also published in 1651. The anonymous *A Memento for Holland or A True and Exact History of the Most Villainous and Barbarous Cruelties Used on the English Merchants Residing at Amboyna* was printed in 1653, as was the anonymous *The Second Part of the Tragedy of Amboyna,* which I analyze below.

16. Benjamin Schmidt, *Innocence Abroad: The Dutch Imagination and the New World, 1570–1670* (Cambridge: Cambridge University Press, 2001): 298. See also Games, "Anglo-Dutch Connections," 460, for a brief description of the colonial context of the tract.

and political authorities and the man on the street, perhaps gearing up for Shrovetide street protests. When the events at Amboyna actually took place in the 1620s, East Indian trade was considerably more lucrative than that of the paltry few plantations in the Americas.[17] But by the 1650s England's Atlantic colonies were well on their way to being the sugar-fueled economic engines they would become later in the century. And though New England was not nearly as important a colony, the tract's title generalized the Dutch threat to all of America. The loss of American plantations would have been crippling. Moreover, by invoking Amboyna and prophesying murder, the tract transforms national trade and colonial competition into potential English martyrdom. The tract thus calls for England to mobilize its military in defense of its American colonial investments, wrapping the call up in predictions of bloody attacks on English planters.

To accomplish its ends, the tract takes particular care in its representation of a victim-aggressor hierarchy. In the published accounts of Amboyna, the Dutch are presented as acting aggressively and alone. Indeed, we see the Dutch treating other nationalities just as harshly as they treated the English. Japanese men in particular are described as victims, though admittedly the publication's focus is squarely on the English. For instance, A True Relation makes it clear that the English know that Japanese nationals are being tortured but ignore the sights and sounds of their torture. The Englishmen's disregard of the Japanese men's sufferings becomes a perverse defense. The Dutch had accused the English of colluding with the Japanese on the island to overthrow Dutch rule. But pro-English writers offered the English indifference to their supposed allies' arrest and torture as proof of their innocence: since the English had done nothing to deserve torture and execution, why should they be concerned if others were being harshly treated?

Indigenous residents of Amboyna are also presented as involved in the events of 1623, but they receive even less consideration in the description of the events (though they do figure in broader descriptions of Dutch crimes in the East Indies). On Amboyna, these residents are at most deep background: references to Dutch and English competition over the spice trade rarely mention that they are negotiating with Native peoples to effect the clove trade. At most, A True Relation, in both its 1624 and 1651 versions, makes fleeting references to a Native presence; the tracts mention "three or foure hundred Mardikers (for so they usually call the free Natives) in the towne."[18]

But whatever relations these hundreds of people had with the Europeans on their island, in the tracts they are cast along with other, indigenous

17. Jamestown, 1607; Somers Isles (Bermuda), 1615; Plymouth, 1620.
18. *True Relation* (1624), 3, and *True Relation* (1651), 4. The tracts also mention "burgers," who may be Native peoples or those with mixed ethnicity.

residents as mere spectators to the treatment the Dutch give their English competitors. Among the humiliations heaped on the English prisoners is one last indignity. As they are marched to the execution site, they are taken "not the ordinary and short way, but round about in a long procession, thorow the towne; the way guarded with five Companies of Souldiers, Dutch and Amboyners, and thronged with the Natives of the Island, that (upon the summons given the day before by the sound of the Drum) flocked together to behold this triumph of the Dutch over the English."[19]

The New England take on Dutch-English competition in America differs sharply from the Amboyna accounts. In *The Second Part of the Tragedy*, indigenous peoples are not silent background observers but key players in an American colonial drama. They are allied with the perfidious Dutch, and the anonymous merchant authors insist that a Christian-heathen binary characterizes not only colonial political relations but essential identities as well. That the Dutch refuse to ally themselves with the English and instead enlist with Indians marks them as savage others, and the spread of violence from the East to the West is imagined in terms of an essential difference of "blood."

The Second Part of the Tragedy argues that in America, English settlers are the stronger colonial power and notes that in contrast to the Dutch treatment of their relatively weaker European brethren in the East Indies, the English have acted beneficently to their European competitors, compelled by a sense of ethnic and religious kinship. When earlier the Dutch were "reduced to a great exigence and strait by the Indians," John Underhill, an English military captain married to a Dutch woman and living among the Dutch, defended them against Indian attack, even when offered a large bribe: "Captain Underhill, a Gentleman of spirit, experience, and conduct, who prizing Christian Blood beyond Indian Wealth and Treasure (being proffered a hogshead of their Wampampege [wampum] to withdraw the English Forces) fell on these Heathens."[20]

The tract explains just how mistaken Underhill was in the next paragraph—not about prizing Christian blood but about whether such blood runs in Dutch veins: "But Ingratitude overclouding these Heroick Actions, and Amboyna's treacherous Cruelty extending it self from the East to the West Indiaes [*sic*], running in its proper channel of Dutch blood, quickly sought their Neighbors, their Friends, their Noble Defenders, the English, Destruction."[21] This description of the English as neighbors, friends, and defenders papers over the recent history of these noble English in the colonies.

19. *True Relation* (1651), 45.
20. *Second Part*, 4.
21. *Second Part*, 4

Indeed, by using the Amboyna incident as historic context for New England's relationship to the Dutch, and in particular as a discursive context for John Underhill's involvement in their relations in the 1650s, the tract represents colonial axes of power in new England ahistorically, at least in terms of local events, which lurk just outside the margins of the tract. By midcentury, New England's colonial authorities had consolidated their power in the region thanks to its victory in the 1636–1637 Pequot War, in which Underhill played a significant role, and to the establishment of the United Colonies in 1643. Yet *The Second Part of the Tragedy* extends the rhetoric of powerlessness and violence found in the tracts detailing East Indian circumstances to imply that the English were everywhere victims rather than aggressors, from the East Indies to the West.

As is well known to scholars of seventeenth-century New England, John Underhill was a logical choice to defend the Dutch against Indians; he had made a name for himself as an Indian fighter in the Pequot War of the 1630s, when he was among the instigators of the infamous Mystic Fort massacre, in which the English attacked a Pequot fort inhabited mostly by noncombatants, old men, women, and children. Underhill and his comrades set fire to the wigwams in the fort, ordering their forces to shoot any who tried to escape the flames. Estimates of the dead ranged to the hundreds. For any New England colonist, mention of Underhill's name would have resonated with accounts of extreme violence against Native people. Indeed, in a 1638 tract that Underhill published after the massacre, *Newes from America; or, a New and Experimentall Discoverie of New England; containing, A True Relation of their War-like Proceedings these Two Yeares Past, with a Figure of the Indian Fort, or Palizado,* he felt compelled to defend the colonists against charges that they had acted too precipitously and harshly: "It may bee demanded, Why should you be so furious (as some have said) should not Christians have more mercy and compassion?" His answer turns God himself into a torturer: "But I would referre you to *Davids* warre, when a people is growne to such a height of bloud, and sinne against God and man, and all confederates in the action, there hee hath no respect to persons, but harrowes them, and sawes them, and puts them to the sword, and the most terriblest death that may bee."[22] Terrible words, terrible deeds. But at least we can say for Underhill in this passage that he acknowledges the horror—Pequot people have been "harrowed" and "sawed." They have died "the most terriblest death that may bee." This is no "ordinary torture," as the apology for the Dutchmen's actions in Amboyna put it. This is genocide, the utter destruction of a

22. John Underhill, *Newes from America; or, a New and Experimentall Discoverie of New England; Containing, A True Relation of their War-like Proceedings these Two Yeares Past, with a Figure of the Indian Fort, or Palizado* (London, 1638), 40.

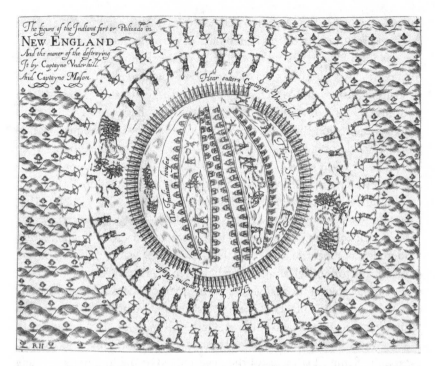

Figure 4.2. "Figure" of the Mystic Fort attack, John Underhill, *Newes from America,* 1638. Photo Courtesy of the Newberry Library, Chicago, Ayer 172.U5 1638.

people because they competed for land and resources, because they imagined themselves sovereign, because they were not English.[23]

Underhill's narrative is especially well known for its "figure" of the Mystic Fort attack, a stylized representation of the fort and the battle (fig. 4.2). If we consider this image in comparison to the widely circulated image of torture in Amboyna, we may illuminate the logic of colonial violence that links these seemingly disparate representations. In both instances, the publications aim to control their viewers' responses to reports of colonial violence and manage their viewers' understanding of the victim-aggressor hierarchies. But if we consider the other actors who appear in the images or texts—or are carefully elided—we can see how these images, together with their texts, create fantasies of English colonial righteousness that shore up larger nationalist and protoimperial claims.

Several scholars have made the case that Underhill's deceptively simple image carries significant representational weight. Ann Kibbey's study of Puritans and violence reads the image through the lens of Puritan iconography

23. For a discussion of levels of violence in the Pequot War and the scholarly debate over its meaning, see Ronald Dale Karr, "'Why Should You Be So Furious': The Violence of the Pequot War," *Journal of American History* 85.3 (December 1998): 876–909; see especially 877–878.

and iconoclasm. She sees the Puritan-Protestant distaste for religious (read Catholic) imagery as extending, through the classical concept of *figura*, to human bodies and actions. Her reading suggests that the image freezes a moment of righteous violence against the *figura* of Pequot blasphemy represented by the Indian possession of land in the English colonies. The Pequot, as other Native peoples in colonial New England seem to have done, may actually have used Christian blasphemy as a wartime tactic against the English. But Kibbey argues that the English are not concerned with real anti-Christian words or deeds on the part of the enemy. Rather, English writers render blasphemous the Pequot in and of themselves. It is not what they do but who they are that matters.[24] And so their utter extirpation is rationalized.

In his study of early American media, literary historian Matt Cohen calls Underhill's image schematic, with its depiction of an orderly, regularized battleground, a "spatial fantasy."[25] In the center of the engraving is a round fort—a palisaded space in which we see depicted neat rows of Pequot houses, all aflame, that frame hand-to-hand male combat. No women or children are shown. The fort is encircled by English soldiers firing at the palisade walls or engaged in small skirmishes. Surrounding them is a circle of Narragansett and Niantic fighters allied to the English, all with arrows notched. Finally, the whole scene is centered in a repeating landscape of small hills and trees.

Cohen makes a persuasive argument that the figure of the fort attack is *not* static as Kibbey suggests—it does not freeze the scene in order to instantiate Puritan ideology (although, as I will discuss, even the figure in motion finally does make that ideology concrete) Rather, the image is put in motion by its reader. The original image is a large fold-out contained in an octavo book, a presentation Cohen calls "another spatial fantasy," and its details inscribe multiple perspectives.[26] In particular, he notes that the off-center orientation of the image suggests "that the image is meant to be read in a circle."[27] Thus "the reading practice it encourages reanimates the combat"—Underhill's particular, self-interested version of that combat, in which he emerges as the clear hero, the leader of English forces waging a just war. Cohen notes as well that the figure, as it visually manipulates events

24. Ann Kibbey, *The Interpretation of Material Shapes in Puritanism: A Study of Rhetoric, Prejudice, and Violence* (Cambridge: Cambridge University Press, 1986). See Kristina Bross, *Dry Bones and Indian Sermons: Praying Indians in Colonial America* (Ithaca: Cornell University Press, 2004), for a discussion of blasphemy as a tool of war during the conflict that came to be known as "King Philip's War," 174–176.

25. Cohen, *Networked Wilderness*, 155.

26. "The spatial fantasy of the Indian village, surrounded by a fantasy of how space is allocated in war... is made possible by another spatial fantasy, the figure, contained within the tight space of a small (octavo) book." Cohen, *Networked Wilderness*, 155.

27. Cohen, *Networked Wilderness*, 156.

toward a singular reading of the battle, also manipulates the reader: "performatively, too, a reader trying to interpret this map will call attention to him or herself in the act of examining it in a spectacular way."[28] In order to view the image, the reader will need to unfold the map and juggle the suddenly unwieldy book, rendering the reader himself or herself subject to interpretation.[29] In addition to the way the image creates the reader as spectacle for other observers, I want to consider the reader's own sensations as he or she "reads" the image. In demanding that the reader twist and turn either his or her own body or the fold-out in order to decode it, the map forces the reader to encounter the image physically. If (as Cohen argues) the image "induces a visual frenzy and confusion that weave a clear, heroic chronology into a hectic sensory experience reminiscent of that of combat," the reader must physically enact that "frenzy," at least on a small scale.[30]

However frenzied the act of reading, it is absolutely clear what the reader's perception ultimately should be: the image of the battle and the reader's physical response to the image simultaneously right themselves as the circular reading concludes. Moreover, our perspective as readers is exactly that of the English soldiers. Like them, we are focused on the center of the figure, toward the fort, so we are never in doubt about where our allegiances should lie. At no point does the image figure what Underhill describes as the much more disorienting sight—the reports of which apparently sparked English concern about the levels of violence being perpetrated by their countrymen in America. Just before he records his response to the question "Why should you be so furious," Underhill reports that in particular the young soldiers in his company were amazed by the destruction: "Great and dolefull was the bloudy sight to the view of young souldiers that never had beene in Warre, to see so many soules lie gasping on the ground so thicke in some places, that you could hardly passe along." The young soldiers reacted to the total destruction of this battle: "many were burnt in the Fort, both men, women, and children, others forced out, and came in troopes to the *Indians* [who were allied to the English], twentie, and thirtie at a time, which our souldiers received and entertained with the point of the sword; downe fell men, women, and children." By contrast, whatever the chaos and confusion of the fight as it was immediately experienced, as we encounter the image of the battle tipped into Underhill's published account, we do not see the burnt and bleeding bodies of Pequot men, women, and children. Rather, details in the image are widely and regularly spaced. There is plenty of room to maneuver in this imagined battle scene, with no danger of

28. Cohen, *Networked Wilderness*, 157.
29. Cohen, *Networked Wilderness*, 155.
30. Cohen, *Networked Wilderness*, 157.

tripping over fallen bodies or slipping on spilled blood. Indeed the image does not represent dead bodies at all.

Cohen argues that Underhill is a master "of information management tactics." His frenzied but ultimately sanitized image of the fort scene suggests that he judges his readers to be easily swayed by blood. In this instance his mastery ensures that readers react to the battle as properly seasoned veterans would do, with an eye to the whole battle rather than to the immediate, bloody hand-to-hand horrors that so rattled the green recruits. The visual image powerfully contains and redirects our sympathies to align with his. Underhill and his men are presented as descendants of Reformation-age enthusiasts, and we might even see them as forerunners of Cromwell's New Model army, clearing the land of sin and blasphemy. The burning fort thus becomes an icon of just war that redirects the question "Why should you be so furious?" Given the simultaneously frenzied representation of battle and its static moral judgment to which a circular reading of the illustration ultimately returns us, Underhill suggests that the better question is "why not"?

"A MORE HORRID RECEPTION"

The logic of this representation becomes especially clear when we compare it to the image most closely associated with the events at Amboyna. Underhill's map returns the viewer to stasis; it walks the viewer through the frenzy of battle to render him or her accepting of the wholesale killing of the fort's inhabitants as the necessary outcome of the encounter. By contrast, the image produced to represent the Amboyna incident, more conventional in its visual elements than the figure in Underhill's account, was meant to provoke anger and action.

When English authors, beginning in 1624 and throughout the century, produced a series of pamphlets retelling the story of Amboyna, they included a detailed description of exactly how ten Englishmen were beaten, burned, and waterboarded before they were executed, and they prominently featured a frontispiece illustrating their torture (fig. 4.1). Whereas Underhill's figure captures a particular moment, the Amboyna image collapses linear time by representing the scene of torture at the top, recovery in the bottom left, and then execution at the bottom right. The main figure of torture has Christic resonances, and as others have noted, the image draws on the popularity and tropes of John Foxe's *Acts and Monuments*, his book of Protestant martyrdom.[31] Unlike Underhill's image, there is no attempt in this engraving

---

31. As Steven Pincus puts it, "the bloody tale of torture and murder was written in the language of Foxe's *Acts and Monuments.*" *Protestantism and Patriotism: Ideologies and the Making of English Foreign Policy, 1650–1668* (Cambridge: Cambridge University Press, 1996), 59.

to represent the various scenes in their historical or spatial context, however stylized. All three victims of Dutch aggression seem present in the same room, with all stages of torture and suffering occurring simultaneously. Whereas the text describes the action over several days and in several locales (the torture rooms, the prison cells, and ultimately the outdoor scene of execution), these details of time and place are omitted in the frontispiece in favor of a compressed representation of atrocity. Everything from torture to execution is seen at a glance.

Although the figure is, unlike Underhill's map, conventional in its orientation, it has the power to excite a physical as well as an emotional response, as attested by William Sanderson in his 1658 essay *Graphice*. In that text, Sanderson examines the force of visual over written expression:

> Picture insinuates into our most inward affections: Things by the *Eare*, doe but faintly stirre the mind, but captivate the *Eyes*; as being the more accurate witnesses of the two: *Gods* may be conceived by *Poesie*, but are made by *Painters*.
>
> So did they well; who, to enforce a more horrid reception of the *Dutch*-cruelty upon our *English* at *Amboyna* in the *East Indies*, described it into *Picture* (after that it had been, most eloquently urged, by Sr. *Dudly Digs* and imprinted,) [*sic*]³² to incense the Passions, by *sight* thereof.... it wrought this strange effect upon the widow of one of the Martyrs; who, upon former relations, prosecuted her complaint; but when she saw the *Picture*, lively describing her Husband's horrid execution, she sunck down, in a dead swound.³³

However "eloquently urged," it seems, the bare description of the events at Amboyna was not enough to spark appropriate outrage and action. Verbal descriptions prompted legal action but did not move the emotions. Sanderson's description of the power of the visual image begs the question: what exactly would constitute a "horrid reception" of the news? The sense is surely that a viewer would respond to the news *with* horror, but the curious phrasing suggests as well that the viewer is contaminated, is herself made "horrible" as she receives the news through "picture" rather than "relation."³⁴ Early modern usage of the related words "horrid" or "horrible" assumed the physical reaction of one exposed to horror; one shudders, shivers, or thrills in horror. Because our use of the term today is to describe events or others,

32. The anonymously published tract *A True Relation* is variously attributed to Dudley Digges and John Skinner.

33. William Sanderson, *Graphice: The Use of the Pen and Pensil. Or, the Most Excellent Art of Painting* (London, 1658), 14. Ironically enough, *Graphice* has almost no illustrations of its tenets and advice, the plates having been lost at sea. Sanderson describes this same effect, though in less detail, in an earlier publication, *A Compleat History of the Lives and Reigns of, Mary Queen of Scotland, and of her Son and Successor, James the Sixth* (London, 1656).

34. See the *Oxford English Dictionary*'s second entry for "horrid" and first entry for "horrible."

not our own reception of the terrible, we may miss the way these seven-teenth-century authors and artists theorized the effect of imaging atrocity. The relationship sketched out by Sanderson between the narrative of an event and its visual representation is that of intellect to emotion. When the "horrid execution" is described in print, the widow is motivated to seek rep-aration. When it is figured, the impression is more intense, provoking a horrid—that is, a shuddering, shivering, physical—reaction that causes the widow to swoon, an extreme but seemingly conventional response.

However effective the representation, as with any art of sensibility, its creators cannot control the way a viewer acts on his or her physical response and awakened emotions. Consider Sanderson's description of his own reac-tion to the image, "which truly," he writes, "appeared to me so monstrous, as I then wished it to be burnt." Whereas the widow faints, he is moved to vio-lence—a particularly fraught reaction because of what it implies: the image of an English martyr being tortured and executed creates within Sanderson the desire to burn it—to destroy the martyr (again). It seems impossible for Sanderson *not* to see himself as lighting an execution pyre himself in this desire to rid himself of a representation of torture and death that affects him so deeply. He desires to act in some way in response to the emotions the image evokes, but if the creators of the image hoped that by turning the ex-ecuted Englishmen into new martyrs the viewer's ire would be directed against the Dutch, Sanderson's tract suggests that his anger is directed toward the would-be martyr figure itself.

In fact, Sanderson's description of his reaction suggests that it is political. As Sanderson reports his emotions, his desired destruction of the image re-flects the Crown's fears in the 1620s about the reaction of the English public to the Amboyna incident. Authorities feared that mobs would channel their horror in politically or diplomatically unacceptable ways, such as at-tacks on Dutch residents in London. In wishing to suppress the image of torture, Sanderson's reaction mirrors that of the authorities thirty years ear-lier: "And so belike it seemed prudentiall to those in power, who soon defac'd it; lest, had it come forth in common, might have incited us then, to a nationall quarrell and revenge; *though we have not wanted other just provo-cations since to make them our enemies.*"[35] Politically, Sanderson walks a care-ful line. He is writing during the Interregnum, and he is a Royalist, or at the very least, he was firmly in the camp of James I early in the century. So he cannot help but approve of the Crown's decision in 1625 to suppress the

---

35. Original emphasis. Helpfully, Sanderson inserts the date "1653" in the margin just at this point, in case his audience needs reminding of the First Anglo-Dutch War, concluded in 1654. I am not yet sure to what exact event of the war (if any) he is pointing, but several major battles were fought 1653.

painting. But as he goes to print, England is at war with the Dutch, and he patriotically supports the anti-Dutch feelings that the painting—now engraving—represents. And however right he judges the rationale behind the 1624 decision to "deface" the image, in 1658 he cannot avoid the implications: burning or mutilating the image suggests the threat of iconoclasm run wild, when even good, Protestant images are subject to destruction and suppression.

The East India Company's own account of the oil painting's suppression, written a few years earlier than Sanderson's, pulls no such punches. The notion that the destruction of the figure of torture is, iconographically speaking, making new Protestant martyrs is clear in the 1651 edition of *A True Relation*, which accuses the Dutch community in London, in league with English authorities, of martyring English sensibilities. In the "Advertisement to the Reader," a preface written specifically for this edition, the author reports: "The *East-India* Company seing [*sic*] themselves obstructed in the prosecution [of their legal case against the Dutch East India Company], thought fit to preserve the memorie of such a butchery, by getting the several Tortures done at large in Oyl, but the Table was scarce sooner hung up, but the Murderers began to fear it would bleed at the nose; so that *Buckingham* was appeased by another sacrifice, and the Picture commanded to be taken down."[36] The passage suggests both the volatile political situation of London in the 1620s and the vividness of the oil painting. The "murderers" are members of the Dutch community in London, those who were meant to be protected by the government's Shrovetide preparations. The Company is obviously still piqued, nearly thirty years later, by the notion that the Duke of Buckingham, King James's favorite and an extremely powerful member of the Privy Council, would choose to appease that community—and would himself be appeased—with another English sacrifice rather than supporting their efforts. Finally, the passage suggests the power of the image—the notion that the tortured figure would "bleed at the nose" references an ancient test for murder; when a corpse was touched by its murderer, it was believed that it would begin to bleed afresh. Here, there is no need for the actual body, but merely the vivid representation of one, and the easy substitution of paint for flesh makes the "sacrifice" of the painting all the more terrible, and the preservation of the image of English martyrdom through engravings and woodcuts all the more important.

Although the 1650s tract doesn't make clear what an appropriate response to the image it contains should be, exactly, the description of problematic responses suggests that the image is meant to provoke action. If Underhill's map is meant to return the viewer to stasis, to subject the

36. *True Relation* (1651), 5r.

reader to the frenzy of battle in order to render him or her calm and accepting of the massacre that ends it, the image of Amboynan torture is meant to arouse the viewer, to affect the senses and sensibility, to overwhelm them, in order to create a climate in which political or military action against the Dutch is possible. The danger of an inappropriate response is clear—one can act against the image itself, as Buckingham does and Sanderson fantasizes doing, rather than against the perpetrators of the actual violence. But perhaps even wrong action is better than none at all. By widely distributing the image through the press, the authors of *A True Relation* sought to counter those who had taken too calm or too pragmatic a view of the secular martyrdom of the English traders and to whip their readers up into an anti-Dutch frenzy.

For all its force, as I have noted, the image compresses the events on Amboyna in the 1620s into its most evocative elements—evocative for the English, that is—and elides a wider view that might introduce other atrocities, other politics of pain, into the discourse. In this, the images of both the Amboyna and Mystic Fort incidents function as examples of a "species of rhetoric" in the sense that Sontag ascribes to photographs. As rhetoric, the images "reiterate. They simplify. They agitate. They create the illusion of consensus."[37] But to assume consensus around the reception of such images is, as Sontag argues, "to dismiss politics."[38] Indeed, as I have shown, because Sanderson has a very different political stance from those circulating the Amboyna image at midcentury, he takes pains to describe his very different reception of the image. In order to sound fully the meaning of this image and its accompanying texts, we must return to Susan Sontag's injunction to remember those *not* pictured, to remember the people who are left completely out of the discussion, whose pain has gone unrecorded or ignored, whose deaths are, in Judith Butler's evocative term, "ungrievable."[39] I've discussed the presence of Japanese troops on the island and the way English authors described and immediately dismissed their torture by the Dutch. They do not appear in the frontispiece of the 1624 *True Relation* or the reprints of 1632 or 1651. So too the enslaved men reported to be tasked with the labor of removing the English from the torture rooms and returning them to their cells are absent from this early image, despite the fact that the man who was in charge of slaves was among those tortured and executed.[40]

Aside from the Japanese and enslaved men, at least one other group is erased by a focus solely on the English and their sufferings, a group that can

---

37. Sontag, *Regarding the Pain of Others*, 6.
38. Sontag, *Regarding the Pain of Others*, 9.
39. Judith Butler, *Frames of War: When Is Life Grievable?* (reprint, London: Verso, 2010).
40. Enslaved people *do* appear in later versions of the image.

be seen if we re-place the figured English in their full global-colonial context. Although the image in *True Relation* suggests that the Dutch torturers and their victims were the only witnesses to the executions of the English, in fact, as I've noted, the written text describes how the "Natives of the Island" were mustered to witness the passage of English merchants to their execution. They were called to the parade route and execution grounds "upon the summons given the day before by the sound of the Drum."[41] Although *A True Relation* and other English accounts of the Amboyna events do little more than note the presence of indigenous people on the island, the American contribution to the discussion, *The Second Part of the Tragedy*, along with Underhill's map, is a stark reminder that although they are often "not pictured," indigenous actors—the Amboyna islanders in this case—were regularly witnesses to events of colonial violence. An intertextual reading of texts from both the East and West Indies should lead us to question the meaning of the roles assigned (or not assigned) to such witnesses in colonial and overseas writings and in the images that accompanied them.

What kind of terror—or perhaps celebration—was caused by the public display of the bruised and mangled bodies of the Englishmen, the Japanese, and the Portuguese overseer of slaves? What did the "sound of the Drum" summoning them to the site of the executions mean to the indigenous witnesses before that day? What might it have meant afterward? In the English accounts of Amboyna, writers emphasize that the spectacle of torture was an important facet in their countrymen's abusive treatment—they account it part and parcel of their torment that the English victims were forced to hear their fellow prisoners "roar" in pain as they were questioned and then to see their rent and bloodied bodies afterward as they were dumped in the cells. But these writers passed over in silence the terrible summons of Native residents to witness the parade of tortured prisoners and their deaths, a witness that was implied by the text but was not allowed to make any impression on the figure of torture that was circulated in so many images throughout the seventeenth century. If we consider the discursive techniques that these propaganda tracts employed to create virtual witnesses to the events on Amboyna or in New England that they purported to record, we can see that these texts admitted of some degree of nuance, or at least included the possibility of other points of view: the enslaved and the Native islanders, the question put to Underhill about the colonists' "fury." But the written texts are in contrast to the visual images that channel that nuance into a message that is meant to provoke a particular affective response to colonial violence or atrocity—to the New England image, acceptance; to the Amboynan image, outrage.

41. *True Relation* (1651), 45. The summons is also described in the 1624 edition, 27.

Underhill's map, which does figure Native witnesses to atrocity, cues us that the exclusion of East Indian colonized subjects from the literature of the Amboyna incident is purposeful. The East India Company authors of *A True Relation* focused attention on their compatriots and in their images of atrocity rendered their struggle with the Dutch stark, uncomplicated by the figures of the Native trading partners who witnessed the executions. Did they refuse to represent Native witnesses because they understood them to be Dutch allies, because they were indifferent to the Native experience of the incident, experiences that might, for instance, have prompted questions about the validity of European claims to Amboyna in the first place? Or were they silent simply because they wanted to keep the focus on the English alone, on their suffering and Dutch guilt—eliding and rendering unimportant any "collateral" violence directed at indigenous residents? Asking these questions, even if we cannot fully answer them, helps keep the suffering of the "not pictured" in the picture, at least to some extent.

Once again, a close consideration of Underhill's justification of the burning of Mystic Fort can shed light on the representation of violence, even in a very different colonial time and place. The Underhill figure reminds us that archival silence does not equal historical absence. As I've discussed, a key moment in Underhill's account is his response to an imagined question: "Why should you be so furious?" Underhill presents this question and his answer almost as a theoretical exercise—a philosophical debate about just war and acceptable levels of violence. He poses the question and answers it just after he describes the appalled reaction of new soldiers to battle, contrasting their confusion with his calm response as a combat veteran and his cool reflection as a theologian, and implying that he considers the question in response to English reactions to the battle. Indeed, the moment is usually read as Underhill working to justify the burning of Mystic Fort to a critical English audience, either real or imagined.

Indeed, he does pose the question in the subjunctive, clearly imagining a future conversation in which New England colonists might be called to account: "It may bee demanded, Why should you be so furious?" But we would do well to note that the question was not, in fact, hypothetical, as he himself notes in an aside—"Why should you be so furious (as some have said)."[42] The question is a real one, and because of its placement in his text, it is easy to assume that the "some" of his aside refer to the English—perhaps to the young soldiers so affected by scenes of gore. However, the question seems not to have been put to him by English interlocutors but by his Narragansett and Niantic allies, or at least he credits them with introducing the idea that English military action was out of proportion to the threat.

42. Underhill, *Newes from America*, 40.

Those who witnessed the destruction of the fort judged it *"mach it, mach it"* a phrase that Underhill glosses as "it is naught, it is naught" but that might better be defined as bad or evil. And in Underhill's tract his allies call the English "furious"—it is their term applied to the English practice of war.[43] If they were too politic or too polite to put the question "why should you be so furious" directly to Underhill or their other English contacts, they were nonetheless able to convey their negative judgment of the English troops' actions at Mystic. So much so that Underhill seemingly internalized the critique, rendering it through the imagined query of more distant observers. Nevertheless, in his answer to the hypothetical question he quickly dismisses Narragansett or Niantic challenges to colonial practices of war. He makes clear that he and his torturer God hold the line on a static colonial front in which wigwams always burn, Englishmen always shoot, and Indian allies remain silent, threatening observers rather than, as the text implies, cogent interlocutors.

But the challenge that the Narragansett and Niantic pose to him is not so easily contained, either by his answer or by the image of the attack on the fort. Underhill offers scriptural support for the extreme violence of the attack but cannot quite issue a blanket apology for all such action: "sometimes the Scripture declareth women and children must perish with their parents; some-time the case alters: but we will not dispute it now. We had sufficient light from the word of God for our proceedings."[44] Although Underhill may have thought (or hoped) that the query "why should you be so furious" was asked and answered, the question continues to resonate, both for Underhill, as he imagines a "some-time" in which such fury is not to be admitted, and certainly centuries later, as new atrocities challenge our assumptions and beliefs.

As is clear from the many references in both Dutch and English archives and publications, the descriptions and images of atrocity at Amboyna were a powerful "species of rhetoric" well after the governments and companies involved had officially come to terms with the incident itself, and despite the best efforts of governments to contain them. Dutch colonial governors believed their actions necessary to protect life and livelihood. If Dutch authorities found the actions of their factors in the East Indies distressing, it was less because of the human toll of torture and more because of the way they disrupted larger political and economic concerns, though there is little to suggest that they saw the torment and execution of ostensible English allies as unsupportable. Nevertheless, the Netherlands recalled the accused

43. Underhill, *Newes from America*, 43.
44. Underhill, *Newes from America*, 36.

agents to put them on trial, convening the court in the late 1620s. The defendants were found not guilty in 1630, when relations between the English and the Dutch had soured in Europe as well as in the Indies.[45]

To English observers, outraged at what they saw as the breaking of international agreements and the transgression of natural law, it mattered little that the Dutch authorities brought in their agents from the field or put them on trial. Long before the verdict was announced, and for more than a century afterward, the Amboyna incident was discussed, debated, resurrected, and decried. As the figure of Mystic Fort and of the executions at Amboyna make clear, however satisfactory (or not) the official resolution of violence and response to torture may be, the initial outrage lives on, and then as now, the government that would put it to rest must needs recognize the effects on minds and hearts, no less than on bodies.

---

45. The English political context of the incident and the trial are well documented in Chancey, "Amboyna Massacre in English Politics."

Coda: "Wicked Weed"

Read a bit about the publication of the Calendars of State Papers and you realize just how transformative that massive project was for anyone interested in England's past. There's a reason that editor W. Noel Sainsbury was a corresponding member of so many historical societies in the United States. With the publication of the calendars, we can see a step toward democratization of information and scholarship.[46] The impact of the calendars is not unlike that which accompanies each new innovation in information technology—microfilm, for instance, or especially our more recent digital revolution.[47] In writing this book I've relied on a number of digital resources, perhaps none more so than Early English Books Online. Because my university has the means to subscribe to this database, I could limit in-person trips to the British Library or the Huntington. Instead, I could read Peter Heylyn's *Cosmographie*, Henry Parker's *Altar Dispute*, or John Underhill's *Newes from America* right in my faculty office in Heavilon Hall, West Lafayette, Indiana. At times my assumption that EEBO was the best way to research got in my way, when its flattening of all texts into two-dimensional, same-sized representations occluded the materiality of John Underhill's fold-out figure of Mystic Fort or when, most dramatically for me, I assumed the primacy of EEBO and relied on a digital copy of William Lilly's *Monarchy or No Monarchy* before I realized that my library had a physical copy of the text in its vaults just a block away.[48]

But at times EEBO was revelatory. Because I was interested in the recycling of the news about Amboyna in the early seventeenth century, I used the database search tools to find all its texts between 1624, when the news first reached London, and midcentury. There were plenty of hits—some

46. Consider the *Calcutta Review*'s review of *Calendar of State Papers, Colonial Series; East Indies, China, and Japan, 1617–1621*, which expressed excitement over the "novel and most interesting historical and antiquarian treasures that have been already unearthed for us by Mr. Sainsbury [the editor]," most especially because those archival treasures would enable a "revolution" in the history of British rule. "*Calendar of State Papers, Colonial Series; East Indies, China, and Japan, 1617–1621*," *Calcutta Review* 53.106 (October 1871), 47.

47. In her discussion of the uses of sources such as the microfilm collection Early English Books Online beyond straightforward access, Diana Kichuk notes that "its major scholarly contribution may be to preserve primary sources and distribute them to a broad swath of scholars who could never hope to travel and examine the original print." "Metamorphosis: Remediation in Early English Books Online (EEBO)," *Literary & Linguistic Computing* 22.3 (2007): 294. And of EEB digitized, Stefania Crowther et al. note that the online source "serve[s] an immediate and much needed pragmatic function, making early printed texts accessible to a broader range of readers"; "New Scholarship, New Pedagogies: Views from the 'EEBO Generation,'" *Early Modern Literary Studies* 14.2/Special Issue 17 (September 2008), 3.1, http://purl.oclc .org/emls/14-2/crjowenu.html.

48. For a succinct discussion of the limitations of EEBO see Sarah Werner, "When Is a Source Not a Source?," *MLA Commons*, conference paper (2015), doi:10.17613/M6PG6F.

eighty-two records. Most were unsurprising, if interesting. Generally, I could figure out why the authors of geographical surveys, histories of English royalty, or agents of the East India Company mentioned the incident. But from the title alone, I could not figure out why the moment was referenced in *Helps for Suddain Accidents* (1633) by Stephen Bradwell. Sermons, I could understand. Reprints of the 1620s propaganda, certainly. But a first-aid manual? I couldn't imagine the interest.

It turns out that Bradwell wasn't so much interested in the global politics of the Amboyna incident as he was simply an Englishman paying attention to the news and trends that reached him in London. EEBO led me to a text illustrating how banal globalism was becoming in the seventeenth century, or at least how unsurprising it was for the everyday English man or woman to encounter global ideas, news, and goods. Very early on in his book, in fact, Bradwell invokes a global metaphor to describe human illness and accidents: "the maine motive which made my Pen for this work, was my observation of *Man*; who is called *A little World*.... Yet withall, those boundlesse Oceans of fatall Accidents (whose mercilesse and suddain billowes threaten still to confound him) make his but *A World of Miserie*."⁴⁹ The preface is a wonder of piled-up metaphors for health and medicine, so I will not argue that Bradwell's is a "global" English medical treatise on account of this single, Shakespearean image, although the metaphor is perhaps more extended than the others he employs and, as the first metaphor in his preface, serves as something of a ruling figure for the rest.⁵⁰ Rather, I came to understand that an analysis of this text fits a study of the early modern global imagination not because of its attention to a world of medicine but because of the way such sensibilities are taken for granted. England's overseas experiences have been incorporated into the text—into medical practice—almost without comment, suggesting how thoroughly global systems of trade and belief took hold of English imaginations in the seventeenth century.

If the integration of colonial knowledge in medicine is significant in Bradwell's text, of equal note—and equally taken for granted—is the way that violence is woven into medical practice throughout the text. While it can be argued that violence is inherent in all medical practice and no more so in medieval and early modern medicine than today, the violence of Bradwell's practice is particular to his time and place.⁵¹ He incorporates

---

49. Stephen Bradwell, *Helps for Suddain Accidents* (London, 1633), A2v.

50. Bradwell begins with the image of man as a "globe in plano" and then runs in quick succession through images of time as dispatching footmen on "sandy arrands." Our "gloryes" are as "Sunne-beames but of a waterish shining." Our lives are measured by "Clocks of Health" that "seldome goe true" (A2v–A3r).

51. One need only consider the effects on the body of chemotherapies or what one healthcare practitioner calls the "brutally invasive" practices of intensive care. Andrew Ellner, "First,

new and potentially dangerous products and practices culled from English colonial and overseas experiences into his prescriptions, and his work sheds additional light on the reception and influence of products, information, and news from the East and West Indies and the myriad uses to which they were put in the metropole.

American colonization and the exportation of American products to London make up one significant West Indian context for *Helps for Suddain Accidents*. Bradwell published his text twenty-six years after the settlement of Jamestown in Virginia, thirteen years after the establishment of Plymouth Colony, five or six years after Barbados was planted, and just three years after the Massachusetts Bay Colony was founded. His first-aid manual reflects the keen interest that metropolitan consumers had in American products, in this case, particularly in tobacco. Although tobacco was held to be a potentially dangerous substance (both physically and morally), by the time Bradwell documented his best practices, it had become a customary addition to daily life in England, though not without risk.

Another important context for the handbook is East Indian. Once again, the Amboyna incident crops up in texts not otherwise interested in East Indian colonial affairs. The Amboyna tortures took place in 1623. Bradwell published in 1633, a year after the incident found political-legal settlement in a not guilty verdict in the trial of the Dutch colonial factors in the Netherlands, and a year after the East India Company republished accounts of the Amboyna incident, including a reissue of *A True Relation* with, as frontispiece, an engraving of the water torture, somewhat modified from the one in the 1624 imprint.[52]

Finally, Bradwell was also writing during the Thirty Years War, the sweeping continental conflict in which wartime atrocities were regularly and sensationally reported both in Europe and in England. The war coincided with a communications revolution in the Holy Roman Empire, resulting in a regular, swift post, the rise of newspapers, a boom in pamphlet printing, and so on, developments that spread to the rest of western Europe.[53] The rapid spread of information was correlated with a shift in the understanding of violence. Peter H. Wilson notes in particular a shift from a medieval sense of violence as a moral failing to an early modern sense of violence as a

Do No Harm," *n+1*, issue 4 (Spring 2006), https://nplusonemag.com/issue-4/politics/do-no-harm/, accessed 6 August 2015.

52. For a discussion of the legal and diplomatic negotiations surrounding the trial, see Chancey, "Amboyna Massacre in English Politics."

53. Judith Pollman and Mark Greengrass, introduction to part 4, "Religious Communication: Print and Beyond," in *Religion and Cultural Exchange in Europe, 1400–1700*, ed. Heinz Schilling and István György Tóth (Cambridge: Cambridge University Press, 2006), 232.

disorder that could be settled only by stronger systems of authority, of stronger government. Such views would come home to England in the wake of its Civil Wars, with Hobbes's *Leviathan* as perhaps their most celebrated articulation.[54] We can see something of this sensibility at work in Bradwell's handbook of emergency medical treatment, especially in his own "invention" for treating hydrophobia, an invention inspired by the water torture on Amboyna. In his short account of how this moment of East Indian violence inspired him to speculate on a new medical treatment, he seems to subscribe to the notion that violence, properly handled, is a legitimate tool of the state and recourse to violence is acceptable if it is wielded by those properly trained and authorized. *Suddain Helps* offers potentially dangerous colonial remedies—questionable treatments and pharmacopoeia that may hurt or heal—but maintains that the threat can be controlled and redirected by properly trained and authorized metropolitan authorities, tobacco and torture alike.

Stephen Bradwell was third in a line of men practicing medicine in early modern England. His maternal grandfather was John Banister, a celebrated doctor; his father was also named Stephen Bradwell. Both men were writers—Banister published several translations of medical treatises, while the elder Bradwell penned a detailed account of a case of witchcraft in which he was a consulting physician. Both eventually became licentiates of the Royal College of Physicians. The younger Bradwell did not, though he seems to have enjoyed a respectable reputation at a time when a sizeable minority of London's health practitioners also worked off the rolls.[55] *Helps for Suddain Accidents* reflects his somewhat marginalized status—few other physicians, it seems, were interested in providing laypeople with medical instruction. Norman Gevitz affords the book "isolated priority" as a first-aid manual. That is, it seems to have been the first such publication devoted to giving laypeople instruction over a wide range of illnesses and accidents, and none like it followed for several decades.[56]

One reason why more such manuals were not produced may be the careful line they needed to tread between lay and professional knowledge. As Gevitz notes, some doctors were concerned that giving untrained people instruction in medical care could have disastrous results. Bradwell

---

54. See Peter Wilson, "Perceptions of Violence in the Early Modern Communications Revolution: The Case of the Thirty Years War, 1618–1648," in *War and Violence in the Media: Five Disciplinary Lenses*, ed. Athina Karatzogianni (Hoboken: Taylor and Francis, 2013), 26.

55. For the family's biography and medical practice, see Norman Gevitz, "'Helps for Suddain Accidents': Stephen Bradwell and the Origin of the First Aid Guide," *Bulletin of the History of Medicine* 67.1 (Spring 1993): 51–73.

56. Gevitz asserts that the book was the first of its kind in England and may have been first in Europe more generally; "'Helps for Suddain Accidents,'" 71.

acknowledges the danger; he provides some medicinal recipes in Latin so that only educated apothecaries could make the compounds.[57] And he takes care to recommend recourse to educated professionals for difficult procedures or after a patient had been stabilized. One such instance is (happily) his recommendation that laypeople employ qualified surgeons for tracheotomies: "But this is not to be attempted by any but some skillful *Chirurgion* indeed, that knoweth perfectly the situation of the parts."[58]

Despite his care to present the text as a supplement to professional health care in seventeenth-century England, the book blends erudition with down-to-earth approaches. As the full title suggests, Bradwell understood that not everyone would have access to professional help. His book is directed toward "those that live farr from Physitions or Churgions" so that they "may happily preserve the Life of a poore Friend or Neighbour, till such a Man may be had to perfect the Cure." And because he and his family practiced in one of London's poorer neighborhoods, he knew that not everyone could afford professional care. He makes that distinction plain at one point, suggesting two courses of treatment depending on income.[59]

His recommendations for tobacco use exemplify his approach. By the 1630s, tobacco was a regular part of metropolitan English culture. As Susan Campbell Anderson explains, upon tobacco's introduction to English markets it received attention first from scientists and then from novelty seekers.[60] By the first decades of the seventeenth century, tobacco's reputation as an effective medicinal plant changed from benevolent cure-all to somewhat dangerous substance requiring "appropriate supervision of a physician."[61] Yet its use for pleasure was steadily increasing. We can see in Bradwell's tract how in 1633 the plant by turns judged a noxious weed and a lucrative crop had become a fairly commonplace product and a fairly unremarkable ingredient in his early modern first-aid kit. What his several references to the use of tobacco to cure—and in one memorable case to wound—demonstrate is how taken-for-granted this colonial American product had become in the English pharmacopeia.

57. Gevitz, "'Helps for Suddain Accidents,'" 64; Bradwell, *Helps for Suddain Accidents*, 78.

58. Bradwell, *Helps for Suddain Accidents*, 90. Bradwell acknowledged the danger of the procedure by repeating an instance of black bedside humor. A surgeon, on being asked what to do in the case of a crushed windpipe, gives this remedy "briefly and wittily": "Cut a throat to save a life."

59. Bradwell, *Helps for Suddain Accidents*, 90. Gevitz says that the family practiced on Silver Street in North London, just within the city wall, "'Helps for Suddain Accidents,'" 57.

60. Susan Campbell Anderson, "A Matter of Authority: James I and the Tobacco War," *Comitatus* 291 (1998): 141. Marcy Norton, *Sacred Gifts, Profane Pleasures: A History of Tobacco and Chocolate in the Atlantic World* (Ithaca: Cornell University Press, 2008), provides an excellent extended discussion of the encounter by Europeans of tobacco. Her book offers a "history of empire...from the periphery to the center" (12).

61. Anderson, "Matter of Authority," 145.

Bradwell recommends tobacco to his readers several times. The way he prescribes it suggests that his recommendations are his own contribution to remedies culled from other sources, and thus he uses colonial ingredients or techniques to improve on the traditions he has inherited. For instance, he suggests blowing "powder of a strong Tobacco" up the nose of a patient who has ingested poison to "make him neeze [sic] often."⁶² Sneezing is also recommended to aid those who are "Suffocated with Stinking Smells."⁶³ He suggests that tobacco is a particularly useful innovation on an older remedy for those who have been choked with coal smoke in a closed room. If these patients come down with fever after the initial treatment, they should have "powder of Euphorbium" blown up their noses to clear their brains (no explicit mention of neezes).⁶⁴ But in an aside, he advises that helpers should swap out the "dangerously violent" purgative euphorbium for the "powder of good Tobacco" to elicit a milder reaction.⁶⁵

Bradwell elsewhere recommends blowing tobacco smoke into the ear to rid it of earwigs, and he adds "two or three leaves of green Tobacco" into his personal recipe for burn salve. Although the tobacco is optional, he counsels that the concoction "will be the better" for the addition.⁶⁶ Lady Hasting's recipe for burn salve, which Bradwell includes as his last entry in the book, is a case in point of the ubiquity of tobacco-based medicine. Its three main ingredients are "Thorny-Apple of Peru," better known to us as *Datura stramonium* or jimsonweed, a highly toxic plant found throughout North America, "English Tobacco," which I take to reference tobacco grown specifically in English colonies, and "Ground-Ivie," a plant native to Europe.⁶⁷

What is remarkable about all these remedies is not the use of tobacco as some kind of exotic colonial wonder drug, as it might have been understood earlier in the century, but its unremarkability. Bradwell assumes the ready availability of tobacco in its various preparations as well as ready access to the accouterments for using it. Here we see prescribed tobacco powder, smoke, whole green leaf, and (by inference) cured leaves. The medical delivery systems are quotidian—blow snuff with a quill—and specialized: that pesky earwig gets a dose of smoke blown through a pipe. Bradwell

---

62. Bradwell, *Helps for Suddain Accidents*, 23.

63. Bradwell, *Helps for Suddain Accidents*, 113.

64. Bradwell, *Helps for Suddain Accidents*, 110.

65. Euphorbium, derived from a Moroccan plant, was "widely used" in the Renaissance to provoke sneezing. But, as one contemporary study of the plant's properties explains, physicians avoided it "on account of the severity of its action." The authors go on to note that a twentieth-century text listed "Euphorbium as a drastic purgative." Giovanni Appendino and Arpad Szallas, "Euphorbium: Modern Research on Its Active Principle, Reseniferatoxin, Revives an Ancient Medicine," *Life Sciences* 60.10 (1997), 683, 684.

66. Bradwell, *Helps for Suddain Accidents*, 30, 87.

67. Bradwell, *Helps for Suddain Accidents*, 125. See L. F. Haas, "*Datera Stramomium* (Jimsonweed)," *Journal of Neurology, Neurosurgery & Psychiatry* 58 (1995), 654.

obviously believed that tobacco in all its forms, as well as the technology to make use of it, would be at hand in average households. After all, as Anderson notes, in the seventeenth century young men went about town equipped with cases kitted out with two or three clay pipes.[68]

Scientists and gallants: these are the groups Anderson identifies as most interested in tobacco as it was introduced to England. Bradwell definitely identifies himself with the first group but also gives us a vivid anecdote concerning the second. Near the end of the book, as its last example in fact, he describes his memory of an accident at a "place" (a home? a tavern?) in 1626 when a young girl got a bit of burning tobacco in her eye. The account illustrates once again that this colonial export had become a usual and customary part of European culture. The story is obviously meant to illustrate his own quick thinking. He "ran into the garden, where I found some ground Ivie, whereof I gathered some, which I stamped, and strayned, and putting a little fine powdred Sugar to the Juice, I dropped some of it into her eye; upon which she received suddain ease."[69]

His decisive action makes for a solid medical anecdote, but the cavalier way those who caused the accident were consuming their tobacco is what turns the account into a vivid story: "some Gentlemen were taking Tobacco; and as one had knocked out the snuffe or coale of it on the Table; another in jest blew it toward him, he also blew it at him againe. This began to be pursued from one to the other, till a little Girle looking on (whose height was little above the Table) received the evill of their jesting; for some of the burning-coale of Tobacco was blown into her eye. It tormented her extreamely (as nothing burneth more terribly)."[70] The detail of his account makes for a good plot—we have the villains of the piece, gallants acting badly; the innocent victim in a very small girl child; and the hero, Bradwell himself. But one wonders why the details need be here at all. The story could simply begin with the cinder in the eye and proceed to the cure, like so many other descriptions in the book.

We can speculate on Bradwell's reasons for detailing this particular accident and its cure, but the effect of the anecdote is to throw into relief the risks—perhaps even the "structural violence" of his medical practice.[71] By including it he acknowledges and then contains the inherent violence of early modern medicine. In 1633, tobacco may have been a common ingredient of metropolitan pleasures and cures, but English readers would have

68. Anderson, "Matter of Authority," 144.
69. Bradwell, *Helps for Suddain Accidents*, 123.
70. Bradwell, *Helps for Suddain Accidents*, 122.
71. "Structural violence is violence exerted systematically—that is, indirectly—by everyone who belongs to a certain social order." See Paul Farmer, "An Anthropology of Structural Violence," *Current Anthropology* 45.3 (June 2004), 307.

remembered concern over—and outright attacks on—the use of tobacco from earlier in the century, and those debates about tobacco's moral valence linger in Bradwell's representation. Perhaps the most influential statement was that of James I, whose authorship of *A Counterblaste to Tobacco* (1604) was an open secret. Certainly his "blast" against tobacco pulls no punches: tobacco use is "lothsome to the eye, hatefull to the Nose, harmefull to the braine, daungerous to the Lungs and in the blacke stinking fume thereof, neerest resembling the horrible Stigian smoke of the pit that is bottomlesse."[72] Ben Jonson supported his patron's view of tobacco in his masque *Gipsies Metamorphosed,* in which tobacco is a "wicked weed" in which Satan delights.[73] By incorporating tobacco into medical remedies, doctors used a substance that was potentially both politically and physically dangerous, subjecting their patients to a local threat in order to bring about a greater good. By including the anecdote of the girl with the spark in her eye, Bradwell suggests that tobacco still had a rather mixed reputation, and he firmly places himself on the right side of the debate about its use. The full context of this particular "suddain accident" effectively contrasts his cool professionalism with the "evill" of the men's jesting. His own earlier use of tobacco in the text is thus revealed as a judicious use of the American plant by a health professional. The substance itself may be unsavory, but the physician's use of it wholesome.

Bradwell's recourse to potentially dangerous treatments and his assertion of professional control over those dangers are even more marked in his description of another colonial inspiration for his practice. He adapts the Amboyna torture apparatus that the Dutch used to waterboard their English prisoners in order to treat hydrophobia, that is, rabies. If the use of tobacco in medicine was somewhat controversial, Bradwell acknowledges that his use of a torture technique on an innocent sufferer to be as nearly unsupportable—he knows that the treatment is flat-out "inhumane." Nevertheless, he justifies employing the torture to cure by claiming that the ends justify the means: "thus have I out of a wicked weed sucked Honey for Health."[74] One could argue that Bradwell's recommendation to waterboard rabies patients is some improvement over the description, just a page earlier, of the "general Remedie is by *Celsus* and others" to cure rabies by throwing the patient into deep water and allowing him almost to drown. Indeed, if the patient knows how to swim, the "general Remedie" recommends that he be held "under water a little while till he have taken in some prettie quantitie."[75]

72. James I, King of England, *A Counterblaste to Tobacco* (London, 1604).
73. Ben Jonson, *Selected Masques*, ed. Stephen Orgel (New Haven: Yale University Press, 1970), 244.
74. Bradwell, *Helps for Suddain Accidents*, 70.
75. Bradwell, *Helps for Suddain Accidents*, 69.

In context, his hydrophobia treatment isn't unusual in its brutality. Throughout the book we hear of less extreme, more regularly used, and definitely still painful medical treatments—emetics, purges, bloodletting, cauterization, not to mention the countless animals jointed, skinned, roasted, gutted, scarified, or otherwise used to compound medicines or effect cures.

Then, again, Bradwell may have come to accept aggressive medical treatment not as a usual and customary element of early modern medicine but as a familial legacy. Consider that he may have read his father's manuscript of a witchcraft case of 1602 in which both the accused and the afflicted girl were subjected to what in another context would be considered outright torture. Mary Glover, a fourteen-year-old girl, had been struggling for weeks with paralysis, fits, and other strange symptoms. The first doctors called in treated her natural ailments but eventually were forced to admit defeat and diagnose supernatural causes.[76] Elizabeth Johnson, a neighbor with whom Mary Glover had had a falling out, was accused of bewitching the girl. The outcome of the trial depended on the testimony of several physicians who testified both for and against a natural diagnosis, with the elder Bradwell testifying that the causes of Glover's distress were not natural. Johnson was found guilty, but when Edward Jordan published a defense of the natural diagnosis, the elder Bradwell wrote a detailed rebuttal, which survives in manuscript but seems never to have been printed.[77] One of the details of the trial that Bradwell recounts is the testing of Mary Glover to be sure that she is not feigning her insensible paralysis. The test takes the form of a physical ordeal typical of criminal inquisitions through torture: trial by fire. As the case made its way up levels of authority, repeated exhibitions of Glover's suffering were required. The recorder of the city of London made this attempt:

> Mr Recorder sent for a candle, made a pin hot in the flame, and applyed it to her Cheeke and after that (with a new heating) neere unto her eye, to see, if she would drawe togeather her eyebrowes, or liddes, or make any semblant of feeling, but she did not. Then he tooke paper somwhat [*sic*] writhed, and setting fyre thereon, put the flame to the inside of her right hand, and there held it, till the paper was consumed. In like maner he

---

76. Glover's was a celebrated case. Hers was the first witchcraft trial in England in which medical experts were called in to diagnose. See Daniel Walker, *Unclean Spirits: Possession and Exorcism in France and England in the Late Sixteenth and Early Seventeenth Centuries* (Philadelphia: University of Pennsylvania Press, 1981), 79; Joanna Levin, "Lady MacBeth and the Daemonologie of Hysteria," *ELH* 69.1 (Spring 2002): 21–55; and Michael MacDonald, editor's introduction to *Witchcraft and Hysteria in Elizabethan London: Edward Jorden and the Mary Glover Case* (London: Tavistock, 1991).

77. The "natural causes" tract is Edward Jordan's *A briefe discourse of a disease called the suffocation of the mother* (London, 1603), which argued that Glover was suffering from hysteria.

proceeded with a second, and a third paper, so as her hand (as well appeared afterwards) was effectually burned, in five severall places.[78]

One can only assume that the elder Bradwell saw the burns afterward in the course of treating them—and one hopes that he had access to Peruvian Thorny Apple and tobacco to treat her. Later, during Johnson's trial, Glover was again suspected of dissembling. She had been carried in a fit to a nearby chamber, into which the recorder, several justices, and the town clerk charged, "with thundering voyces crying; bring the fyre, and hot Irons, for this Counterfett; Come wee will marke her, on the Cheeke, for a Counterfett."[79] Glover passed the test by not responding to the threats. The elder Bradwell evidently approved of this treatment of a fourteen-year-old girl as an efficient means to get at the truth of the case.

It is impossible to know how familiar young Stephen would have been with this celebrated case or if he ever read his father's account. But it seems likely that he would have paid attention in 1602. He was eleven or twelve years old himself at the time, and surely the supernatural and juridical torment of a girl near his own age would have interested him. So perhaps it is not surprising that Stephen Bradwell, grown and practicing medicine for himself, would upon encountering the image of Amboyna look on it with dispassionate interest and, rather than seeing only a means of martyring English heroes, would see instead a technique that in the right hands could be a promising medical treatment: "My selfe (upon sight of a picture of the *Water-Torture* in Amboyna) have conceited [*sic*] this invention."[80]

He cannot, of course, escape the violent implications of the scene. Patients so treated will seem emblematic of Christian martyrs; the visual is inescapable: "Let the Patient bee bound fast to some post or stake, and tie about his necke a linnen cloth doubled and cast into the forme of a hollow Bason (as you would make him looke like the signe of St. *John Baptists head in a platter*)." Nevertheless, the treatment must procced, no matter how the patient resists: "the cloth must first be dipped in Oyle and Waxe well mixed together, that it may hold water like a Bason: Then let one with an Ewer or Pitcher poure water gently into the cloth, till the water rise up to his nostrills, where through it may enter into his body (if he will not open his mouth) whether he will or no…onely sometimes forbeare so much as to maintaine his breathing."[81] As I've suggested, his invention perhaps "improves" on the classical treatment of hydrophobia. In the original treatment, care

78. Stephen Bradwell, "Mary Glovers Late Woeful Case," in MacDonald, *Witchcraft and Hysteria in Elizabethan London*, 21.
79. Bradwell, "Mary Glover," 23.
80. Bradwell, *Helps for Suddain Accidents*, 70.
81. Bradwell, *Helps for Suddain Accidents*, 70.

must be taken to simulate drowning, whereas here at least, care is taken to allow the patient to breathe.

As I discuss in chapter 5, others who viewed the pictures of the Amboyna torture reacted much differently. As noted, one victim's widow was said to have swooned at the sight. Bradwell's reaction, by contrast, is a measured, "rational" application of its lessons to effect a medical cure, much like his judicious use of tobacco. Here, Bradwell illustrates Susan Sontag's point in *Regarding the Pain of Others* in which she notes that images of atrocity do not affect us all equally: "there are many uses of the innumerable opportunities a modern life supplies for regarding—at a distance, through the medium of photography—other people's pain. Photographs of an atrocity may give rise to opposing responses."[82] Bradwell's description suggests that he himself has competing reactions to the image of the Amboyna torture. His dispassionate description of the torment includes the fanciful comparison of the patient's head swaddled for treatment to John the Baptist's head on Salome's platter. The odd image registers the violence of the treatment, perhaps an acknowledgment of illegitimate desires on the part of Bradwell as a medical practitioner, and gestures toward the horror of the colonial inspiration for this new prescription. The technique of waterboarding may be, as Bradwell says in an (unconscious) echo of Jonson, a "wicked weed," but Bradwell does not doubt his ability to control its effects.[83] It's worth quoting his assertion again: "Thus have I out of a wicked weed sucked Honey for Health; and from an inhumane torture extracted ease in a grievous sickness."[84]

What he does not acknowledge, despite his use of the past tense, is that this horrific water cure is neither tested, nor in his experience even needed. Hydrophobia was for Bradwell in 1633 an entirely hypothetical affliction. He prefaces his description of his invented water treatment with a caveat: "Although in this our countrey of *England,* I have neither seene nor heard or

---

82. Sontag, *Regarding the Pain of Others* 13.

83. It's possible that Bradwell took the phrase from Jonson directly. Though it was not published until 1640, *Gipsies Metamorphosed* was performed in August 1621. At that time, Richard Brome was one of Jonson's servants. Brome would go on to become part of a coterie of minor poets and playwrights that included Humphrey Mill, Thomas Heywood, and Nathaniel Richards. Bradwell wrote prefatory poems to various of their works (Humphrey Mill, *A Nights Search*; Thomas Heywood, *The Nine Worthy Women*; Nathaniel Richards, *Messaline*). He also probably wrote a prefatory poem for Richard Brome himself, in *The Northern Lass*. See Julie Sanders, "Textual Introduction" (2010), in *The Northern Lass,* ed. Julie Sanders, in *The Complete Works of Richard Brome-Online,* gen. ed. Richard Cave, http://www.hrionline.ac.uk/brome/. Ben Jonson also contributed a prefatory poem to Brome's work. As one of Brome's friends, it is possible that in 1621 Stephen got a glimpse of the court masque. The tobacco-burning gentlemen nearly blinded the little girl in 1624, and one can imagine that Bradwell describing a game gone wrong among his own coterie. Else why was he so near at hand?

84. Bradwell, *Helps for Suddain Accidents,* 70.

any such terrible dangers happening to people by a mad-dogs biting, as in other Regions: yet I have seen Dogs mad."[85] Here we see that his knowledge of the best way to cure a case (imagined) of rabies is utterly secondhand, culled from classical texts. He takes pride, then, in fantasizing an extreme cure, invented from his contemplation of images of colonial torture, and applied to a terrible illness he has neither witnessed nor likely will witness in his career. A "wicked weed," indeed.

85. Bradwell, *Helps for Suddain Accidents*, 53.

CHAPTER 5

"Would India had beene never knowne"

Wives Tales and the Global English Archive

I magine little William Sanderson, just seven years old, welcoming great-uncle Walter Raleigh, come to consult with young William's father. William Sanderson the elder was handling the explorer's accounts for his voyage to Guiana in 1595.[1] Or picture him at the baptismal font—three times!—as his younger brothers were christened "Ralegh," "Drake," and "Cavendish," the last two in recognition of the explorers' accomplishments in "compassing the Earth."[2] In 1592 we can imagine that William got a close-up view of the first globes ever printed in England, for which his father had paid a thousand pounds. As Ruth A. McIntyre notes, Sanderson the elder was "one of the merchants who . . . were renewing their interest in the most alluring geographical concept of the late sixteenth century, namely, that England could be linked with the rich commerce of Asia by a route running northward."[3] The Sanderson family, though not the most celebrated, belonged to a cohort of early modern Englishmen interested in and intimately involved with supporting England's extension into the world.

---

1. Anita McConnell, "Sanderson, William (1547/8–1638)," in *Oxford Dictionary of National Biography* (Oxford: Oxford University Press, 2004), http://www.oxforddnb.com/view/article/52001, accessed 4 September 2016.

2. McConnell, "Sanderson, William." Sanderson the younger also gives an account of his family in *An Answer to a Scurrilous Pamphlet* (London, 1656), 3.

3. Ruth A. McIntyre, "William Sanderson: Elizabethan Financier of Discovery," *William and Mary Quarterly* 13.2 (April 1956), 189. She goes on to note that Sanderson the elder was "the most consistent single supporter of the three voyages of discovery sailing from England from 1585 to 1587 with orders to find a passage to China." Three surviving narratives of these voyages were written by his servants (190).

Figure 5.1. Sir Walter Raleigh and son, artist unknown, 1602. Used by permission of the National Portrait Gallery, London.

How profound must have been William Sanderson the younger's disappointment, then, when the promise of his early years was met by tragedy and loss. A brother accompanied Captain George Weymouth on a voyage to find the Northwest Passage, and when his family learned of that young son's death William was about sixteen. He was in his twenties when Raleigh's family brought suit against his father for mishandling the explorer's funds, and he was in his late twenties when he would have received news that his brother Drake had died while accompanying Raleigh on his last American voyage (though another brother returned safely). Nor was the family's fate all westward. A decade later, his brother Hugh died in the East Indies, and Thomas Sanderson was shot in Russia by a Scottish rival after serving as an officer with distinction not only in the East and West Indies but also in Ireland, Scotland, Sweden, and Germany.[4] Moreover, we know many of these details through the works William Sanderson himself published when he was in his seventies, a man grown old, but still loyal to the idea of an English king and royal succession, forced to navigate the hostile political waters of

4. As reported by Sanderson, *Answer to a Scurrilous Pamphlet*, 3.

the Interregnum. In the 1650s, he published his views not of future history but of recent past and present in a series of polemical tracts, royal histories, and even a treatise on visual art. In all these works, we can see him inscribing his family's history onto the nation, and if we look closely we can see how he shapes a particular vision of the English world, one that is invested in martyrdom rather than millennialism and that celebrates a muscular, masculine English identity.

It's fair to say that England's performance on a global stage brought sorrow to the Sandersons: at least four sons dead overseas, legal complications and financial losses from their support of voyages of discovery. But it's also fair to say that, judging from the younger Sanderson's writings, the family took pride in their contributions to England's expansion abroad: the globes, the sons' christening, even the sacrifice of so many sons, among them Thomas, whom William Sanderson the younger called a man "of some note," taking care to record his feat of being the first "that ever carried a double Reigment [sic] of 2000. men by Sea, about the Norway Cape, to the Emperor of Mosco."[5] If there was pain, there was also profit.

But for others, there was little such pride to be had. For many lower-class English and indigenous actors on the global stage, for most women caught up in global events, such endeavors resulted in outright misery. The disaffection of such people is dramatized in the 1632 play *The Launching of the Mary, or The Seaman's Honest Wife*, written by Walter Mountfort, an East India Company employee, on board ship as he returned to England from Persia. The main plot of the play is described by Matteo Pangallo as consisting of "extremely long and dramatically uncompelling exchanges."[6] Its subplots, however, are much more interesting. One plotline follows workers employed by the East India Company complaining about (among other things) the bloody treatment of the English in Amboyna. A second centers on women, not those who might be involved in East Indian trade, exploration, or settlement directly, but those left behind by their husbands who, employed by the Company, traveled for months or years on Company business. As Dorotea Constance, the one honest wife in the play, contemplates her state without the protection of her husband, she wishes away England's overseas endeavors: "would I had never known a maryed state or else would India had beene never knowne."[7] Dorotea's fantasy that the Indies had

5. Sanderson, *Answer to a Scurrilous Pamphlet*, 3.

6. Matteo Pangallo, "Seldome Seene: Observations from Editing *The Launching of the Mary: Or the Seaman's Honest Wife*," in *Divining Thoughts: Future Directions in Shakespeare Studies*, ed. Peter Orford with Michael P. Jones, Lizz Ketterer, and Joshua McEvillia (Newcastle: Cambridge Scholars), 1–16.

7. Walter Mountford, *The Launching of the Mary*, ed. John Johnson (Oxford: Oxford University Press, 1933), 33.

"beene never knowne" is a reminder that the benefits of England's overseas exploration and colonial settlement did not extend to all.

Yet women appear regularly in the printed and archival record of English extension into the world, just not often because of their own interests or endeavors. It's true that some women, as did William Sanderson the elder, supported England's global enterprises directly; for example, Lady Mary Armine was considered the financial patron of the Indian mission in New England. But more often, accounts of women were used to generate support—financial or otherwise—for the plans of the various joint-stock companies organized in England to settle and exploit the colonies and trading factories. In the literature of colonial and overseas expansion, women serve as both witchy threats to Christian order and symbols of the righteousness of the colonial enterprise. In metropolitan writings, they are the ground of "proper" family and economic order, sexual threats to that order, and even at times wielders of serious political power. But even when women's voices are hard to hear, as I've shown in the case of the unnamed Algonquian woman described and quoted in the mission tract *Of the Conversion of Five Thousand Nine-Hundred East Indians*, by reading the documents closely, sometimes with and sometimes against the grain, and by using an interdisciplinary approach to those records, we can not only analyze the worlding of the imaginations of those with access to print and authority in record keeping but also consider those who did not have as celebrated a position in England's colonial or overseas order.

To return to the Amboyna incident: rather than focusing only on the men who suffered and who took center stage in the accounts from the 1620s to the 1670s, it behooves us as well to consider the "wives' tales" that were conjured out of fleeting, seemingly incidental references in the manuscript and print records of the Amboyna incident. Consider, for instance, the English widow of one of the men executed by the Dutch in 1623, a story recounted by William Sanderson. In two publications in the 1650s, he describes an Amboyna widow who, self-possessed enough to sue for reparations for her martyred husband, swooned when confronted with the painting of the Amboyna torture. In brief anecdotes, Sanderson inscribes an image of an intrepid woman who is nonetheless sentimental and susceptible.[8] His accounts suggest several questions: What would her experiences grappling with Company courts have been? How difficult was it for a woman to seek such reparations? What kind of life did she face as a Company man's widow in London, and why did an oil painting of a scene she must have often imagined and heard described so unnerve her?

---

8. Sanderson briefly describes this woman and her reaction twice: in *A compleat history of the life and raigne of King Charles*, published in 1656, and in his 1658 publication *Graphice*.

A different set of questions is prompted by another version of an Amboynan wife. She too may be counted a widow—of sorts. The East India Company court records reference an enslaved woman who had been given to the "Captain of the Slaves," and whose fate therefore was uncertain after his execution. The archival traces of this woman seems to have inspired John Dryden to reimagine her for *Amboyna*, his jingoistic play of English national pride and Dutch villainy. Among literary scholars, Dryden's turn at representing the Amboyna incident is fairly well known, certainly better known than any other representation of the events written in the seventeenth century. While his play, written in 1673, was not, strictly speaking, a product of Cromwell's world of the 1650s, which was the historical context of the other Amboyna texts I have considered, and which has been my primary focus throughout this book, Dryden himself surely was. As we shall see, Dryden's created two characters from the historical records of this woman, though he makes one, the beautiful and innocent Ysabinda, the focus of the main plot. She, like her husband Gabriel Towerson, is betrayed by the Dutch and made to suffer in service to the moral of the play.

Sanderson's swooning and Dryden's tragic widow should prompt us to ask how and why these writers chose to represent Towerson's wife as they did. What can their version of events tell us about their understanding of the world—and of England as a nation with global pretentions—in the 17th century? Moreover, by comparing the fantasies that Sanderson and Dryden constructed to other print and archival traces of Amboyna and of women's lives in early modern England more generally, we can speculate on the meaning women themselves made of their experiences, however seemingly minor their roles. The result is a fuller picture of English overseas life and a useful corrective to a records-driven picture of a male-dominated colonial world.

A COMPANY WIDOW

On 9 March 1623, ten Englishmen on the island of Amboyna were led to the scaffold to be executed by the Dutch merchants in control of the island. As the sword severed head from neck, head from neck, down the line, the sky darkened and the earth shook—or so the English accounts read. Moreover, when a Dutch leader later inadvertently stumbled into the English gravesite, he promptly went mad. Thus, reports of the incidents were wrapped in wondrous, even Christic elements, and the executed men became instant heroes, martyrs of the English nation.[9] Given such potent signs of cosmic

9. Among the wonders catalogued in response to English deaths, *A True Relation of the Unjust, Cruell, and Barbarous Proceedings Against the English at Amboyna in the East-Indies*

disturbance at the death of England's merchant sons, surely we should learn that the families and widows of the victims were somehow instantly struck by the news of their loved ones' deaths. There should have been premonitions. There should have been apparitions.[10]

Instead, news of the men's' deaths limped into port weeks later, brought by an East India Company memo to East India Company men. The news came by way of Texel—the perpetrators' own port. And in the absence of supernatural instruction, the survivors had to determine their own responses to their personal and familial tragedies. Whatever the survivors' immediate reaction to the news—weeping, shock, indifference, grim determination—the archives show that in fairly short order they had to tackle the task of living—and without the support of husbands, fathers, or brothers.

Before the deaths of their husbands, the wives of the men executed in Amboyna would have enjoyed a measure of financial security as the spouses of gainfully employed Company men. These women inhabited an interesting demographic. They ran their households and exercised a degree of independence during their husbands' long absences in the East on cruises that could run from many months to years.[11] As married women they had the status of wives, but during their husbands' absences they would have been functionally in the position of widows, raising families, making decisions on their own. According to Company apologist Thomas Mun, wives received up to two months' advance pay for every year of their husband's service, a stipend only, to be sure, but it must have been a welcome one.[12] Often, wives petitioned the Company court for additional funds. Wives left behind while their husbands were away on Company business could also have taken in lodgers or engaged in small trade. Mun further suggests in his 1621 *Discourses of Trade* that although many East India Company employees were taken from the ranks of the poor, if crafts- or tradesmen signed on, their wives might have continued the family business. In short, they occupied the role of what Laurel Thatcher Ulrich calls the "deputy husband."[13]

(London, 1624), lists sudden darkness, a tempest, a plague, and a Dutch official driven mad upon falling into the grave of the English martyrs (29–30).

10. John Dryden agrees. In his play *Amboyna*, an English boy who has been subjected to torture threatens just such a supernatural visitation: "I have a little Brother in *England*, that I intend to appear to, when you have kill'd me; and if he do's not promise me the Death of ten *Dutchmen*, in the next War, I'le haunt him instead of you." *Amboyna*, in *The Works of John Dryden*, vol. 17, ed. Vinton A. Dearing (Berkeley: University of California Press, 1994), 5.1.204–207.

11. *The Launching of the Mary* proclaims that "the voyages are thirty monthes or more"; Walter Mountford, *The Launching of the Mary*, ed. John Johnson (Oxford: Oxford University Press, 1933), 66.

12. Thomas Mun, *A discourse of trade, from England vnto the East-Indies answering to diuerse obiections which are vsually made against the same* (London, 1621), 42. Mun's tract is partially dramatized in Mountford, *The Launching of the Mary*.

13. See "Deputy Husbands," chapter 2 of Laurel Thatcher Ulrich, *Good Wives: Image and Reality in the Lives of Women in Northern New England, 1650–1750* (New York: Knopf, 1982).

Although they were legally *femmes couvert*, wives did engage with the Company's court in their husbands' absence. In 1624, the year that survivors of the men executed on Amboyna began to ask the Company for financial compensation or relief, more than 400 petitions in total were made to the Company's General Court.[14] Of these, forty-four are clearly marked as having been made by wives of Company men. The majority of wives' petitions were for part of their husbands' wages; thirty of the forty-four petitions by wives asked for set amounts or for half of their husbands' wages.[15]

But what became of these quasi-independent women when the fiction of their man-less existence became fact? William Sanderson's story of one widow's reaction to the news underscores the ways that the legal system in seventeenth-century England did make a place for (some) widowed women. In two of his midcentury publications, *A Compleat History of the Lives and Reigns of, Mary Queen of Scotland, and of Her Son and Successor, James the Sixth*, published in 1656, and *Graphice: The Use of the Pen and Pensil*, published in 1658, he recalls the Amboyna incident. In *Graphice*, he digresses from his main argument to recall one of the Amboyna widows, who "upon former relations" of her husband's torture had "prosecuted her complaint."[16] His word "complaint" conveys the sense of both lamentation and going to law for redress, as if her grief and her legal action are inextricable.

But what did it mean to "prosecute her complaint"? How did she do so, and why? The economics of her situation suggest one answer: before the news from Amboyna reached England, the wives of the East Indies merchants employed in the East Indies had certain rights and resources, and East Indian court records of 1624 offer a fascinating glimpse of how they deployed those rights. Some cases suggest women's dependence on their husband's income. For instance, in late August, Jane Mason requested the

---

14. See "East Indies: Miscellaneous, 1624," in *Calendar of State Papers Colonial, East Indies, China and Japan*, vol. 4, *1622–1624*, ed. W. Noel Sainsbury (London, 1878), 477–493, British History Online, http://www.british-history.ac.uk/cal-state-papers/colonial/east-indies-china-japan/vol4/pp477-493, accessed 25 November 2015.

15. To be sure, the Company court dealt with wives only if they felt that their husbands had authorized their legal voices. Petitions were denied because the court wasn't convinced that a wife was actually acting in partnership with her husband and not on her own behalf. Consider the case of Mary Bradley, whose 26 September 1624 petition was denied as "contrary to husband's wishes"; East India Company Court Minutes, 2 July 1624–14 April 1625, India Office Records, Asia and Africa Collections, British Library, IOR/B/9. At 26 September 1623, the *Calendar of State Papers* summarizes two petitions from men who had lost money to women posing as their wives: "John Heath, quartermaster of the London, for 5l. paid in his absence to one that pretended to be his wife; and Nicholas Sneering, for two months' wages paid in the same way: the Court ordered payment, but charged Mr. Hurte to be more careful hereafter." "East Indies: September 1623," in *Calendar of State Papers Colonial, East Indies, China and Japan*, vol. 4, *1622–1624*, 147–155, http://www.british-history.ac.uk/cal-state-papers/colonial/east-indies-china-japan/vol4/pp147-155, accessed 3 December 2015.

16. Sanderson, *Graphice*, 14.

wages of her husband, a runaway. On 13 August, the wife of Cuthbert Atkinson asked for relief for her husband, who had broken his leg at Blackwall, the company's shipbuilding yard. Other petitions demonstrate women's involvement in trade and the general business of the company. Emma, wife of Edward Raven, petitioned the company to receive a parcel of the trade good "aloes ciccatrine" (possibly aloe succotrina) due her. The record also suggests the difficulties inherent in being a woman without male supporters— Margaret Newton petitioned on December 24 for the maintenance of a child fathered by John Flippery.[17]

Widows had as large a presence as wives in the court in 1624. Another forty-six women who are named petitioners are clearly identified as widows (or "relicts")—though some have remarried, and their new husbands have joined them in the suit to claim money from their late husbands' legacies or other considerations from the Company. Of the remaining thirty-five women who petitioned the court in 1624, some few were acting in their roles of daughter or sister. The rest are not identified in terms of family connection; presumably the number of women who petitioned the court as deserving widows and wives is larger than I have accounted here.

The end of September 1624 was a particularly active period for the court to deal with its constituents' needs. Two sessions in September were devoted to dealing with petitions, and women petitioners were conspicuous in their numbers. Of the thirty petitions heard during the special sessions dated September 25 and 26, half were brought forward by women, including seven wives or widows requesting part of their husbands' wages and one woman asking for her late husband's share in the ship's clove shipment. Did these women know one another? Did they discuss their cases and their strategies before they appeared in the court? It seems likely that the court grouped the September petitioners together in order to dispense with the large number quickly, but did the women get to know one another while waiting for their turn to speak? What might their experiences have been during those two early autumnal days in 1624?

The archives allow us to speculate and so to gain some purchase on the experiences of an Amboyna widow moved to "prosecute her complaint." As Company records show, women regularly appeared before the General Court. Indeed, historian Tim Stretton notes that during this period, "women were no strangers to courts of law" in general, and his research finds women (widows particularly) "participated in legal actions, either as plaintiffs or defendants, in every major court for which records survive."[18] Women regularly

---

17. Both cases are catalogued in "East Indies: Miscellaneous, 1624," 477–493.

18. Tim Stretton, "Widows at Law in Tudor and Stuart England," in *Widowhood in Medieval and Early Modern Europe*, ed. Sandra Cavallo and Lyndan Warner (London: Routledge, 1999), 195, 194.

appeared in the various courts of early modern England, but it must still have been a difficult undertaking. As Stretton points out, "law courts were confrontational arenas where litigants spoke their minds in public."[19] However intimidating the scene, women asserted themselves in the courts, quite simply because they had to do so. The General Court of the East India Company was not a court of law; even so, it must have been daunting for a woman to consider pursuing economic justice there. Yet on their own, perhaps with dependent children, widows of Company men needed both the justice and charity of the East India Company court to survive.[20]

Consider the case of Thomazin Powell who petitioned the court in 1623 for the money and goods her son lost (along with his life) when his ship, the *Solomon*, was captured by the Dutch. The Calendar *of State Papers* gives this short description of her argument: "Her son [William Powell] about six years since was employed to the East Indies in the Swan, served in the great fight with the carrack in which the General [Benj. Joseph] was slain, and was afterwards taken in the Solomon, with many hundreds more at the Moluccas by the Hollanders, who spoiled him of all his goods and starved him to death in prison. She has long been a suitor to the East India Company for recompense. Prays their Lordships mediation with the Company or the States of Holland."[21] We can imagine not only that this comprehensive loss wiped out individual income streams but also, because the women likely had networks of support linking the family members of the Company, particularly those connected to a single crew, that the loss of the ship with most of its men left widows more than usually vulnerable. Powell (who is called "Widow Powell" throughout the court minutes) and her compatriots were insistent on their rights. The company had awarded her and her fellow petitioners some amount of money, but the full claim was rebuffed by the East India court (who argued that the Dutch had the goods, so the Company couldn't pay out). Powell then petitioned the Privy Council and the House of Lords. Twice.[22] Ostensibly she was looking for high-level assistance in forcing reparations from Holland, but it seems likely that the tactic was aimed more at embarrassing the Company into awarding the widows

19. Stretton, "Widows at Law in Tudor and Stuart England," 197.

20. Stretton notes the "concentration of legal activity associated with the onset of widowhood" that "serves as a reminder that restored independence, symbolically so important from a modern perspective, was not always a welcome acquisition for widows" ("Widows at Law in Tudor and Stuart England," 199).

21. "East Indies: May 1623," in *Calendar of State Papers Colonial, East Indies, China and Japan*, vol. 4, 1622–1624, http://www.british-history.ac.uk/cal-state-papers/colonial/east-indies-china-japan/vol4/pp118-119, accessed 25 November 2015.

22. "East Indies: May 1623," and 'East Indies: December 1623, 1-10', in *Calendar of State Papers Colonial, East Indies, China and Japan, Volume 4, 1622-1624*, 185-190. *British History Online* http://www.british-history.ac.uk/cal-state-papers/colonial/east-indies-china-japan/vol4/pp185-190 [accessed 14 March 2017].

additional funds. It's difficult to reconstruct from the brief records what actually happened when Powell appeared before the Lords or the men of the Company court, but the authorities seem aggravated by her litigiousness.

On 8 December 1623, the court records note that Company representatives were called to the Privy Council to give their account about these claims—at that time, two other women had joined the petition. Another document dated 1623 but lacking a month is catalogued after the Company was summoned. This time, the petition comes from Powell and thirty other women. It seems that word had spread that Powell was gaining traction in her suit. On 12 December the court retaliated. From the Company's point of view, they had already addressed the complaint, dispensing some funds and giving another of Powell's sons a ship's posting. They resolve "to send for her sonne home again" because "she is become so troublesome."[23] Still, the Company had to satisfy the Privy Council, and its agents, having waited on the Lords and explained the Company's actions to compensate Powell—including a 40-shilling charitable gift. The Lords apparently were satisfied, and the agents report that they were told that "if those women did further trouble them they shall be whipt."[24] The threat at least impressed W. Noel Sainsbury, the editor of this volume of the *Calendar*; it is the only passage that he quotes directly from this set of minutes.[25]

Apparently Powell was less impressed. She is back in February, petitioning the Company court for 6 pounds. On 9 April 1624, the court throws up its hands and agrees to pay her, rather "than be troubled by her dayly clamor."[26] On 14 April, she signs a release and ends her appeals. The court minute book and the *Calendar* summaries alike suggest that her claims—her importunities—took a larger share of the court's attention than her status would ordinarily have claimed. It certainly seems that her continual presence in the minutes caught Sainsbury off guard. He had to play catch-up in his summary of the minutes for 11–13 February. In order to explain her appearance at that court, he brings up details from 8 December 1623 that had not been previously summarized. Perhaps he expected to treat her as he did most other petitioners. Rather than summarizing their claims as they were made to appear in the minutes, the *Calendar of State Papers* collects them annually into a table that appears in each year's "Misc." section. Such an editorial treatment does not suffice for Thomazin Powell. Her insistence on being heard is transhistorical.

Powell seems to have had an extraordinary amount of determination—or perhaps of desperation—enough to lead thirty other women into court

23. East India Company Court Minutes, 2 July 1624–14 April 1625, India Office Records, 307.
24. East India Company Court Minutes, 2 July 1624–14 April 1625, India Office Records, 316.
25. Though Sainsbury does clean up the spelling.
26. East India Company Court Minutes, 2 July 1624–14 April 1625, India Office Records, 411.

and risk the wrath of important men and institutions. She succeeded, at least to some degree. Her exceptional story begs several questions. Without such force of personality, what strategies might a widowed woman have employed in approaching the Company for assistance? What might her court experiences have been like?

In the 1620s, the main offices of the East India Company were in Crosby House, on Bishopsgate. This street, in northeast London, ran into the city wall just a short walk from the Company headquarters. In *The Launching of the Mary*, Company wives are spread across greater London; they can be found in Wapping, Ratcliff Highway, Limehouse Corner, Six Windmills, Mile End, Blackman Street, Whitechapel, Little Minories, West Smithfield, and Blackwall, site of the Company shipyards. Approaching the Company headquarters in Bishopsgate from the north, beyond the city wall, a petitioner would have passed through more sparsely populated areas—the "Agas" map, circa 1560, depicts farms and fields just outside the wall, and the area was still less developed in that direction even years later. Petitioners from south or west would have traveled through more densely built lanes, passing churches and guild halls. If a widow were coming from the Company's yards at Blackwall, as one Jane Garroway did to seek redress for her husband's broken leg, she would have had a considerable trip. Early yard workers complained of the commute from their homes closer to London (and Company officials complained about the time workers took leaving the yard for their midday meal). In response, residences and taprooms were constructed. Garroway may have lived in one of the newly constructed homes.[27]

As John Stowe described Bishopsgate Ward in 1603, visitors to the area would have been confronted by the typical seventeenth-century London stew of savory and repulsive ingredients: "faire houses for Marchants, and artificiers, and many fayre Innes for trauellers" but also "a quadrant called Petty Fraunce, of Frenchmen dwelling there and to other dwelling houses, lately builded on the banke of the [Town Ditch] by some Cittizens of London, that more regarded their owne priuate gaine, then the common good of the Cittie: for by meanes of this causeye raysed on the banke, and soylage of houses, with other filthines cast into the ditch."[28] On the one hand a petitioner walking to Crosby House through Bishopsgate Ward would encounter churches, priories, and Gresham College, a house "most spatious of all other thereabout, builded of Bricke and Timber, by Sir *Thomas Gresham*, knight." On the other hand she might have encountered Bethlehem

27. John Marriott, *Beyond the Tower: A History of East London* (New Haven: Yale University Press, 2011), 26.
28. John Stow, "Bishopsgate warde," in *A Survey of London: Reprinted from the Text of 1603,* ed. C. L. Kingsford (Oxford, 1908), 163–175, British History Online, http://www.british-history.ac.uk/no-series/survey-of-london-stow/1603/pp163-175, accessed 24 November 2015.

Hospital, better known today as Bedlam, with its long reputation for dark disorder.

As she stood before the Company offices in Crosby House, the Amboyna widow would have looked up on an imposing building that dated back to the times of Richard II, when it was a royal residence.[29] Part of the building still stands today in London; it was moved from Bishopsgate to Chelsea in the early twentieth century, where the section that houses the great hall still looms large.[30] Court proceedings were held in the great hall, a large room of royal proportions with a vaulted ceiling, supported by an elaborate system of decorative timbering.[31] A woman approaching the dozen or so men seated at the table for any particular court would have been dwarfed by the proportions of the room. It's even possible that—for a time at least—women entering the court might have faced the display of Robert Greenbury's large canvas depicting the Amboyna torture. We know that it was displayed in the Company's house, and such a large a work as this would have been hard to accommodate in lesser rooms. As Anthony Milton notes, "clearly this was no small portrait but a major canvas that might have covered an entire wall."[32]

So a woman, recently bereaved, approaches the most powerful of her late husband's employers in a room notable for its majestic feel to ask for recompense or at least charity. She may have been driven by concern for dependent children; she may have been inspired by righteous, nationalistic outrage at her husband's treatment. She may simply have been hungry. Perhaps her decision to petition was bolstered by other women similarly bringing suit. Or perhaps she had heard of Thomazin Powell's treatment. If so, did her experience convince the Amboyna widow that she had as good a case? Did the Lords' threat of a whipping give the new petitioner pause? Is it possible that the Amboyna widow who fainted—if indeed there was such a woman—was reacting as much to the imperious surroundings of the company's main hall as to the subject of the painting itself?

We can never excavate from the archives the particular emotions an Amboyna widow felt, but it is possible to imagine at least some details of

29. From 1621 to 1638 it served as the East India Company headquarters. Sir George Birdwood, *Report on the Old Records of the India Office* (2nd reprint, London: W. H. Allen and Co., 1891), 39.

30. See Walter H. Godfrey, "Crosby Hall (re-erected)," in Survey of London, vol. 4, Chelsea, pt. 2 (London, 1913), 15–17, British History Online, http://www.british-history.ac.uk/survey-london/vol4/pt2/pp15-17, accessed 5 September 2016.

31. See William Foster, "The East India Company at Crosby House, 1621–1638," in *London Topographical Record*, vol. 8 (London, 1913), 106–139.

32. Anthony Milton, "Marketing a Massacre: Amboyna, the East India Company and the Public Sphere in Early Stuart England," in *The Politics of the Public Sphere in Early Modern England*, ed. Peter Lake and Steven Pincus (Manchester: Manchester University Press, 2012), 178.

Figure 5.2. Crosby House Great Hall, drawing by Frederick Nash (1782–1856). Bishopsgate Institute, London, Collection Manuscripts/63, n.d.

her experience. Thomazin Powell's example points us to the successful tactics employed by women petitioning the court, but if Powell's attempts to badger the courts into submission were effective, they risked playing into the stereotype of the haranguing, grasping widow. Stretton points out that many other widows performed gender norms of weakness and frailty in their addresses to courts, even exaggerating their status as women left with small children to raise, playing the part of the poor, defenseless widow.[33] If Sanderson's account corresponds to a real case, it seems that the widow in question was initially more aggressive—she was determined to "prosecute her complaint" rather than collapse under it.

But in reporting her reaction to the depiction of Amboyna torture, Sanderson places her squarely in the realm of the "poor widow," the kind of woman most often rewarded by the court. As Sanderson explains it in *Graphice*, the painting "wrought this strange effect upon the widow of one of the Martyrs; who, upon former relations, prosecuted her complaint; but when she saw the Picture, lively describing her Husband's horrid execution,

33. Stretton, "Widows at Law in Tudor and Stuart England," 206–207.

she sunck down, in a dead swound."[34] Overcome by the sight of torture, she no longer prosecutes her grief; she is rendered helpless by it. With one stroke, then, Sanderson both proves his larger "graphic" point about the relative power of image over verse and illustrates his own ideas about gender roles. He imagines this woman as a normative, conservative figure, a poor widow who needs the protection of the court, the state, and Sanderson himself. If Matthew T. Jenkinson is correct in identifying Sanderson as the author of *Rebels No Saints; Or, A Collection of the Speeches, Private Passages, Letters, and Prayers of Those Persons Lately Executed* (1661) and a follow-up published the same year, Sanderson was keenly interested in who was—and in the case of the regicides he lambasted in *Rebels No Saints,* who was not—a martyr.[35] The Amboyna widow he imagines is a figure worthy of reward, the "relict" of a national martyr.

Up to this point, I have been treating "the Amboyna widow" as an anonymous individual, someone whom we can never definitively identify from archival sources, and indeed, she is not named in Sanderson's *Graphice.* But Sanderson is clear in his *Compleat History of the Lives and Reigns of, Mary Queen of Scotland* that the widow who faints before the painting is Captain Gabriel Towerson's wife. In order to identify her so, he has to disregard the very evidence he brings to bear on the topic. He quotes at length the description of torture that had been circulating in the tracts describing the incident, a quotation that explicitly identified Samuel Colson as the suffering victim. But he introduces the quotation by identifying the description of a trussed and tortured man not with Colson but with Towerson. Gabriel Towerson was a Company employee with a rather checkered record. For instance, he was accused by the Company of private trading in 1614.[36] But whatever the vicissitudes of his career, upon his execution he became a martyr, a catalyst for English national pride and anger against the Dutch. For reasons that I will discuss, even if Sanderson was acquainted with an Amboyna widow suing for compensation after her husband's death, his claim that this woman was Towerson's widow is a flat-out fabrication. But rather than solving the possible historical mystery (who was that fainting woman?), I want to ask why Sanderson made the claim. When Sanderson, some thirty years after the Amboyna incident, recalled this story as an anecdote to illustrate both a point in his history of English royalty and a point in his treatise on art, what primed the imaginative pump?

We know that William Sanderson and his family were immersed in visions of a worldly empire from the time of Elizabeth and Raleigh and

---

34. Sanderson, *Graphice,* 14

35. Matthew T. Jenkinson, "A New Author," *Notes and Queries* 52.3 (September 2005): 311–314.

36. See J. D. Alsop, "Towerson, Gabriel (bap. 1576, d. 1623)," in *Oxford Dictionary of National Biography* (Oxford: Oxford University Press, 2004), http://www.oxforddnb.com/view/article/27591, accessed 18 November 2015.

throughout the seventeenth century. Although Sanderson the younger was in his seventies when he wrote down the story of the Amboyna widow, he may have had good reason to remember it. His brother Hugh died in the East Indies in 1624, the same year that news of the Amboyna incident reached London and the year that the East India Company commissioned the painting that so disturbed the widow. It does not seem too much of a stretch of the imagination to posit that the two tragedies—one personal and one national—were entwined in Sanderson's memory, perhaps not even too much of a stretch to see in his description of the woman's sorrow some reflection of the grief of his own brother's widow, a "what if" fantasy of his brother among the executed on Amboyna.[37]

Sanderson may have had aesthetic as well as personal and political reasons to create this figure of a grieving, "sensible" woman overcome by art. Caroline Anne Good argues that Sanderson saw good art as engendering an emotional relationship between viewer and painting: "Sanderson's account offers a tentative introduction to the favoured components of a way of seeing that powerfully sought in its characteristics to identify both an emotional connection and a meaningful response from the portrait, one that should inspire in the viewer that passion which in turn dominates and informs the subject itself."[38] He makes the relative force of the visual over the textual even clearer in his treatment of the Amboyna widow in his *Compleat history of the lives and reigns of Mary Queen of Scotland*. There, the widow seems likely to be martyred herself by the power of the painting: *"So great force and resemblance hath that Art with Nature that the effects thereof fell upon Towersons Widow, who at sight of the Picture fell down in a Swound, with hazard then in that Trance, to follow her Husband, which the often Relation before, did not so much astonish."*[39]

Whatever Sanderson's reasons for identifying the swooning woman as the widow of Gabriel Towerson, the English national martyr of Amboyna, it is clear that this anecdote belongs not to the historian but to the fabulist. Towerson's widow, Mariam Towerson, was not a petitioner of the East India Company in the 1620s or 1630s.[40] Rather, if we dig deeper, we find that she *was* a petitioner to the East India Company General Court, but a decade earlier and for very different reasons. Mariam (sometimes Maryam) Towerson, nee Kahn, was born to a Christian Armenian family in Agra,

37. To be clear, I have not been able to trace Hugh, and he may not have had a wife.

38. Caroline Anne Good, "Lovers of Art: English Literature on the Connoisseurship of Pictures" doctoral diss., University of York, 2013, 51.

39. Sanderson, *Compleat History*, 578. He goes on to conclude: *"The disparity of a Political pen, with the powerful art of painting, may thereby be distinguished."*

40. The Towerson family was represented in petitions before the court, but they were presented by Towerson's brother, not his widow, who by this time was not in the country, as I discuss below.

India, and married an Englishman, William Hawkins.[41] She probably met Towerson in 1611, when she and her husband sailed to England with him. Hawkins died on the voyage, and by the time the ship made port, she and Towerson were affianced. They married soon after landing in England in 1613. Nevertheless, she petitioned the East India Company as Hawkins's widow; when he died he owed his brother 300 pounds. The East India Company court arbitrated the dispute, cleared her late husband's debts, and awarded her 250 pounds "as a token of their love."[42] As it turns out, she wasn't as hard up as she had represented to the Court; apparently she affected the "poor widow" posture Stretton identifies as useful to widows in the period. In reality she was worth some 6,000 pounds.[43] Nevertheless, at this point the Company treated her with a kind of avuncular generosity.

Her subsequent fate was less happy, certainly less financially secure. She left England in 1617, sailing with Gabriel Towerson to Agra, where he hoped to trade on her familial connections; when his plans did not pan out, he left her with her mother. According to Fisher, "by late 1619 she had incurred debts of several hundred rupees, and was reduced to daily petitions to the Company's agents in Agra for aid."[44] Company reports from Agra claim that Mariam Towerson remained there despite her husband's wishes, and though she received some funds from the Company, it is clear that officials felt caught in a domestic dispute, reporting in December 1619 that by remaining with her mother in Agra, "shee stayeth behind hir husband, not much to his likinge." Moreover, though in this instance the Company representatives did give her 200 rupees, they doubted that they would see it repaid, as Gabriel Towerson "hath not given warrant to releeve hir."[45] While we might speculate that Mariam Towerson faced difficulties because of her ethnicity, the Company's exasperation with her seems entirely on account of her financial woes.[46] Nonetheless, by the time Gabriel Towerson set sail

41. My account of Mariam Towerson's biography relies on Michael Fisher, *Counterflows to Colonialism: Indian Travellers and Settlers in Britain 1600–1857* (Delhi: Permanent Black, 2004), 22–29, and Bindu Malieckal, "Mariam Khan and the Legacy of Mughal Women in Early Modern Literature of India," in *Early Modern England and Islamic Worlds*, ed. Bernadette Diane Andrea and Linda McJannet (New York: Palgrave Macmillan, 2001), 97–122.

42. Quoted in Fisher, *Counterflows*, 26. Fisher has also described Mariam Towerson's life in "Seeing England Firsthand: Women and Men from Imperial India, 16141–769," in *Europe Observed: Multiple Gazes in Early Modern Encounters*, ed. Kumkum Chatterjee and Clement Hawes (Cranbury, NJ: Associated University Presses, 2008), 143–171.

43. Fisher, *Counterflows*, 26.

44. Fisher, *Counterflows*, 28.

45. "Thomas Kerridge, Thomas Rastell, and Giles James at Surat to William Biddulph . . . Dec [8?], 1619," in William Foster, *The English Factories in India, 1618–1621* (Oxford: Clarendon Press, 1906), 155.

46. Indeed, Michael Fisher argues in *Counterflows* that Mariam's marriages to the two Englishmen, alliances that "in later centuries might be considered 'inter-racial,'" did not raise eyebrows in London.

for Amboyna, his wife was an embarrassment, and the complaints she and her mother lodged against him marked them as disloyal and foreign. William Biddulph reported in a letter to the Company that the two women "rayled uppon hir husband and nation." Did they mount their attacks in public as officials passed to their offices? In formal Company settings? It's difficult to know exactly when and how they "rayled" against Gabriel Towerson, but the results are clear: their complaints were "noe smale discreditt to our nation." Unless something was done to curb her, Mariam Towerson would, Biddulph warns, "breed much trouble to your factors at Agra and the court." They counsel an appeal to Gabriel Towerson "for hir mayntaynnance, or send for hir to him to avoyd expense, trouble and scandall."[47]

Obviously, this is *not* the wife that a national martyr-hero should have (nor, perhaps, is a wife-abandoning Gabriel Towerson all that an English hero should be). In these reports, Mariam is akin to the widow figure made stock in late-century drama, the "Litigious She-Pettyfogger, who is at Law and difference with all the World."[48] I am not suggesting that William Sanderson invented this story to cover up the more uncomfortable reality; there is no evidence to suggest that he knew of Mariam Towerson's financial history or of her more recent trouble with her husband and the Company. Rather, Sanderson describes the widow that his experiences and his politics demand. Sanderson was a supporter of Charles I, rewarded for his loyalty by a knighthood from Charles II. His few publications—aside from *Graphice*—are histories of and apologies for the Crown.[49] Small wonder, then, that in 1658, the waning years of the protectorate, he would represent the widow of a man so universally understood in England as a national martyr from James I's time as a woman performing her appropriate role.[50] And the appropriate role for the widow of a national hero is that of a susceptible widow, swooning at the sight of her beloved husband suffering torture for his country, not a Thomazin Powell, importuning the court for compensation, however richly deserved. Global fantasies must needs be populated by the appropriate characters.

---

47. "William Biddulph and John Willoughby at the Mogul's Camp to the company, December 25, 1619," in Foster, *English Factories*, 169. This moment is discussed in Fisher, "Seeing England Firsthand," 154.

48. William Wycherley describing the Widow Blackacre in *The Plain Dealer*, quoted in Stretton, "Widows at Law in Tudor and Stuart England," 196.

49. D. R. Woolf, "Sanderson, Sir William (1586–1676)," in *Oxford Dictionary of National Biography* (Oxford: Oxford University Press, 2004), http://www.oxforddnb.com/view/article/24630, accessed 18 November 2015.

50. Note that he was writing during a time when the issue of compensation for widows whose husbands were lost in national service was hotly debated. See Geoffrey L. Hudson, "Negotiating for Blood Money: War Widows and the Courts in Seventeenth-Century England," in *Women, Crime and the Courts in Early Modern England*, ed. Jennifer Kermonde (Chapel Hill: University of North Carolina Press, 1995), 146–169.

UNMANNING THE ARCHIVE

Few writers at the time understood the need for national plots driven by appropriate characters better than John Dryden, who began his authorial and political career at the midcentury, at about the time Sanderson was describing his Amboynan widow. He wrote occasional verse "extolling Cromwell's victories" in Ireland and against the Dutch in the First Anglo-Dutch War.[51] He may have served officially in Cromwell's government. Certainly he had a prominent role in the spectacle of Cromwell's funeral and the following period of mourning. He walked in the funeral procession with Milton, and perhaps his first truly successful poetic publication was his "Heroic Stanzas" in praise of Cromwell.[52]

His career survived the Restoration, and he went on to inhabit a role as a "national" poet and writer by serving royal government ends through both his verse and dramatic productions, becoming poet laureate in 1668 and historiographer royal in 1670.[53] Indeed, Laura Brown argues that politically Dryden "favored royal absolutism and Stuart succession."[54] Elizabeth Maddock Dillon sees his dramatic efforts after 1660 as borne out of innovations in the public dramatic performances that he witnessed during the Interregnum, particularly in William Davenant's offerings: "Dryden, like D'Avenant, uses the stage as a location in which imperialism and nationalism are coarticulated in such a way as to give new force and meaning to the English as a (benevolent, imperial) people."[55] By the 1670s, Dryden's political perspective had been formed and his pen sharpened by the tumultuous events of the preceding years.[56]

We can see such energies at work especially in Dryden's portrayal of women in his play *Amboyna*. This tragedy, clearly an effort to shape public opinion about the Third Anglo-Dutch War of the 1670s, draws directly on the earlier "true relation" accounts of the Amboyna merchants' torture and

51. James Anderson Winn, *John Dryden and His World* (New Haven: Yale University Press, 1987), 80.

52. Winn, *Dryden and His World*, 80.

53. On the role of historiographer royal, see Edward Saslow, "Dryden as Historiographer Royal: The Authorship of *His Majesties Declaration Defended*, 1681," *Modern Philology* 75.3 (1978): 261–272. Saslow says that the role was perhaps "meant to distinguish him as the king's 'prose writer'" as a match to his role as royal poet (264).

54. Laura Brown, "The Ideology of Restoration Poetic Form: John Dryden," *PMLA* 97.3 (May 1982), 404.

55. Elizabeth Maddock Dillon, *New World Drama: The Performative Commons in the Atlantic World, 1649–1849* (Durham: Duke University Press, 2014), 65.

56. His experiences in the Interregnum and his role after the Restoration made him keenly aware that no rank or privilege was secure. Winn asserts that in the 1670s, "he was not only re-thinking his aesthetic principles but struggling to survive" and his art reflected the times: "he could hardly ignore the political and theatrical crises through which the nation and the King's Company were passing"; *John Dryden and His World*, 243.

death, several of which were published in the 1650s, when Dryden was a young man and writer looking about himself for government patronage. Like Sanderson writing about the Amboyna widow in the 1650s, Dryden fabulates from the archival records an appropriate, heroic wife for his idealized version of Gabriel Towerson as English national hero.

Dryden's play follows the story of Gabriel Towerson, chief of the English factors on Amboyna, and Ysabinda, a Native Amboyna woman who marries Towerson in the course of the action. From the start we see that the Dutch forces on the island are jealous of the English, competing with them for trade and for women. The son of the Dutch governor on the island, Harman Junior, is in love with Ysabinda. When she rejects him, he abducts, binds, gags, and rapes her. Towerson avenges her in a duel, during which he kills Harman Junior. Subsequently, a Dutch official named only "the Fiscal" accuses Towerson of murder; the other English men on the island are rounded up and collectively accused of treason. We witness their torture by water and by fire before they are led offstage to their deaths, but not before Towerson prophesies doom against the Dutch:

> Heav'n has bid me prophesy to you th'unjust contrivers of this Tragick Scene; *An Age is coming, when an* English *Monarch with Blood, shall pay that blood which you have shed: to save your Cities from victorious Arms, you shall invite the Waves to hide your Earth, and trembling to the tops of Houses fly, while Deluges invade your lower rooms: Then, as with Waters you hae swell'd our Bodies, with damps of Waters shall your Heads be swoln;*
> *Till at the last your sap'd foundations fall,*
> *And Universal Ruine swallows all.*[57]

Most critical attention focuses on the representation in the play of Company men—Dutch and English alike—which makes sense when we read the work for its 1670s propaganda value. But a somewhat different focus emerges if we consider the play through the generic lens of historic fiction. Towerson's directive from heaven is a moment in which Dryden channels his historic sources—while his relation to prophecy and millenarianism is not quite that of his predecessors, he would have encountered the millennial register in the earlier works—and a moment when he uses his knowledge of events that have come to pass and gives Towerson a powerful speech that the audience knows will come true.[58]

57. John Dryden, *Amboyna*, in *The Works of John Dryden*, vol. 12, ed. Vinton A. Dearing (Berkeley: University of California Press, 1994), 5.1.452–461. All quotations from *Amboyna* hereafter are from this edition.) As many scholars have pointed out, Towerson's prophecy refers to the deliberate breaching of the dykes by the Dutch in 1672 in an attempt to hold off French forces. See Dearing's headnote, 263.

58. Jan Wojcik argues that Dryden was not a millennialist himself but saw prophecy and "millenialist allusions" as instrumental for his art. "John Dryden's Interest in Prophecy," in *Poetic*

We can see more tangible influences of Dryden's sources if we look more closely at the archival inspiration for this play. One of the most striking elements of the work is his retelling and reimagining of Towerson's wife. The characters of Ysabinda and the other women in the play are revealing about the role of gender, particularly about the intersections of gender with nation and violence. I am, perhaps, putting a lot of weight on a play that Sir Walter Scott, in an early edition of Dryden's works, introduced as "beneath criticism; and I can hardly hesitate to term it the worst production Dryden ever wrote."[59] Candy Schille calls it "relatively inconsequential," while Marjorie Rubright terms it "Dryden's most underexplored play."[60] But in recent years, scholars have seen its significance as a commentary on and representation of English colonial ideology, an ideology laid bare, perhaps, by the play's lack of polish.[61] In conjunction with Dryden's other "American" and "Eastern" plays, *The Indian Emperour, Indian Queen, Aureng-Zebe,* or even his revision of Shakespeare's *The Tempest,* the play can be understood as straightforward imperial apology, but it is also a play that, as Markley puts it, stages "the instabilities within the discourses of nationalism, free trade, and gentlemanly civility that the play overtly champions."[62]

Clearly the play, whatever its value as a work of drama, performs some heavy-duty cultural work.[63] My approach here will be to bring several aspects of the play together, but in particular I consider how Dryden's representation of Amboyna women "completes" Sanderson's earlier, brief suggestions about gender in which the national martyr Gabriel Towerson is married to an idealized, fragile, and susceptible woman. In short, the play takes seriously the role of colonial women in the seventeenth-century English imagination as symbols of the righteousness of English imperial actions and colonizing claims. Moreover, an aspect of the play that some have

---

Prophecy in Western Literature, ed. Jan Wojcik and Raymond-Jean Frontain (London: Associated University Presses, 1984), 81.

59. *The Dramatic Works of John Dryden,* new ed., ed. George Saintsbury, vol. 5 (Edinburgh, 1882), 3.

60. Candy B. K. Schille, "With Honour Quit the Fort: Ambivalent Colonialism in Dryden's *Amboyna,*" *Early Modern Literature Studies* 12.1 (May 2006): 1–30. Marjorie Rubright, *Doppelgänger Dilemmas: Anglo-Dutch Relations in Early Modern English Language and Culture* (Philadelphia: University of Pennsylvania Press, 2014).

61. See especially Robert Markley, "Violence and Profits on the Restoration Stage: Trade, Nationalism and Insecurity in Dryden's *Amboyna,*" *Eighteenth-Century Life* 22.1 (February 1998): 2–17, and Schille, "With Honour Quit the Fort" for just two examples of the reassessment of this play.

62. Markley, "Violence and Profits on the Restoration Stage," 19.

63. Schille, "With Honour Quit the Fort," 1. And may have done some heavy-duty literary work as well. On the treatment of English torture on the island of Amboyna, including Dryden's play as a source of images of torture for Aphra Behn's *Oroonoko,* see Richard Kroll, "Tales of Love and Gallantry: The Politics of *Oroonoko,*" *Huntington Library Quarterly* 67.4 (December 2004): 596.

seen as still resonant centuries after the moment of its production is its general condemnation of rape and torture as tools of the state. Dryden's play, as a work of historical fiction, points us (once more) to the archives and what they tell us (or fail to tell us) about the subjects of the English global fantasies inscribed in the literature and other print records of the seventeenth century.

Dryden derives all of the main male characters from the historical record save one, Harman Junior, the son of Amboyna's Dutch governor. Both of the two women central to the play, Jane, the wife of Perez, a "Spanish captain," and Ysabinda, the fiancée and later wife of Gabriel Towerson, seem inspired in part by the enslaved wife of Augustine Perez, identified in the English records as the Portuguese captain of the slaves. English readers could have first encountered Perez and his wife in a 1632 reprint of *A Remonstrance of the Directors*, the Dutch East Indian Company's account of the events on Amboyna.[64] *A True Relation* (1651) reports that Perez testified that he deserved his fate, because though married "in his own Countrey," he had "by the perswasion of the Dutch Governor taken another in that Countrey, his first being yet living."[65] Hendrik E. Niemeijer suggests why Perez might have identified this relationship as the cause of his troubles: "Calvinist burgher society was sternly disapproving of sexual liaisons between married Europeans and local women, not so much because of racial differences but because they defied the monogamy of Christian marriage. Sometimes the Bench of Aldermen convicted Dutchmen for secretly marrying a concubine in Batavia when they had left a wife in Holland; from the Church's viewpoint, bigamy was a more serious crime than adultery."[66] Dryden draws on the historical record, and his character Perez disavows his wife, Julia, in language exactly parallel to the historic reports of his repudiation of her: "I am guilty of a greater crime; For, being married in another Countrey, The Governors perswasions, and my love to that ill Woman, made me leave the first, and make this fatal choice. I'm justly punish'd, for her sake I dye."[67]

However much Perez believed this woman to be the cause of his demise, the records contain scant details about her. This woman has such a slight

64. *A Remonstrance of the Directors* (London: 1632).

65. *A True Relation of the Unjust, Cruell, and Barbarous Proceedings Against the English at Amboyna in the East-Indies* (London, 1651), 46. See J. A. Van der Welle, *Dryden and Holland* (Groningen: Netherlands, 1962), for a point-by-point comparison of *True Relation* and Dryden's play.

66. Hendrik E. Niemeijer, "Slavery, Ethnicity and the Economic Independence of Women in Seventeenth-Century Batavia," in *Other Pasts: Women, Gender and History in Early Modern Southeast Asia*, ed. Barbara Watson Andaya (Honolulu: Center for Southeast Asian Studies, 2000), 183.

67. Dryden, *Amboyna*, 5.1.442–445.

presence in the English accounts that she does not even merit a name in them. Moreover, *A Remonstrance of the Directors* notes that after Perez's execution, the Dutch East India Company repossessed the woman as its property.[68] Nevertheless, she obviously looms large in Dryden's imagination, for she is doubled here. She serves as the historic ground for the character of Julia, who is listed as "wife to Perez" in the dramatis personae, and, less directly, for Ysabinda. Unlike Julia, the wife Dryden creates for his Gabriel Towerson is not his hero's moral downfall but is "beauteous, rich, and young" and a native of the island.[69] His main concern is obviously to stage a dramatic and sympathetic romance, drawing on antecedents such as Shakespeare's *Othello* and his own earlier effort *The Indian Emperour*, in which Cortez courts a Native woman. But artistic effect does not fully account for the doubled characters of Ysabinda and Julia. Dryden's characters are avatars of historic figures who meant something to their own communities and to the men who more regularly find voice in Company documents. Augustine Perez's enslaved wife, by virtue of her position, and surely as well by virtue of her personality and character, provoked Perez in his extremity, at a moment when he believed he was soon to be judged by God, to point to her as the prime mover of his fate (however we might understand the irony of his casting an enslaved Native woman in that role).[70] Some of that powerful significance attaches to Dryden's historic fiction; although he easily could have ignored or recast this moment in the record of the Amboyna incident, as I've noted, he imports Perez's self-accusation directly into the final act.

Dryden does, in fact, invent whole cloth a shipwrecked English woman who arrives on the scene to deliver another indictment of Dutch cruelty, so he could have peopled the island with other women, ignored their presence altogether, or made their roles much less central to his plot. He insists, however on making this drama a colonial romance, or—as one editor, Vinton A. Dearing, terms it—a "domestic tragedy."[71] At the same time, as Dillon

---

68. According to "An Authentic Copy of the Confessions and Sentences Against M. Towerson, and Complices," in *A Remonstrance of the Directors*: "the wife of Augustine Peres which hath been a slave of the honourable *Dutch East India* Company, who was given to the said *Augustine* in hope of his good carriage, for the present, shee shall returne to her ancient Maisters of the said Companie, untill such time that she shall be otherwise disposed of by the Governour" (35).

69. Dryden, *Amboyna*, 1.1.124.

70. It has been difficult to decide how to refer to this woman. She's considered both a wife and a slave, and each term casts some doubt on the lived experiences of inhabiting the other role. Her dual role can remind us of what Behn illustrated so well in *Oroonoko*: in the early modern period, these roles were, if not interchangeable, certainly implicated in one another. I've compromised on a hybrid term, "enslaved wife," as a reminder that she inhabited a complex identity in her time and place, even as I cringe at the reductive nature of even a doubly generic title.

71. See his "Commentary" on *Amboyna* in Dryden, *Amboyna*, ed. Dearing, 274.

argues in *New World Drama,* he has constructed a work of national public theater. At the intersection of these various genres, we can see the figure of the colonial/colonized woman as offering not just historical verisimilitude but colonial critique through its dramatic function. Rubright, one of the few scholars to attend to the character of Julia, argues that "together the women of Dryden's *Amboyna* breathe life into the gaps of the historical narrative, expanding the imaginative framework of social relations on the island while complicating the binary structure and adversarial national stance of the pamphlet literature."[72] If, as Hayden White argues succinctly, the historical real "would consist of everything that can be truthfully said about its actuality plus everything that can be truthfully said about what it could *possibly* be," then Dryden's attention to the possibilities for women under colonization reminds us (once again) of the archives' real limitations.[73]

The character of Julia allows us to assess most easily Dryden's reimagination of the historical figure, as she can be closely mapped onto the documentary record. Julia is desired by three men on the island: her husband, the Fiscal, and Beaumont, an English factor. Perez suspects the other two of cuckolding him; his rivals know the score and openly compete for Julia's favors. Julia herself seems by turns to use her sexual power for her own ends and to be carried away by forces beyond her control. In the last act, for instance, she accuses the Fiscal of ruining her by persecuting her husband, using the conventional language of seduction narratives: "Oh you have ruin'd me, you have undone me, in the Person of my Husband!"[74] Despite this moment of despair, her character is fundamentally comic, so elsewhere in the play the emphasis is on her knowing manipulation of her sexuality. Indeed, just after her lament, she elicits a promise from the Fiscal that in exchange for marrying him, he will save the life of Beaumont, her other lover, who has been swept up in the treason charges leveled against the other Englishmen. Thus we see the limitations of Dryden's critique—despite the language of sexual violence implicit in Julia's "you have ruin'd me," in the end, she accepts the notion of her body as transferable from one male partner to another, and she uses that transferability to force a form of limited negotiation with the colonial authorities. While it may be the case that the actual woman attached to Perez negotiated her status and that of loved ones in this way, Dryden, in his light-handed treatment of the character Julia, carves out an accepted space for sexual violence—or at least for sex as capital—that he presents as business as usual in the English East Indies. In no way does the play mean us to understand Julia to be martyred for the

---

72. Rubright, *Doppelgänger Dilemmas,* 216.
73. Hayden White, "Introduction: Historical Fiction, Fictional History, and Historical Reality," *Rethinking History* 9.2/3 (June/September) 2005: 147.
74. Dryden, *Amboyna,* 5.1.223–224.

English cause.[75] Indeed, Julia herself talks of replacing Perez: "Farewel my dearest, I may have many Husbands, but never one like thee," reinforcing the legal ambiguity of her position.[76]

This pat conclusion to Julia's story—it's really quite jarring to see her so quickly accede to the Fiscal's demands as Perez and the noble Englishmen are executed—might be chalked up to the overall aesthetic failure of the play. But it is striking that Dryden backs away from the violent implications of Julia's fate in the last scene. In doing so, he creates a nonviolent sexual economy that Bridget Orr suggests serves as a synecdoche for European fantasies of East Indian colonization and trade exploitation.[77] In act 3, scene 1, the comic interlude in the play, as has been noted by many critics, Julia and her three lovers are clearly positioned as figures signifying colonial competition. Julia, a character built on the archival scaffold of an indigenous enslaved woman, nameless to an English audience, understands herself to be sexually available, willing to cuckold Perez for pleasure or for gain, but also sees her choices and her body as participating in and making possible imperial ambition: "If my *English* Lover *Beaumont*, my *Dutch* Love the *Fiscall*, and my *Spanish* Husband, were Painted in a piece with me amongst 'em, they wou'd make a Pretty Emblem of the two Nations, that Cuckold his Catholick Majesty in his *Indies*."[78] Now there's a canvas never meant to hang in the East India Company headquarters. However much the governing board might approve of its anti-Spain symbolism, it smacks too much of manipulation or at least agency on the part of the colonized. If the Indies/Julia can cuckold Spain, what's to stop her from cheating on other European states?

It may be that Dryden so casually depicts Julia as an East Indian colony ripe for (sexual) exploitation in order to reserve the bleaker, much more violent implications for his heroine, Ysabinda. Like Sanderson's anecdote of a fainting Mrs. Towerson, it's clear that Dryden's play demands a virtuous wife as the proper consort for its English hero. But unlike Sanderson, whose manipulation of the historic record mutes or erases Mariam Towerson's ethnicity, Dryden wrote the character as an Asian woman, though not the Christian Agra-born woman of the archives. Rather, he drew on the same historic figure who inspired Julia to create Ysabinda. He turns her into an

75. However, Rubright, *Doppelgänger Dilemmas,* does argue that Julia is "forced to withdraw herself from the circuit of desire," in which she had been agent, not just subject (231).

76. Dryden, *Amboyna*, 5.1. 437–438.

77. Bridget Orr, *Empire on the English Stage, 1660–1714* (Cambridge: Cambridge University Press, 2001), 158.

78. Dryden, *Amboyna*, 2.1.226–230. Julia is Spanish in the play. However, on seeing Julia and the Fiscal embrace, Beaumont comments: "You've the Indie's in your armes," a comment I take to be both a confirmation of Julia's sense of herself as an "emblem" of the Spice Islands and an oblique reference to the historical "Julia" as an East Indian. Dryden, *Amboyna*, 2.1.282–283.

indigenous Amboynan woman, and by so doing, he creates another entry in the seventeenth-century English tradition of Indian-English romantic fantasy. But the play takes a step further in its manipulation of the record of violence and gender. If Ysabinda's romance with Towerson is Pocahontas–John Smith redux, then her attack by the Dutch factor resonates with the story of the twelve-year-old Japanese girl purchased as a sex slave by English trader Richard Cocks that I discuss in chapter 2. Ysabinda is raped by Harman Junior and her husband is tortured by Harman Senior. Their sufferings are twinned as Towerson is "unmanned," as he is feminized. In short, the transgression by the Dutch in the main plot of the play is as much about how gender and torture are concomitant constructions as it is about making the English, their erstwhile allies, the subject of that torture.

To create his exotic character of Ysabinda, Dryden draws on various elements of the historical record. The dramatis personae calls Ysabinda "an Indian Lady," a description ambiguous enough to reference any non-European woman, from the Americas to the Spice Islands to Agra.[79] Later in the play, however, the scheming Fiscal dismisses her as "an Amboyner," which suggests a potential connection to the historical record of Perez's East Indian enslaved wife.[80] The name "Ysabinda" (some editors use "Isabinda") seems to be adapted from the list of Japanese soldiers who served in the castle at Ambon and were the first to be suspected of treason and tortured for their confessions, one of whom is identified as Tsabinda. These men are discussed in the play, though they never appear on stage, so the name is fully appropriated to Dryden's heroine, a striking gender reassignment considering that these men had a fearsome reputation as warriors, but of a piece with the English disinterest in the Japanese men's role in this English national tragedy.

The archival inspiration of Ysabinda's name is an early indication of the gendered work to come, work that is directly evidenced in the sexual assault on Ysabinda and the parallels to Dutch attempts to control and subdue Towerson's masculine puissance. Consider this exchange between Harman Junior and Ysabinda in the scene leading up to her rape. He has lured her alone into the wood with the promise of helping her to find Towerson:

> Ysab.   Come, Sir, which is the way? I long to see my love.
>
> Harm. Jun. You may have your wish, and without stirring hence.

---

79. The opening scene's reference to the three-year separation of the fictional lovers may be an allusion to the historical break between Towerson and his wife. It is perhaps an attempt to rehabilitate their reported rancor to one another in order to create a properly heroic couple.

80. Dryden, *Amboyna*, 4.4.54. On the Japanese soldiers, see Adam Clulow, "Unjust, Cruel and Barbarous Proceedings: Japanese Mercenaries and the Amboyna Incident of 1623," *Itinerario* 31.1 (2007): 15–34.

Ysab.　　My Love so near? sure you delight to mock me.

Harm. Jun. 'Tis you delight to torture me; behold the Man who loves you more then his
　　　　　own Eies...[81]

Many in the play's audience would have known the Amboyna story, as it
had been fodder for propaganda for decades, and so Harman Junior's conventional assertion that, by rejecting him Ysabinda did "torture me" makes
the language of unrequited love horribly wrong.[82] Those familiar with
English versions of the Amboyna story know too well what real torture is—
or if not, torture will soon be presented to us graphically on stage.

Thus the figurative appropriation of physical violence by a man lusting
after a woman who does not reciprocate adds to the horror of what's to come.
Similarly, in the scene immediately following, Harman Senior, Beaumont,
and the Fiscal engage in verbal raillery that collapses figural with literal violence. Like a debased version of Shakespeare's *Midsummer Night's Dream,*
the men are wandering the woods in search of the missing bride and groom,
Ysabinda and Gabriel Towerson. Harman suggests they would find that the
pair simply retired early to enjoy their marriage bed, whereas "a good honest
Dutchman wou'd have been plying the Glass all this while...till 'twas Bed-
time."[83] In response, Beaumont labels Dutchmen drunks and cowards (and
possibly impotent when sober): "In my Conscience you *Hollanders* never
get your Children, but in the Spirit of *Brandy*; you are exalted then a little
above your Natural Phlegm, and *only that which can make you fight and destroy Men, makes you get 'em.*"[84] To this, the Fiscal replies, in heavy-handed
foreshadowing: "You may live to know, that we can kill Men when we are
sober." Beaumont's crude jest that the Dutchman's impulse to fight or to get
children comes from the same drunken place confirms what we have just
witnessed in the exchange between Ysabinda and Harman Junior. Sex and
violence are conflated in Dryden's East Indies.

However debased the various Dutch characters, the real villain of the
play is the Fiscal, and Dryden plumbs the depths of his depravity in the next
scene, as Harman Junior and the Fiscal debate what to do with Ysabinda.
Harman has raped her and left her gagged and bound to a tree, and the
Fiscal urges him to kill her so as to remove her as a threat. Despite his
wretched character, it's clear that the Fiscal is no irrational villain, no Iago
acting out of personal enmity or individual flaw to incite Harman Junior to

81. Dryden, *Amboyna,* 4.1.1–6.
82. Blair Hoxby affirms "the audience could be expected to hear the play's many instances
of verbal foreshadowing"; *Mammon's Music: Literature and Economics in the Age of Milton* (New
Haven: Yale University Press, 2002), 187.
83. Dryden, *Amboyna,* 4.4.6–8.
84. Dryden, *Amboyna,* 4.4.17–20, my emphasis.

murder Ysabinda. Rather, his villainies are coldly calculated according to national interest and shaped by his colonial setting. To Harman's stirrings of remorse for the rape, the Fiscal responds: "Wou'd you degenerate, and have remorse? Pray, what makes any thing a sin but Law; and, What Law is there here against it? Is not your Father Chief? Will he condemn you for a petty Rape? The Woman an *Amboyner*, and what's less, now Marry'd to an *Englishman*."[85]

Most provocatively, he asserts a clear difference between metropolitan and overseas mores: "Come, if there be a Hell, 'tis but for those that sin in *Europe*, not for us in *Asia*; Heathens have no Hell."[86] This line certainly is meant to indicate the amorality of the Fiscal specifically and the Dutch he represents more generally—in one breath he both flirts with atheism ("if there be a Hell") and asserts a legal and moral relativism that we are surely meant to recognize as a cynical manipulation of the distance between the Dutch factors and their authorities. Nonetheless, by articulating a relativism mapped onto ethnic difference and colonization, the Fiscal's words invite the audience to consider systemic abuses of Native women and of European laws more generally. After all, Julia's imagined emblem situates all three European powers in a tableau of a sexualized competition over the Indies. The implied critique is underscored by Ysabinda's injunction to Towerson, which generalizes her wrongs to all of Europe and ironically echoes the Fiscal's sophistry. She urges Towerson to "fly this detested Isle, where horrid Ills so black and fatal dwell, as *Indians* cou'd not guess, till *Europe* taught."[87]

I don't want to get carried away with the notion that Dryden's play carries a subversive critique of English overseas expansion.[88] The play is definitely a partisan effort, and Dryden makes clear that although the English are not error free on Amboyna, unlike the Dutch (or even the Spanish), they commit venial never mortal sins. In his drama the English practice is a benevolent colonization. Moreover, they heroically oppose Dutch abuses, and however confident the Dutch are that they can act counter to the laws of God and man on Amboyna, they still have to contend with the strength and heroism of Englishmen. Indeed, when Harman Junior and the Fiscal encounter Towerson in the woods, Harman Junior, enraged by his discovery of the attack on Ysabinda, agrees to duel him alone, warning the Fiscal to "stand back." The Fiscal sarcastically rejects his directive: "thank you for

85. Dryden, *Amboyna*, 4.4.51–55.
86. Dryden, *Amboyna*, 4.4.55–57.
87. Dryden, *Amboyna*, 4.5.15–17.
88. Schille thinks this moment is exemplary of Dryden's "characteristic complexity of mind" and does see this moment as encoding Dryden's more general critique of colonialism, even of English colonialism.

that; so if he kills you, I shall have him single upon me."[89] Despite the two-on-one odds, Towerson does kill Harman Junior and—with Ysabinda's help—fights the Fiscal to a surrender. But he is taken by the governor's forces when the Fiscal, who has been spared by Towerson, accuses him of cold-blooded murder. It is at this point that the full force of the Dutch plot against the English is loosed. The Fiscal accuses the whole contingent of English factors of treason, and they are all carried to prison, with Towerson's final words of encouragement and instruction ringing in their ears: "remember yet that no unmanly weakness in your sufferings disgrace the Native Honour of our Isle."[90]

Towerson's words encouraging manly fortitude are underscored a scene later by Harman Senior's threats. If to succumb to torture is to be unmanned, the Dutch method of torture exploits the fear of this outcome. Van Herring, a merchant, and Harman Senior sadistically draw out the revelation of how the English will be tortured, describing the waterboarding in gendered terms:

> *Van Her.* In a few words Gentlemen confess. There is a Beverage ready for you else, which
> you'l [sic] not like to swallow.
> *Collins.* How's this?
> *Harm.* You shall be muffl'd up like Ladies, with an Oyl'd Cloath put underneath your
> Chins, then Water pour'd above; which either you must drink or must not breath.[91]

Note that the phrase "muffl'd up like Ladies" is Dryden's own wording; the original accounts of the torture do not describe the torture apparatus in this way. And as we have seen, the method of torture can be gendered differently—Stephen Bradwell likens the "muffling" of the victim to martyrdom, to the presentation of the Baptist's head on a platter.[92]

Attempts to unman the English are perhaps underscored by the staging of the scenes of torture, in which they are made helpless and attacked by their enemies, their sufferings suddenly presented to the audience. Just as in act 4 the "*Scene drawn Discovers* Ysabinda *bound*," so in the middle of act 5, scene1, the "*Scene opens, and discovers the English Tortur'd, and the* Dutch *tormenting* them." The parallels suggest a conflation of sexual and other forms of violence. And corresponding anxiety about their English manhood is evident throughout the last act. Beaumont and Towerson are concerned before and during the torture that they will lose "the shapes of

89. Dryden, *Amboyna*, 4.5.119–121.
90. Dryden, *Amboyna*, 4.5.238–239.
91. Dryden, *Amboyna*, 5.1.137–142.
92. See my discussion of Stephen Bradwell in the coda to chapter 4.

Men."[93] Mental and physical torment are equally sharp and require equally gendered responses to resist, as Towerson has "summon'd all I had of Man" in order to bear up during his farewell from Ysabinda.[94] As he takes his leave from Beaumont, who is being sent to England, Towerson charges Beaumont to "tell my friends I dy'd so as became a Christian and a Man."[95]

The measure of the play's anxiety about unmanning may be taken when we consider the scene in which Dryden most departs from the historical record. The thread and threat of unmanning is mitigated by the interrogation on stage of two English boys and an English woman—all three Dryden's invention. While the express intent of the Dutch is to feminize the Englishmen, and the English fear that they will be unmanned by torture, these three assert that English endurance of torture evidences English masculine courage. Towerson's young page protests his innocence: "I have told your Hangman no, twelve times within this hour; when I was at the last Gaspe, and that's a time I think, when a Man shou'd not dissemble."[96] Harman Senior responds only to the seeming boast in his words: "A Man, mark you that now; you *English* Boys have learn't a trick of late, of growing Men betimes, and doing Mens Work too, before you come to twenty."[97] The unnamed Englishwoman refuses to confess to save herself from torture, though she is, as Harman urges, "of a softer Sex."[98] "But," she retorts, she is "of a Courage full as Manly; there is no Sex in Souls; wou'd you have *English* Wives shew less of Bravery then their Children do? to lie by an *English* Man's side, is enough to give a Woman Resolution."[99] Here, then, is yet another imagined wife, one whose fortitude comes directly from her physical relationship with an Englishman and who serves to counter the threat of unmanning that the English victims of torture face.

However, despite this staging of English manliness, for the most part, women are both literally and figuratively the site of violent penetration, and Englishmen are vulnerable to similar violence insofar as their gender roles shift and they are feminized by their Dutch attackers. Throughout the play, women represent European colonization and trade; or rather, they represent the East Indies themselves, similar to the image of a naked, recumbent America welcoming Europe in the well-known engraving of Vespucci in the New World (see fig. 1.1).

---

93. Beaumont, *Amboyna*, 5.1.157–158; Towerson says to Beaumont "Let me embrace you while you are a Man, now you must lose that form" (5.1.346–347).
94. Dryden, *Amboyna*, 5.1.410.
95. Dryden, *Amboyna*, 5.1.398.
96. Dryden, *Amboyna*, 5.1.181–183.
97. Dryden, *Amboyna*, 5.1.184–186.
98. Dryden, *Amboyna*, 5.1.209.
99. Dryden, *Amboyna*, 5.1.210–213.

If woman is the colonial space ripe for exploitation, she is vulnerable to violent treatment of all kinds. Annette Kolodny has discussed how the metaphor of the "virgin land," of "land as woman," leads to the justification of violent penetration of the Americas.[100] Dryden's endgame in his play partakes of that colonial "logic" and pushes the symbolism even further. Dryden's Dutch have created on Amboyna what Italian philosopher Giorgio Agamben calls a "state of exception" in order to justify their extralegal seizure and torture of the Englishmen. They have suspended the rule of law as a response to dire threats to the state.[101] Once they have done so, and following the logic of colonization in which the proper object of imperial penetration is the woman, Ysabinda is raped and English men are feminized in order that they, too, can be penetrated and destroyed.

The full implication of the intersection of gender and violence can be seen when we contextualize the play's plotline, in which women synecdochically positioned as the East Indian Spice Islands are despoiled with Amboyna's history. When the Dutch conquered the island from the Portuguese in 1605, they undertook the full eradication of all clove trees not under their direct control. Neighboring islands' trees were clear cut and trade was strictly regulated in order to consolidate Dutch control.[102] Similarly, as symbols of the islands and territories over which Europeans assert control, Native women possess "bare life" (Agamben's phrase is *Homo sacer*). They can be killed, but not sacrificed, and their deaths do not subject their killers—or their colonizers—to punishment: "Pray, what makes any thing a sin but Law; and, What Law is there here against it?"

Dryden's presentation of Amboyna can be mapped quite closely to Elaine Scarry's analysis of the structure of torture and the "fiction of power" that it creates. In particular, Dryden stages the unbearable appropriation by the torturer of intimate spaces and bodily functions (as I will discuss), but he sees them as horrifying primarily as they pertain to Englishmen's bodies, to their "unmanning," penetration, and destruction. If we extend his presentation beyond the bounds of his fiction and into the documentary record, we can speculate about the fuller application of Scarry's theory to the English overseas world.

While the records of the Amboyna torture—both in published midcentury accounts and in Dryden's rendering of it—describe several ways that the Dutch inflicted pain on the Japanese and English men they arrested, the

---

100. Annette Kolodny, *The Lay of the Land: Metaphor as Experience and History in American Life and Letters* (Chapel Hill: University of North Carolina Press, 1984).

101. Giorgio Agamben, *State of Exception*, trans. Kevin Attell (Chicago: University of Chicago Press, 2005).

102. Donald F. Lach and Edwin J. Van Kley, *Asia in the Making of Europe*, vol. 3, *A Century of Advance* (Chicago: University of Chicago Press, 1998), 68.

ways that the Dutch treat the water torture in particular confirm Scarry's account of the relation of torture to power. As Scarry describes it, the un-making of the victim's world progresses through the piece-by-piece trans-formation of the mores and tools of civilization—that which in ordinary times allows the individual to extend himself or herself into the world—into weapons. Thus, the most quotidian of objects, of actions, of move-ments, are used to inflict pain: "The room, both its structure and its content, is converted into a weapon, deconverted, undone. Made to participate in the annihilation of the prisoner, made to demonstrate that everything is a weapon, the objects themselves, and with them the fact of civilization, are annihilated."[103]

This contrast—between the torturer, with his ability to insist on the "in-contestable reality" of his world, and the sufferer, every element of whose world is being unmade—is illustrated in Dryden's play by the governor's twisted wordplay in the moments before torture is inflicted.[104] We have seen how Harman Senior describes the torture apparatus as muffling the Englishmen "like ladies." Further, he jocularly promises Beaumont and Collins (another English factor) "a beverage...which you'll not like to swal-low." Upon learning the nature of this "beverage," Beaumont calls out Harman for wanton sadism: "You are inhumane, to make your Cruelty your Pastime: Nature made me a Man, and not a Whale, to swallow down a flood."[105] In reply, Harman begins to construct the irreconcilable difference between the two of them that he will confirm in the torture chamber, a dif-ference that turns on the unmaking of the world that Beaumont will shortly experience and that will confirm the Dutchmen's power. Beaumont has re-fused Harman's words, refused to accept the way that he domesticates the tool of torture. Beaumont instead makes his torment a world-altering disas-ter. Doggedly, however, Harman returns to the quotidian register. He matches Beaumont's accusation that Harman will turn him into an animal with his own, sadistic jocularity, asserting that Beaumont is already less than a man. The water torture, Harman promises, will force Beaumont to "grow a Corpulent Gentleman like me; I shall love you the better for 't; now you are but a spare rib," not only a reference to their relative sizes, but a facile allusion to the Genesis story in which Eve is constructed out of Adam's rib. Beaumont is, Harman suggests, a woman to Harman's own fine figure of a man.

That Dryden's play represents the structure of torture in ways similar to Scarry's powerful descriptions is especially striking when we consider the

103. Elaine Scarry, *The Body in Pain: The Making and Unmaking of the World* (Oxford: Oxford University Press, 1985), 41.

104. Scarry, *Body in Pain*, 27.

105. Dryden, *Amboyna*, 5.1.148–150.

prelude to this scene. The function—as well as the sadism—of the governor's words to Beaumont and Collins illustrates the ineluctable distance between torturer and victim, a distance that is insisted upon, even before the prisoners arrive, in the twisted badinage Harman exchanges with a member of the Dutch Company. The apparatus of torture has been assembled; the Dutch know to what torments they will put the Englishmen—as should the audience—and they indulge in a kind of boasting hedonism in which an excess of drink is an essential element of civilized ritual:

> *Har.*   Boy, give me some Tobacco, and a stope of Wine, Boy.
>
> *Boy.*   I shall Sir.
>
> *Har.*   And a Tub to leak in Boy; when was this Table without a leaking Vessel?
>
> *Van Her.* That's an Omission.
>
> *1 Dutch.* A great Omission. 'Tis a Member of the Table, I take it so.
>
> *Har.*   Never any thing of Moment was done at our Counsel Table, without a leaking Tub;
>   at least in my time; great affairs require great Consultations, great Consultations
>   require great Drinking, and great Drinking a great leaking Vessel.
>
> *Van Her.* I am e'en drunk with joy already, to see our godly business in this forwardness.[106]

We could read Harman as simply a callous, even evil man, taking perverse pleasure in trivializing the weapons of torture about to be used against his enemies, but as Scarry has shown, such perversities are part and parcel of the way torture has been constructed in Western cultures: "it is naturally not the acts of eating or moving themselves, but the self-consciously civilized elaborations of these acts, the dinner party or the dance, that the torturer's words reach out for."[107]

Scarry's phrase "the self-consciously civilized elaborations of these acts" points us out and away from Dryden's fiction both to the documentary record and to the effects of the torture on the larger Amboynan community. A final "civilized elaboration" of an act—the execution itself—serves as a bridge to the wives' tales Dryden offers about the insular European-Amboynan community to my own speculation about that community. In moving the analysis from the spectacle of torture to that of the execution, we leave the Dutch-controlled castle and enter the realm of enslaved people, Native Amboynans and Mardikers (freemen), back to the realm of the historical woman who was Perez's enslaved wife.

---

106. Dryden, *Amboyna*, 5.1.76–89.
107. Scarry, *Body in Pain*, 44.

Coda: Un/Making the World

In *The Body in Pain*, Scarry argues that the relationship of torturer to victim unfolds as a way for the torturer to assert the reality of his world by "unmaking" the world of the victim. The victim's world is reduced to physical suffering, while the torturer's world remains fully present. The torturer has reason and language, the victim pain and noise. Thus the "point" of torture is not information but power; the questions put to its victims and the answers elicited display that power, create what Scarry calls a "fiction of power."[108] William Sanderson's account of the swooning widow suggests that this power can extend even to those who mourn its victims. So long as the representation of her husband's torture was described in words, the woman could respond in kind. But the graphic representation of pain causes the woman to give over rational response and lapse into unconsciousness.

There are other women who are even more directly affected by the violence on Amboyna—eyewitnesses to the events. The fate of one woman, unnamed in the English print record and archives, intimately connected to one of the men tortured and executed, can be excavated from contemporary accounts, and hers is the last of the "wives' tales" I examine. The archives and the woman's silence within them parallel the treatment of the Amboyna victims. If torture unmade the world of Samuel Colson, James Ramsey, or John Beaumont, who were among those executed, its aftereffects also unmade the world of this woman. The East India Company court records reference an enslaved woman who was given to Augustine Perez, the Portuguese "Captain of the Slaves" who was executed along with the English factors in Amboyna. The records describe her as his wife, but she is far from being able to pursue her rights in court; the Dutch East India Company determines to reclaim her as a company slave until they can decide her fate.

The English Archive gives voice to the Englishmen who were killed, to their Company employers, even to their torturers. This woman is given no voice at all; the Archive contains her within its own "fiction of power." But this fleeting archival moment opens up a line of inquiry: How did this woman come to be the "property" of the Dutch East India Company? What exactly did it mean to be considered Perez's wife? What did she witness and feel at his execution?

The first reports of the Amboyna incident describe the spectacle of the execution as a two-day affair designed to satisfy, impress, or terrify outsiders.

---

108. Scarry argues that "the physical pain [of torture] is so incontestably real that it seems to confer its quality of 'incontestable reality' on that power that has brought it into being. It is, of course, precisely because the reality of that power is so highly contestable, the regime so unstable, that torture is being used"; *Body in Pain*, 27.

Islanders were summoned on the first day; on the next, the condemned were paraded through town before being killed: "they were...carried unto the place of execution...not the ordinarie and short way, but round about in a long procession, through the Town; the way guarded with five Companies of Souldiers, Dutch and Amboyners, and thronged with the Natives of the Island, that (upon the summons given the day before by the sound of the Drum) flocked together to behold this Triumph of the *Dutch* over the *English*."[109] The drums were a traditional signal for gathering; leaders used such drum calls in order to gather and recruit workers for special projects or men for particular military duties.[110] Note as well that the route breaches the boundaries between European and East Indian. The procession is taking a deliberately circuitous path rather than the "customary" route. If we consider the appropriation of this ritual by Europeans through the lens of Scarry's theories on torture, we might understand it as a way of "unmaking" the Native world and turning it colonial. The quotidian—a drum call— becomes a new psychological weapon—a signal that brutal executions are to take place and that Amboyna's people are called on to witness them.

It makes sense that the Dutch stage this spectacle as a means of consolidating power. The Dutch were vastly outnumbered—all Europeans were— in the Moluccas. Augustine Perez is called the "captain of the slaves" in the accounts, a position that had real responsibility, but a role in which authority must have seemed only tenuous, given the disproportionate demographics of Europeans and Others.[111] In the province of Amboyna as a whole, the portion of European "others" was just under 10 percent; moreover, Gerritt Knaap reports that "the proportion of the slaves in the non-indigenous population was more than 50 per cent."[112] However the categories are parsed, it's clear that European rulers in the Indies were the minority.

109. *True Relation* (1651), 45.

110. I'm arguing that this summons was an appropriation of the summons to participate in the practice of *kerahan*, in which a Malay leader summoned "the populace to work on specific projects of benefit to the leaders, as well as to the whole community." Andaya describes *kerahan* as "part of a general concept of mutual assistance, which characterized the cooperative nature of local life in the archipelago" (*World of Maluku*, 73).

111. Gerritt Knaap, "The Demography of Ambon in the Seventeenth Century: Evidence from Colonial Proto-censuses," *Journal of Southeast Asia Studies* 26.2 (September 1995), table 1, 234.

112. Hendrik E. Niemeijer provides early seventeenth-century demographics for Batavia, a larger Dutch settlement, but one that gives some indication of the proportions of Europeans and indigenous people, slave and free, in the Dutch East Indies. Enslaved people made up nearly 40 percent of the population, while Europeans were a mere 3.3 percent. Even if we include the category "Eurasions" (and it's possible that Perez might have belonged to this group, as we know that he was born in Bengal, and after the withdrawal of the Portuguese from the Moluccas, a number of those born from unions of Portuguese men and Native women remained behind), the total number in Batavia is only 4.8 percent. "Slavery, Ethnicity and the Economic Independence of Women," 176. Knaap estimates that in 1673, only around 19 percent of the total population

Thus it is unsurprising that the public and elaborate display of the executions might have been a tactic of shock and awe. D. K. Bassett, drawing on older historians, points out that one of the reasons why the executions were carried out in Amboyna [rather than Jakarta] was to terrorise some rebellious Ternatens."[113] The description here suggests that the spectacle was aimed at the "Natives of that Island," a category distinct from "Amboyners," who are likely Native Christians who had been allied with the Dutch from the time they captured the islands from the Portuguese.[114] Moreover, the emphasis on the unusual route that the condemned took to their executions suggests the particular terror that the scene offered to Native observers: by going "not the ordinarie and short way, but round about in a long procession, through the Town," the Dutch breached the barrier that separated Europeans and East Indians. It seems a risky move, in that the castle walls were meant to protect the Dutch, and this spectacle demonstrated how porous the walls were—both because they had ostensibly come under threat by the English-Japanese alliance and because the Dutch themselves could transport the weapons of violence through them. Thus, the drum penetrates the bounds, calling Native peoples, slaves, and Mardikers to mingle with Europeans to contemplate the spectacle of Dutch power outside the walls of the castle, walls that should have contained them and offered some measure of protection for the customs, cultures, and persons on either side. As Leonard Y. Andaya argues of the Portuguese castle in Ternate, it "created more than simply a physical barrier between the Ternatens and the Portuguese. It reinforced well-entrenched prejudices on both sides. The walls enclosed a separate European world in which the Portuguese could safely maintain their dress, food, and customs unbesmirched by contact with 'uncivilized' society. For the Malukans there must have been a corresponding feeling of relief in viewing the outsiders confined within a specific place which served as a continual reminder of their alienness in the Malukan world."[115] But of course, even if such separation offered a comforting illusion of protection, it was but a fragile one.

Just how fragile can be measured in the story of the death of two enslaved men in 1623, or rather, the story of their killer's request to be compensated for the fines they incurred as a result of the deaths. All we know from the records is that the enslaved men were killed when Thomas Bottes,

---

on the island of Amboyna was other than Ambonese ("Demography of Ambon in the Seventeenth Century," 233).

113. D. K. Basset, "The 'Amboyna Massacre' of 1623," *Journal of Southeast Asian History* 1.2 (1960), 3, n. 8.

114. See Gerritt Knaap, "Headhunting, Carnage and Armed Peace in Amboina, 1500–1700," *Journal of the Economic and Social History of the Orient* 46.2 (2003), 164.

115. Andaya, *World of Maluku*, 117.

a gunner on the *Globe,* fired a "salute." His cannon was fully loaded, and his shot hit the castle on Amboyna, killing "a Couple of slaves."[116] As with so many other colonial stories, we know particulars of these people only incidentally—not their occupations, their names, or even their genders (though we know all these details of their killer). And their deaths are recorded in the archives not as memorial but as a part of a bureaucratic note. The gunner who fired the shot petitioned the English East India Company because he had been fined by the Dutch for their loss of property—the slaves and possibly the structural damage lumped in. Bottes asks the Company to reimburse him, claiming that the deduction of the fine from his wages "would utterly undo him." The Court blamed him entirely for the error, but as the *Calendar of State Papers* summarizes, they were "moved with the poverty of the man" and so "were content to give him freely 10*l.* toward that loss."[117]

At a remove of nearly 400 years, we can analyze the spare record through several theoretical lenses. The enslaved men were considered "socially dead" before their lives ended, by both Dutch and English. Theirs was a "bare life," as Giorgio Agamben would have it; they inhabited the role of the "homo sacer," whose death is not intelligible within the realms of jurisprudence or religious ritual (sacrifice).[118] In Judith Butler's terms, theirs were not "grievable" lives. Indeed, the incident is a near perfect illustration of systematic colonial violence that can be parsed through recent formulations of biopolitics. Yet, however useful such analyses, more is needed. As I see it, our theoretical analyses are productively iterable but inevitably limited to the colonizer's point of view, and thus such analyses risk rendering the lives and deaths of these men inert, victims of my/our own archival violence. Shifting from theory to speculation, we can imagine a quite different response from those who did indeed mourn the men's deaths (assuming any did) or at the very least from those tasked with clearing their remains from the broken castle wall.

In her recent book *'Til Death or Distance Do Us Part,* Frances Smith Foster describes instances of stable love and marriage among African-American enslaved people in the nineteenth century that belie the received notions of the institutional barriers to such deep and long-lasting relationships. In

116. East India Company Court Minutes, 2 July 1624–14 April 1625, India Office Records, Asia and Africa Collections, British Library, IOR/B/9, 116–117.

117. East Indian India Company Court Minutes, 16 September 1623, India Office Records, Asia and Africa Collections, British Library, IOR/B/9, 116–117; "East Indies: September 1623," in *Calendar of State Papers Colonial, East Indies, China and Japan,* vol. 4, *1622–1624,* ed. W. Noel Sainsbury (London, 1878), 147–155, British History Online, http://www.british-history.ac.uk/cal-state-papers/colonial/east-indies-china-japan/vol4/pp147-155, accessed 27 November 2015.

118. Giorgio Agamben, *Homo Sacer: Sovereign Power and Bare Life,* trans. Daniel Heller-Roazen (Stanford: Stanford University Press, 1998).

short, she offers a counter to the easy assumptions that enslaved people themselves had no recourse but to internalize the "social death" that Orlando Patterson argues made their status as disenfranchised chattel-persons tenable in slaveholding societies worldwide.[119] That is, they were subject to the process by which, as Patterson argues, enslaved people are stripped not only of their cultural connections and social relations but also of the ability to forge new relations outside the master-slave structure.[120] To return to the unnamed enslaved wife, given her treatment as a piece of chattel property easily passed from one Company-approved master to another, we might also classify her as "socially dead," and for the English and Dutch alike, such was indeed her position in their colonial society.

It may be true that she was functionally socially dead insofar as under European rule, she could not freely pursue cultural connections and relationships as those Europeans understood and legalized them. But Maluku ideas of slavery and exchange may have meant that this woman understood her position differently. Anthony Reid and Jennifer Brewster argue that Europeans fundamentally misunderstood what their local trading partners, allies, and even enemies in the East Indies meant when they pointed to bonded labor in their communities. Europeans termed these people "slaves," they argue, "because that was how these bondsmen were described by earlier inhabitants in the various languages they used as lingua franca.... The Europeans immediately noticed, however, that most of these slaves were treated as well as servants in Europe, if not better.[121] Just as Foster takes issue with the Western definitions of familial relations that underpin the notion that, for instance, enslaved African-American men could not claim the role of fatherhood, so we might consider in this case that an East Indian understanding of slavery can illuminate the unnamed enslaved woman's experience of bondage differently from a lens trained only on the understanding of her European "owners."

---

119. See Frances Smith Foster, 'Til *Death or Distance Do Us Part: Love and Marriage in African America* (Oxford: Oxford University Press, 2010). Although I am referencing Patterson's older *Slavery and Social Death* (1985), she engages with his *Rituals of Blood* (1998).

120. Orlando Patterson, *Slavery and Social Death: A Comparative Study* (Cambridge, MA: Harvard University Press, 1985).

121. Anthony Reid and Jennifer Brewster seem a bit sanguine about the treatment of and possibilities for such people, noting that "the Portuguese captain in Malacca cited by Manguin is an excellent example, complaining that one had to pamper each slave 'so that he does not run away,' and suggesting that mistreated slaves could simply run away to the "jungle hinterland." *Slavery, Bondage and Dependency in Southeast Asia* (New York: St. Martin's Press, 1983), 14, 15. While the separation of Europeans and others on the island of Amboyna does seem to make such a move possible, European-Asian relations were complicated, and it would be hard to say just where this woman might go to be beyond the reach of intercultural alliances. Moreover, slaves were brought to the island from elsewhere, and slaves had by this time been born into the colonial system. As citizens in a "cosmopolitan" colonial settlement, it would have been no easy thing to hike into the mountains and escape.

The difference in the ways that enslaved people circulated in the Indies compared to the transatlantic Middle Passage is instructive on this point. While I in no way wish to minimize the pain an individual woman might feel if she were uprooted from her immediate family and transported, as so many were, to a new place and especially in a condition of forced servitude to Europeans, Andaya explains that despite such personal distress, she would not be experiencing the anomie of the Atlantic Middle Passage: "The Christian European tradition of the center and the periphery representing moral and spiritual polarities was in sharp contrast to the Malukan idea of complementarity and unity in center/periphery relations.... One consequence of the fluidity of center/periphery relations was the emphasis on the human community rather than on geographic location as a basis of identity.... The frequent movement of populations, and the presence of different transplanted groups within a single community, helped to reaffirm the notion of plurality within a larger Malukan family as depicted in the origin myths."[122] In other words, if she were born to the Maluku culture, transportation alone would not have been enough to effect social death; unlike the Middle Passage of the Atlantic, movement from one island to another (if indeed, this woman was originally from another island) would not necessarily have been the radical break that transatlantic passage from African to the Americas was for enslaved peoples. On Amboyna, she could have understood herself as still connected to the life she had lived before.[123] She likely understood her status and her relationship to Perez in ways we can never recover.

122. Andaya, World of Maluku, 110.
123. Although I have been trying to suggest some alternative ways to speculate on the experience of Perez's enslaved wife, there is no way to escape the fact that for the Dutch and English who documenteded her existence and her fate, she was an inconsequential player in the events on Amboyna. Even if traditional ways of understanding the role of women and of slaves in Amboynan society persisted in the seventeenth century, sweeping changes were under way. Reid and Brewster note that slavery in Southeast Asia was not necessarily assumed to be for the life of the enslaved person but corresponded to the life of the master, and in Batavia "slaves were very frequently manumitted on the death of their masters" (Slavery, Bondage and Dependency in Southeast Asia, 17). However, Augustine Perez's enslaved wife, as I have shown, was not manumitted but was held until she could be given to another, a treatment that seems to suggest that the Dutch saw her only in the position of a sexually available perpetual slave. Such treatment by Europeans is possible in part because of the colonists' policy of separation from their slaves. As Reid and Brewster argue, "the Dutch and British (the Portuguese much less markedly) differed from Southeast Asian urban slaveowners however, in that they maintained a social distance from their slaves and made little effort to incorporate them culturally" (18). Such a distance would have meant that a woman's choices were radically circumscribed—there was no unified Eurasian culture into which she could move. As Niemeijer argues about the situation during the latter part of the seventeenth century in Batavia, the colonial culture experienced a "feminization of poverty" that made certain kinds of servitude and sex work necessary for some women ("Slavery, Ethnicity and the Economic Independence of Women in Seventeenth-Century Batavia," 182). See also his "The Free Asian Christian Community and Poverty in Pre-modern Batavia," in Jakarta/Batavia: Socio-cultural Essays, ed. P. Nas and C. Grijns (Leiden: KITLV

And so I have reached the end of the wife's tale that I can tell, hit the limits of the Archive of this book. Any attempt to shift focus to explore her self-understanding leaves us with many questions but few answers. What remains for this particular wife's tale is to consider what her reactions might have been to the scene of violence—Augustine Perez's execution—that has made her briefly visible in the colonial archives. When the Dutch marched Perez to the place of execution, when they breached their castle walls, entered the province of the Christian Ambonese who lived in the surrounding town, did they process through her family's neighborhood? Could they have passed by the home she shared with Perez, since as a "mixed" couple, they likely were housed outside the fort, in the surrounding, cosmopolitan urban space? Did she obey the summons of the drums? Or did she hide? When she saw Augustine Perez kneel and receive the executioner's stroke, did she cry out? Did she weep? Was she secretly—or openly—glad? The records can only leave us unsatisfied. The last trace of her in the English print record leaves her fate suspended: "shee shall returne to her ancient Maisters of the said Companie, until such time that shee shall be otherwise disposed of by the Governour."[124]

Other scholars, multilingual and better versed in Dutch and Asian sources, may be able to trace this woman in sources I have not located or cannot access. But we are unlikely to uncover many specific details about these women's experiences. Native women, or even English women of the poor to middling sort, rarely attract sustained notice by the chroniclers of colonization and early modern trade. As Betty Joseph argues in *Reading the East India Company*, we rarely even learn the names of women from Company records of their East Indian activities, much less any detail of their individuality and agency.[125] Nevertheless, I agree with Joseph that although we encounter women in early modern archives in at best a piecemeal way, "the partial and fragmented appearance of women can provide the occasion for a new telling that ushers in a new subject of history."[126] In particular, bringing together the stories of English women and Native

---

Press, 2000), 81–98. The foreclosure of choice for women is illustrated by the high percentage of Native Christian women, as Christian status gave unaffiliated women some measure of poor relief.

124. This last glimpse of her is in "An Authentic Copy of the Confessions and Sentences Against M. Towerson, and Complices," 35. Dutch archives may have more information, but I have concentrated on the English circulation of information.

125. Betty Joseph, *Reading the East India Company, 1720–1840: Colonial Currencies of Gender* (Chicago: University of Chicago Press, 2004), 3.

126. She argues as well that "the very presence of these women in the London archives is proof that domains of affect and sexuality were caught up in the everyday governance of the empire and that the historical effects of these domains could never be determined in advance" (*Reading the East India Company*, 10).

women who were associated with the Amboyna incident gives us, in Joseph's words, "a globalized reading of the transnational archive of British rule [that] can enable us to locate intersections and shared histories rather than the separation of national traditions."[127]

Much of my telling of these woman's lives relies on speculation, but (I hope) informed speculation. Taken together, these stories suggest the reach of the East India Companies and their governments (both English and Dutch) into people's lives. Their stories also suggest the limits of that power, as women figure in unexpected ways in Company and colonial history. Such speculation seems a useful approach for reading the messy archives of colonial entanglement, wherever they may be found.[128]

In the women of Amboyna, we have an example of Michel de Certeau's formulation of fiction as the "repressed other of historical discourse,"[129] an other that lurks not just in fiction or drama but also, as I have traced in this book, in the pages, margins, and even the gaps of the colonial Archive. By reinventing, reimagining, recasting Perez's enslaved wife as both Julia and Ysabinda, Dryden, in spite of his own goals, in effect reanimates a figure whom the Dutch and English authorities in the East Indies had rendered socially dead. Dryden's characters are fantasies, to be sure, but they are serious fantasies that call into question imperial and colonial systems. Fantasies such as these, whether they are written in the 17th century or even today should spur us return to the written record of early globalism, to trace the threads that connected the metropole to even the most unlikely places and people worldwide. By doing so, we not only find new ways to read, but also we may better recognize the witness of figures who are also contained within the early modern Archive, "sheltered" there, as Derrida suggests, so that they may be forgotten:[130] figures such as Elizabeth Wilcocks, debating William Lilly in the margins of his own book; Louis, plotting freedom on Guadalupe; the unnamed Japanese girl buying herself back from English traders; the Algonquian mother and basket maker in colonial New England finding a new "Indian place"; the Narragansett warriors expressing their

---

127. Joseph, *Reading the East India Company*, 2.

128. Other threads might lead to a consideration of the wives of New England missionaries or military men—John Underhill's wife, for instance—or to an expanded excavation of the experiences of Algonquian Christian women in the seventeenth century. I explored the experiences of women, both Algonquian and English, who made New England Christian evangelism possible in "The Women of the New England Mission," paper presented at conference "London and the Americas 1492–1812," Society of Early Americanists, Kingston University, London, 17–20 July 2014.

129. Michel de Certeau, "History and Science," in *Heterologies*, quoted in White, "Introduction: Historical Fiction, Fictional History, and Historical Reality," *Rethinking History* 9.2/3 (June/September 2005), 147.

130. Jacques Derrida, *Archive Fever: A Freudian Impression*, trans. Eric Prenowitz (Chicago: University of Chicago Press, 1995), 2.

horror at Underhill's violence; even the girl with a spark in her eye victimized by the carelessness of drunken gallants. The men and women who made the English early modern world continue to offer their challenge to the ways we have told their stories, a challenge that may not quite belong to the era of Lilly, Gage, Cocks, Jessey, Underhill, Bradwell, or Dryden but, that most certainly belongs to ours.

BIBLIOGRAPHY

Note: primary sources consulted through the online database Early *English Books Online* are designated "EEBO."

Agamben, Giorgio. *Homo Sacer: Sovereign Power and Bare Life.* Trans. Daniel Heller-Roazen. Stanford: Stanford University Press, 1998.

Agamben, Giorgio. *State of Exception.* Trans. Kevin Attell. Chicago: University of Chicago Press, 2005.

Alkon, Paul K. *Origins of Futuristic Fiction.* Athens: University of Georgia Press, 1987.

Alsop, J. D. "Towerson, Gabriel (*bap.* 1576, *d.* 1623)." In *Oxford Dictionary of National Biography.* Oxford: Oxford University Press, 2004. http://www.oxforddnb.com/view/article/27591. Accessed 2 October 2016.

Amory, Hugh. "British Books Abroad: The American Colonies." In *The Cambridge History of the Book in Britain,* vol. 4, *1557–1695,* ed. John Barnard and D. F. McKenzie. Cambridge: Cambridge University Press, 2002: 744–754.

Anderson, Benedict. "Exodus." *Critical Inquiry* 20.2 (Winter 1994): 314–327.

Anderson, Susan Campbell. "A Matter of Authority: James I and the Tobacco War." *Comitatus* 291 (1998): 136–163.

Andaya, Leonard. *The World of Maluku: Eastern Indonesia in the Early Modern Period.* Honolulu: University of Hawaii Press, 1993.

Appelbaum, Roger. *Literature and Utopian Politics in Seventeenth-Century England.* Cambridge: Cambridge University Press, 2004.

Appendino, Giovanni, and Arpad Szallas. "Euphorbium: Modern Research on Its Active Principle, Reseniferatoxin, Revives an Ancient Medicine." *Life Sciences* 60.10 (1997): 681–696.

Armitage, David. "The Cromwellian Protectorate and the Language of Empire." *Historical Journal* 35.3 (September 1992): 531–555.

Attebery, Brian. *Strategies of Fantasy.* Bloomington: Indiana University Press, 1992.

Barthes, Roland. *Camera Lucida: Reflections on Photography.* Trans. Richard Howard. New York: Hill and Wang, 1981.

Bassett, D. K. "The 'Amboyna Massacre' of 1623." *Journal of Southeast Asian History* 1.2 (1960): 1–19.

"A Batch of Children's Books." *Athenaeum,* 24 December 1870, 840–841.

Bell, Maureen. "Hannah Allen and the Development of a Puritan Publishing Business, 1646–51." *Publishing History* 26 (1989): 5–66.

Birdwood, Sir George. *Report on the Old Records of the India Office.* 2nd Reprint. London W. H. Allen and Co., 1891.

Boruchoff, David A. "New Spain, New England, and the New Jerusalem: The 'Translation' of Empire, Faith, and Learning (*translatio imperii, fidei ac scientiae*) in the Colonial Mission Project." *Early American Literature* 43.1 (2008): 5–34.

Bowley, A. L. "Foxwell, Herbert Somerton (1849–1936)." Rev. Richard D. Freeman. In *Oxford Dictionary of National Biography*. Oxford: Oxford University Press, 2004. http://www .oxforddnb.com/view/article/33239.

Boyer, Allen D. "Gage, Thomas (1603?–1656)." In *Oxford Dictionary of National Biography*. Oxford: Oxford University Press, 2004. http://www.oxforddnb.com/view/article/10274. Accessed 6 November 2015.

Bozeman, Theodore. *To Live Ancient Lives: The Primitivist Dimension in Puritanism*. Chapel Hill: University of North Carolina Press, 1988.

Bradwell, Stephen. *Helps for Suddain Accidents Endangering Life*. London, 1633.

Bradwell, Stephen. "Mary Glovers Late Woeful Case." In *Witchcraft and Hysteria in Elizabethan London: Edward Jorden and the Mary Glover Case*, ed. Michael MacDonald. London: Tavistock, 1991.

Bragdon, Kathleen. *Indians of Southern New England, 1500–1650*. Norman: University of Oklahoma Press, 1996.

Bragdon, Kathleen. *Indians of Southern New England, 1650–1775*. Norman, University of Oklahoma Press, 2009.

Bremer, Francis. *Congregational Communion*. Boston: Northeastern University Press, 1994.

Brenner, Elise. "To Pray or to Be Prey: That Is the Question: Strategies for Cultural Autonomy of Massachusetts Praying Town Indians." *Ethnohistory* 27.2 (1980): 135–152.

Brewer, John, and Roy Porter, eds. *Consumption and the World of Goods*. New York: Routledge, 1994.

A Brief Description of the Future History of Europe, from Anno 1650 to An. 1710. London, 1650. EEBO.

Bross, Kristina. *Dry Bones and Indian Sermons: Praying Indians in Colonial America*. Ithaca: Cornell University Press, 2004.

Bross, Kristina. "The Women of the New England Mission." Paper presented at conference "London and the Americas 1492–1812," Society of Early Americanists, Kingston University, London, 17–20 July 2014.

Brown, Laura. "The Ideology of Restoration Poetic Form: John Dryden." *PMLA* 97.3 (May 1982): 395–407.

Bumas, E. Shaskan. "The Cannibal Butcher Shop." *Early American Literature* 35.2 (2000): 107–136.

Burnham, Michelle. *Folded Selves: Colonial New England Writing in the World System*. Hanover: University Press of New England, 2007.

Butler, Judith. *Frames of War: When Is Life Grievable?* Reprint, London: Verso, 2010.

Butts, Francis T. "The Myth of Perry Miller." *American Historical Review* 87.3 (June 1982): 665–694.

Calendar of State Papers Colonial, America and West Indies. Vol. 1. 1574–1660. Ed. W. Noel Sainsbury. London, 1860. British History Online. http://www.british-history.ac.uk/cal-state-papers/colonial/america-west-indies/vol1. Accessed 22 September 2016.

Calendar of State Papers Colonial, East Indies, China and Japan. Vol. 4. 1622–1624. Ed. W. Noel Sainsbury. London, 1878. British History Online. http://www.british-history.ac.uk/cal-state-papers/colonial/east-indies-china-japan/vol4. Accessed 15 September 2016.

Calendar of State Papers Colonial, East Indies, China and Persia. Vol. 6. 1625–1629. Ed. W Noel Sainsbury. London, 1884. British History Online. http://www.british-history.ac.uk/cal-state-papers/colonial/east-indies-china-japan/vol6. Accessed 23 September 2016.

"Calendar of State Papers, Colonial Series; East Indies, China, and Japan, 1617–1621." *Calcutta Review* 53.106 (October 1871): 47.

"Calendar of State Papers. Colonial Series. East Indies, China and Japan, 1513–1616." *Athenaeum*, 4 April 1863, 453–455.

"Calendar of State Papers, Colonial Series, East Indies, China, and Japan…" *Edinburgh Review* 152.312 (October 1880): 407.

Calendar of State Papers Domestic Series, Charles I, 1628–1629 (1859). Reprint, Nendeln, Liechtenstein: Kraus Reprint, 1967.

Campbell, Colin. "Understanding Traditional and Modern Patterns of Consumption in Eighteenth-Century England." In *Consumption and the World of Goods*, ed. John Brewer and Roy Porter. New York: Routledge, 1993: 40–57.

Campos, Edmund Valentine. "Thomas Gage and the English Encounter with Chocolate." *Journal of Medieval and Early Modern Studies* 39.1 (Winter 2009): 183–200.

Canny, Nicholas. "The Origins of Empire: An Introduction." In *Oxford History of the British Empire*, vol. 1, ed. Nicholas Canny. Oxford: Oxford University Press, 2001: 1–33.

Capp, Bernard. *The Fifth Monarchy Men: A Study in Seventeenth-Century English Millenarianism.* London: Faber and Faber, 1972.

Chancey, Karen. "The Amboyna Massacre in English Politics, 1624–1632." *Albion* 30.4 (1998): 583–598.

"Christmas Books." *Saturday Review of Politics, Literature, Science and Art,* 24 December 1870, 813–815.

Churchman, Bartholomew. *An Answere to the Hollanders Declaration* (1622). EEBO.

Clulow, Adam. "Unjust, Cruel and Barbarous Proceedings: Japanese Mercenaries and the Amboyna Incident of 1623." *Itinerario* 31.1 (2007): 15–34.

Cogley, Richard. "'Some Other Kinde of Being and Condition': The Controversy in Mid-seventeenth Century England over the Peopling of Ancient America." *Journal of the History of Ideas* 68.1 (January 2007): 35–56.

Cogley, Richard. *John Eliot's Mission to the Indians before King Philip's War.* Cambridge, MA: Harvard University Press, 1999.

Cohen, Margaret. "Literary Studies on the Terraqueous Globe." *PMLA* 125.3 (May 2010): 657–662.

Cohen, Matt. *The Networked Wilderness: Communicating in Early New England.* Minneapolis: University of Minnesota Press, 2009.

Collet, C. E. "Herbert Somerton Foxwell." *Economic Journal* 46.184 (December 1936): 589–619.

A Courante of Newes from the East India. London, 1622. EEBO.

Cowley, Abraham. "Leaving Me and Then Loving Many." In *Poems Written by A. Cowley.* London, 1656. EEBO.

Craft, Peter. "Peter Heylyn's Seventeenth-Century World View." *Studies in Medieval and Renaissance History*, 3rd ser., 11 (2014): 325–344.

Cromwell, Oliver. *To All Persons Whom These May Concern, in the Several Townes, and Plantations of the United Colonies in New-England.* London, 1656. EEBO.

Crowther, Stefania, Ethan Jordan, Jacqueline Wernimont, and Hillary Nunn. "New Scholarship, New Pedagogies: Views from the 'EEBO Generation.'" *Early Modern Literary Studies* 14.2/ Special Issue 17 (September 2008): 3.1–30. http://purl.oclc.org/emls/14-2/crjowenu.html.

Curry, Patrick. "William Lilly (1602–1681)." In *Oxford Dictionary of National Biography*. Oxford: Oxford University Press, 2004. http://www.oxforddnb.com/view/article16661. Accessed 12 July 2016.

The Day-breaking, f Not the Sun-rising of the Gospell with the Indians in New-England. London, 1647. EEBO.

Dee, John. *John Dee: The Limits of the British Empire.* Ed. Ken MacMillan with Jennifer Abeles. Westport: Praeger, 2004.

Delbanco, Andrew. *The Puritan Ordeal.* Cambridge, MA: Harvard University Press, 1989.

Denison, John L. *An Illustrated History of the New World.* Norwich, CT, 1870. Sabin America. Accessed 23 September 2016.

Derrida, Jacques. *Archive Fever: A Freudian Impression.* Trans. Eric Prenowitz. Chicago: University of Chicago Press, 1995.

Dillon, Elizabeth Maddock. *New World Drama: The Performative Commons in the Atlantic World, 1649–1849.* Durham: Duke University Press, 2014.

Dolan, Frances. *True Relations: Reading, Literature, and Evidence in Seventeenth-Century England.* Philadelphia: University of Pennsylvania Press, 2013.

Dryden, John. *Amboyna*. In *The Works of John Dryden*. Ed. Vinton A. Dearing. Berkeley: University of California Press, 1994.

Dryden, John. *Amboyna*. In *The Dramatic Works of John Dryden*, ed. George Saintsbury. Vol. 5. Edinburgh, 1882.

Eilers, Michelle L. "On the Origins of Modern Fantasy." *Extrapolation* 41.4 (2000): 317–337.

Eliot, John. *A Late and Further Manifestation of the Gospel*. London, 1655. EEBO.

Ellner, Andrew. "First, Do No Harm." *n+1* 4 (Spring 2006). https://nplusonemag.com/issue-4/politics/do-no-harm/. Accessed 6 August 2015.

The Emblem of Ingratitude a True Relation of the Unjust, Cruel, and Barbarous Proceedings Against the English at Amboyna in the East-Indies. London, 1672. EEBO.

Engler, Bernd, Joerg O. Fichte, and Oliver Scheiding. "Transformations of Millennial Thought in America." In *Millennial Thought in America: Historical and Intellectual Contexts, 1630–1860*, ed. Bernd Engler, Joerg O. Fichte, and Oliver Scheiding. Trier: Wissenschaftlicher Verglad, 2002: 9–37.

Escobedo, Andrew. "The Millennial Border between Tradition and Innovation: Foxe, Milton, and the Idea of Historical Progress." In *Anglo-American Millennialism, from Milton to the Millerites*, ed. Richard Connors and Andrew Colin Gow. Leiden: Brill, 2004: 1–42.

Farmer, Paul. "An Anthropology of Structural Violence." *Current Anthropology* 45.3 (June 2004): 305–325.

Farrington, Anthony, ed. *The English Factory in Japan, 1613–1623*. Vol. 1. London: British Library, 1991.

Field, Jonathan Beecher. *Errands into the Metropolis: New England Dissidents in Revolutionary London*. Lebanon, NH: Dartmouth University Press, 2009.

Firth, C. H., and R. S. Rait, eds. *Acts and Ordinances of the Interregnum, 1642–1660* (1911). British History Online. http://www.british-history.ac.uk/Default.aspx. Accessed 16 July 2009.

Fisher, Michael. *Counterflows to Colonialism: Indian Travellers and Settlers in Britain 1600–1857*. Delhi: Permanent Black, 2004.

Fisher, Michael. "Seeing England Firsthand: Women and Men from Imperial India, 1614–1769." In *Europe Observed: Multiple Gazes in Early Modern Encounters*, ed. Kumkum Chatterjee and Clement Hawes. Cranbury, NJ: Associated University Presses, 2008: 143–171.

Fitzgerald, Stephanie. "The Cultural Work of a Mohegan Painted Basket." In *Early Native Literacies in New England*, ed. Kristina Bross and Hilary Wyss. Amherst: University of Massachusetts Press, 2008.

Foster, Frances Smith. *'Til Death or Distance Do Us Part: Love and Marriage in African America*. Oxford: Oxford University Press, 2010.

Foster, William. "The East India Company at Crosby House, 1621–1638." In *London Topographical Record*, vol. 8. London, 1913: 106–139.

Foster, William. *The English Factories in India, 1618–1621. A Calendar of Documents in the India Office, British Museum and Public Record Office*. Oxford: Clarendon Press, 1906.

Frank, Andre Gunder. *ReOrient: Global Economy in the Asian Age*. Berkeley: University of California Press, 1998.

Fuller, Randall. "*Errand into the Wilderness*: Perry Miller as American Scholar." *American Literary History* 18.1 (Spring 2006): 102–128.

Gage, Thomas. *The English-American: A New Survey of the West Indies, 1648*. Ed. A. P. Newton. London: Routledge, 1946. EEBO.

Gage, Thomas. *The English-American, His Travail by Sea and Land, or, A New Survey of the West-India's*. London, 1648. EEBO.

Gage, Thomas. *A New Survey of the West-India's, or, The English American, His Travail by Sea and Land*. London, 1655. EEBO.

Gage, Thomas. "Some Brief and True Observations Concerning the West-Indies." December 1654 Memorial to Oliver Cromwell. In *A Collection of the State Papers of John Thurloe*, vol. 3, *December 1654–August 1655*, ed. Thomas Birch. Originally published London: Fletcher Gyles, 1742. British History Online. http://www.british-history.ac.uk/. Accessed 12 March 2015.

Gage, Thomas. *Thomas Gage's Travels in the New World*. Ed. J. Eric Thompson. Norman: University of Oklahoma Press, 1958.

Gage, Thomas. *Tyranny of Satan, discovered by the teares of a converted sinner ... By Thomas Gage, formerly a Romish Priest, for the space of 38 yeares, and now truly reconciled to the Church of England* (London, 1642). EEBO.

Games, Alison. "Anglo-Dutch Connections and Overseas Enterprises: A Global Perspective on Lion Gardiner's World." *Early American Studies* 9.2 (Spring 2011): 435–461.

Games, Alison. Anglo-Dutch Relations in the East Indies and the 'Massacre' at Amboyna, 1623." Paper presented at Symposium on Anglo-Dutch Relations in the Early Modern World, Newberry Library, Chicago, 19 October 2012.

Games, Alison. "Violence on the Fringes: The Virginia (1622) and Amboyna (1623) Massacres in Comparative Perspective." *History* 99.336 (2014): 505–529.

Games, Alison. *The Web of Empire: English Cosmopolitans in an Age of Expansion, 1560–1660*. Oxford: Oxford University Press, 2009.

Geneva, Ann. *Astrology and the Seventeenth Century Mind: William Lilly and the Language of the Skies*. Manchester: Manchester University Press, 1995.

Gevitz, Norman. "*Helps for Suddain Accidents Endangering Life*: Stephen Bradwell and the Origins of the First Aid Guide." *Bulletin of the History of Medicine* 67.1 (1993): 51–73.

Gibson, Kenneth. "John Dury's Apocalyptic Thought." *Journal of Ecclesiastical History* 61.2 (April 2010): 299–313.

Gilliland, Anne J. and Michelle Caswell. "Records and Their Imaginaries: Imagining the Impossible, Making Possible the Imagined." *Archival Science* 16 (2016): 53–73.

Godfrey, Walter H. "Crosby Hall (Re-erected)." In *Survey of London*, vol. 4, *Chelsea*, pt. 2. London, 1913: 15–17. British History Online. http://www.british-history.ac.uk/survey-london/vol4/pt2/pp15-17. Accessed 5 September 2016.

Goldrank, Walter. "Paradigm Regained? The Rules of Wallerstein's World-System Method." *Journal of World-Systems Research* 6.2 (2000): 150–195.

Good, Caroline Anne. "Lovers of Art: English Literature on the Connoisseurship of Pictures." Doctoral diss., University of York, 2013.

Gookin, Daniel. *Historical Collections of the Indians in New England*. Boston: Apollo Press, 1792. Nineteenth Century Collections Online.

Green, Jonathan. "Translating Time: Chronicle, Prognostication, Prophecy." *Renaissance Studies* 29.1 (2015): 162–177.

Green, Margaret R., Walter D. Mignolo, and Maureen Quilligan, eds. *Rereading the Black Legend: The Discourses of Religious and Racial Difference in the Renaissance Empires*. Chicago: University of Chicago Press, 2007.

Greenspan, Nicole. "News and the Politics of Information in the Mid Seventeenth Century: The Western Design and the Conquest of Jamaica." *History Workshop Journal* 69.1 (Spring 2010): 1–26.

Gregerson, Linda. "Commonwealth of the Word: New England, Old England, and the Praying Indian." In *Empires of God: Religious Encounters in the Early Modern Atlantic*, ed. Linda Gregerson and Susan Juster. Philadelphia: University of Pennsylvania Press, 2011: 70–83.

Haas, L. F. "*Datera Stramomium* (Jimsonweed)." *Journal of Neurology, Neurosurgery and Psychiatry* 58 (1995): 654.

Hale, Edward E. "Appendix: Life of Sir Ralph Lane." *Archaeologica Americana; American Antiquarian Society Transactions and Collections* 4 (1860): 317–344.

Hale, Sarah Josepha Buell. *Woman's Record, or Sketches of all distinguished women, from the creation to AD 1868.* 3rd ed. rev. New York, 1870. Sabin Americana. Accessed 23 September 2016.

Hall, David D. *Worlds of Wonder, Days of Judgment: Popular Religious Belief in Early New England.* Cambridge, MA: Harvard University Press, 1990.

Hamilton, Carolyn, Verne Harris, Michele Pickover, Graem Reid, Razia Saleh, and Jane Taylor, eds. *Refiguring the Archive.* Norwell, MA: Kluwer Academic, 2002.

Hanson, Elizabeth. "Torture and Truth in Renaissance England." *Representation* 34 (Spring 1991): 53–84.

Harriot, Thomas. *A Briefe and True Report of the New Found Land of Virginia.* New York: Dover, 1972.

Harris, C. A. "Sainsbury, William Noel (1825–1895)." In *Oxford Dictionary of National Biography.* Oxford: Oxford University Press, 2004. http://www.oxforddnb.com/view/article/24474. Accessed 30 September 2016.

Hartman, Saidiya. "Venus in Two Acts." *Small Axe* 26 (June 2008): 1–14.

Helgerson, Richard. *Forms of Nationhood: The Elizabethan Writing of England in the Early Modern Period.* Chicago: University of Chicago Press, 1992.

Herbert, George. "Church Militant." In *New World Metaphysics: Readings on the Religious Meaning of the American Experience,* ed. Giles Gunn. New York: Oxford University Press, 1981: 36–38.

Heylyn, Peter. *Cosmographie.* London, 1652. EEBO.

Heylyn, Peter. *Microcosmos.* London, 1621. EEBO.

Hilgrath, J. N. *The Mirror of Spain, 1500–1700: The Foundation of a Myth.* Ann Arbor: University of Michigan Press, 2000.

Hoberman, Schell. *Mexico's Merchant Elite, 1590–1660: Silver, State and Society.* Durham: Duke University Press, 1991.

The Hollanders Declaration of the Affaires of the East Indies. Or a True Relation of That Which Passed in the Ilands of Banda, in the East Indies. London, 1622. EEBO.

Holstun, James. *Rational Millennium: Puritan Utopias of Seventeenth-Century England and America.* Oxford: Oxford University Press, 1987.

Hoxby, Blair. *Mammon's Music: Literature and Economics in the Age of Milton.* New Haven: Yale University Press, 2002.

Hudson, Geoffrey L. "Negotiating for Blood Money: War Widows and the Courts in Seventeenth-Century England." In *Women, Crime and the Courts in Early Modern England,* ed. Jennifer Kermonde. Chapel Hill: University of North Carolina Press, 1995: 146–169.

Hunt, Lynn. *Writing History in the Global Era.* New York: Norton, 2014.

Hutchins, Zachary. *Inventing Eden: Primitivism, Millennialism, and the Making of New England.* New York: Oxford University Press, 2014.

James I. *A Counterblaste to Tobacco.* London, 1604. EEBO.

Jehlen, Myra. "History before the Fact: John Smith's Unfinished Symphony." *Critical Inquiry* 19.4 (Summer 1993): 677–692.

Jenkinson, Matthew. "A New Author." *Notes and Queries* 52.3 (September 2005): 311–314.

Jessey, Henry. *Exceeding Riches of Grace Advanced by the Spirit of Grace in an Empty Nothing Creature.* London, 1647. EEBO.

Jessey, Henry. *Of the Conversion of Five-thousand Nine-Hundred East Indians.* London, 1650. EEBO.

Joseph, Betty. *Reading the East India Company, 1720–1840: Colonial Currencies of Gender.* Chicago: University of Chicago Press, 2004.

Jonson, Ben. *Selected Masques.* Ed. Stepen Orgel. New Haven: Yale University Press, 1970.

Jordan, Edward. *A Briefe Discourse of a Disease Called the Suffocation of the Mother.* London, 1603. EEBO.

Kaislaniumi, Samuli. "Early East India Company Merchants and a Rare Word for Sex." In *Words in Dictionaries and History: Essays in Honour of R. W. McConchie*, ed. Tanja Säily and Olga Timofeeva. Amsterdam: John Benjamins, 2011: 169–192.

Karr, Ronald Dale. "'Why Should You Be So Furious': The Violence of the Pequot War." *Journal of American History* 85.3 (December 1998): 876–909.

Katz, David. "Henry Jessey and Conservative Millenarianism in Seventeenth-Century England and Holland." In *Dutch Jewish History: Proceedings of the Fourth Symposium on the History of the Jews in the Netherlands*, ed. Joseph Michman. Jerusalem: Grf-Chen Press, 1987: 75–93.

Katz, David. "Menasseh Ben Israel's Christian Connection: Henry Jessey and the Jews." in *Menasseh ben Israel and His World*, ed. Yusef Kaplan, Henry Méchoulan, and Richard H. Popkin. Leiden: Brill, 1989: 117–138.

Katz, David. "Philo-Semitism in the Radical Tradition: Henry Jessey, Morgan Llwyd, and Jacob Boehme." In *Jewish-Christian Relations in the Seventeenth Century: Studies and Documents*, ed. Johannes van den Berg and E. G. van der Wall. Dordrecht: Kluwer Academic, 1988: 195–200.

Kellaway, William. *The New England Company, 1649–1776*. New York: Barnes & Noble, 1962.

Keynes, John Maynard. "Herbert Somerton Foxwell." In *The Collected Writings of John Maynard Keynes*, vol. 10, *Essays in Biography*. Cambridge: Macmillan St. Martin's Press, 1971: 267–296.

Kibbey, Ann M. *The Interpretation of Material Shapes in Puritanism: A Study of Rhetoric, Prejudice, and Violence*. Cambridge: Cambridge University Press, 1986.

Kichuk, Diana. "Metamorphosis: Remediation in Early English Books Online (EEBO)." *Literary and Linguistic Computing* 22.3 (2007): 291–303.

Killeen, Kevin. *Biblical Scholarship, Science and Politics in Early Modern England: Thomas Browne and the Thorny Place of Knowledge*. Farnham, UK: Ashgate, 2009.

Kim, Julie Chun. "Chocolate, Subsistence, and Survival in Early English Jamaica." *Caribbeana: The Journal of the Early Caribbean Society* 1.1 (2016): 4–33.

Knaap, Gerritt. "The Demography of Ambon in the Seventeenth Century: Evidence from Colonial Proto-censuses." *Journal of Southeast Asia Studies* 26.2 (September 1995): 227–241.

Knaap, Gerritt. "Headhunting, Carnage and Armed Peace in Amboina, 1500–1700." *Journal of the Economic and Social History of the Orient* 46.2 (2003): 165–192.

Kolodny, Annette. *The Lay of the Land: Metaphor as Experience and History in American Life and Letters*. Chapel Hill: University of North Carolina Press, 1984.

Koselleck, Reinhart. *Futures Past: on the Semantics of Historical Time*. Trans. Keith Tribe. New York: Columbia University Press, 2004.

Kroll, Richard. "Tales of Love and Gallantry: The Politics of *Oroonoko*." *Huntington Library Quarterly* 67.4 (December 2004): 573–605.

Krueger, Christine. "Mary Anne Everett Green and the Calendars of State Papers as a Genre of History Writing." *Clio* 36.1 (Fall 2006): 1–21.

Krueger, Christine. "Why She Lived at the PRO: Mary Anne Everett Green and the Profession of History." *Journal of British Studies* 42.1 (January 2003): 65–90.

Kupperman, Karen Ordahl. *The Atlantic in World History*. London: Oxford University Press, 2012.

Kupperman, Karen Ordahl. "The Love-Hate Relationship with Experts in the Early Modern Atlantic." *Early American Studies* 9.2 (Spring 2011): 248–267.

Kupperman, Karen Ordahl. *Providence Island 1630–1641: The Other Puritan Colony*. Cambridge: Cambridge University Press, 1995.

Lach, Donald F., and Edwin J. Van Kley. *Asia in the Making of Europe*. Vol. 3. *A Century of Advance*. Chicago: University of Chicago Press, 1993.

Levin, Joanna. "Lady MacBeth and the Daemonologie of Hysteria." *ELH* 69.1 (Spring 2002): 21–55.

Ligon, Richard. *A True and Exact History of the Island of Barbados*. Ed. Karen Ordahl Kupperman. Indianapolis: Hackett, 2011.

Lilly, William. *Anglicus: Peace or No Peace*. London, 1645. EEBO.

Lilly, William. *Monarchy or No Monarchy in England. Grebner his Prophecy Concerning Charles, Son of Charles, His Greatnesse, Victories, Conquests*. London, 1651. Copy in Virginia Kelly Karnes Archives and Special Collections, Purdue University, West Lafayette, Indiana.

Lilly, William. *A Prophecy of the White King; and Dreadfull Dead-man Explaned*. London, 1644. EEBO.

Loth, Vincent. "Armed Incidents and Unpaid Bills: Anglo-Dutch Rivalry in the Banda Islands in the Seventeenth Century." *Modern Asian Studies* 29.4 (October 1995): 705–740.

MacDonald, Michael, ed. *Witchcraft and Hysteria in Elizabethan London: Edward Jorden and the Mary Glover Case*. London: Tavistock, 1991.

Mack, Phyllis. *Visionary Women: Ecstatic Prophecy in Seventeenth-Century England*. Berkeley: University of California Press, 1992.

Maclear, J. F. "New England and the Fifth Monarchy: The Quest for the Millennium in Early American Puritanism." *William and Mary Quarterly*, 3rd ser., 32.2 (April 1975): 223–260.

Malieckal, Bindu. "Mariam Khan and the Legacy of Mughal Women in Early Modern Literature of India." *Early Modern England and Islamic Worlds*, ed. Linda McJannet and Bernadette Diane Andrea. New York: Palgrave Macmillan, 2001: 97–122.

Maltby, William S. *The Black Legend in England: The Development of Anti-Spanish Sentiment, 1558–1660*. Chapel Hill: Duke University Press, 1971.

Markley, Robert. *The Far East and the English Imagination, 1600–1730*. Cambridge: Cambridge University Press, 2006.

Markley, Robert. "Nothing Was Moribund, Nothing Was Dark: Time and Its Narratives in the Early Modern Period." *Eighteenth Century* 41.3 (Fall 2000): 179–184.

Markley, Robert. "Violence and Profits on the Restoration Stage: Trade, Nationalism and Insecurity in Dryden's *Amboyna*." *Eighteenth-Century Life* 22.1 (February 1998): 2–17.

Marriott, John. *Beyond the Tower: A History of East London*. New Haven: Yale University Press, 2011.

Mayhew, Robert J. "'Geography Is Twinned with Divinity': The Laudian Geography of Peter Heylyn." *Geographical Review* 90.1 (January 2000): 18–34.

McCants, Anne E. C. "Exotic Goods, Popular Consumption, and the Standard of Living: Thinking about Globalization in the Early Modern World." *Journal of World History* 18.4 (December 2007): 433–462.

McConnell, Anita. "Sanderson, William (1547/8–1638)." In *Oxford Dictionary of National Biography*. Oxford: Oxford University Press, 2004. http://www.oxforddnb.com/view/article/52001. Accessed 4 September 2016.

McDonald, Deborah. *Clara Collet 1860–1948: An Educated Working Woman*. London: Woburn Press, 2004.

McIntyre, Ruth A. "William Sanderson: Elizabethan Financier of Discovery." *William and Mary Quarterly* 13.2 (April 1956): 184–201.

McMullen, Ann, and Russell G. Handsman, eds. *A Key into the Language of Woodsplint Baskets*. Washington, CT: American Indian Archaeological Institute, 1987.

A Memento for Holland or A True and Exact History of the Most Villainous and Barbarous Cruelties Used on the English Merchants Residing at Amboyna. London, 1653. EEBO.

Mignolo, Walter. "The Enduring Enchantment: Or the Epistemic Privilege of Modernity and Where to Go from Here?" *South Atlantic Quarterly* 101.4 (Fall 2002): 927–954.

Mignolo, Walter. *Local Histories/Global Designs: Coloniality, Subaltern Knowledges, and Border Thinking*. Princeton: Princeton University Press, 2000; reprint, 2012.

Milton, Anthony. "Heylyn, Peter (1599–1662)." In *Oxford Dictionary of National Biography*. Oxford: Oxford University Press, 2004. http://www.oxforddnb.com/view/article/13171. Accessed 14 July 2016.

Milton, Anthony. "Marketing a Massacre: Amboyna, the East India Company and the Public Sphere in Early Stuart England." In *The Politics of the Public Sphere in Early Modern England*, ed. Peter Lake and Steven Pincus. Manchester: Manchester University Press, 2012: 168–190.

Mohlmann, Nicholas K. "Corporate Poetics and the Virginia Company of London, 1607–1655." Ph.D. diss., Purdue University, 2014.

Morrison, Dane. *A Praying People: Massachusett Acculturation and the Failure of the Puritan Mission, 1600–1690*. New York: Peter Lang, 1995.

Morrison, Kenneth M. "That Art of Coyning Christians": John Eliot and the Praying Indians of Massachusetts." *Ethnohistory* 21.1 (1974): 77–92.

Mountford, Walter. *The Launching of the Mary*. Ed. John Johnson. Oxford: Oxford University Press, 1933.

Mun, Thomas. *A Discourse of Trade, from England unto the East-Indies Answering to Diverse Obiections Which are Usually Made Against the Same*. London 1621. EEBO.

Naeher, Robert James. "Dialogue in the Wilderness: John Eliot and the Indian Exploration of Puritanism as a Source of Meaning, Comfort, and Ethnic Survival." *New England Quarterly* 62.3 (1989): 346–368.

Newes Out of East India of the Cruell and Bloody Usage of Our English Merchants and Others at Amboyna. London, 1624. EEBO.

Niemeijer, Hendrik E. "The Free Asian Christian Community and Poverty in Pre-modern Batavia." In *Jakarta/Batavia: Socio-cultural Essays*, ed. P. Nas and C. Grijns. Leiden: KITLV Press, 2000: 81–98.

Niemeijer, Hendrik E. "Slavery, Ethnicity and the Economic Independence of Women in Seventeenth-Century Batavia." In *Other Pasts: Women, Gender and History in Early Modern Southeast Asia*, ed. Barbara Watson Andaya. Honolulu: Center for Southeast Asian Studies, 2000.

Nixon, Judith M. "Krannert Special Collection: The Story of Treasures in Economics at Purdue University and How They Found Their Way to Indiana." *Journal of Business and Finance Librarianship* 8.1 (2002): 3–25.

O'Brien, Jean. *Dispossession by Degrees: Indian Land and Identity in Natick, Massachusetts, 1650–1790*. Lincoln: University of Nebraska Press, 2003.

O'Flynn, Dennis, and Arturo Giráldez. "Born with a 'Silver Spoon': The Origin of World Trade in 1571." *Journal of World History* 6.2 (Fall 1995): 201–221.

"On the Foxwell Papers at Kwansei Gakuin University Library." http://library2.kwansei.ac.jp/e-lib/keizaishokan/foxwell/english.html. Accessed 21 September 2016.

Orr, Bridget. *Empire on the English Stage, 1660–1714*. Cambridge: Cambridge University Press, 2001.

Pagden, Anthony. Introduction to Bartolomé de las Casas, *A Short Account of the Destruction of the Indies*. London: Penguin, 1992.

Pangallo, Matteo. "Seldome Seene: Observations from Editing *The Launching of the Mary: Or the Seaman's Honest Wife*." In *Divining Thoughts: Future Directions in Shakespeare Studies*, ed. Peter Orford with Michael P. Jones, Lizz Ketterrer, and Joshua McEvillia. Newcastle: Cambridge Scholars, 2007: 1–16.

Parfitt, Tudor. *The Lost Tribes of Israel: The History of a Myth*. London: Phoenix, 2002.

Parker, Henry. *The Altar Dispute, or, A Discourse Concerning the Severall Innovations of the Altar*. London, 1641. EEBO.

Parrish, Susan Scott. *American Curiosity: Cultures of Natural History in the Colonial British Atlantic World*. Chapel Hill: University of North Carolina Press, 2006.

Parrish, Susan Scott. "Richard Ligon and the Atlantic Science of Commonwealth." *William and Mary Quarterly* 67.2 (April 2010): 209–248.

Parrish, Susan Scott. "Rummaging/In and Out of Holds." *Early American Literature* 45.2 (2010): 261–274.

Parry, J. H. "Asia-in-the-West." *Terra Incognitae* 8.1 (January 1976): 59–72.

Patterson, Orlando. *Slavery and Social Death: A Comparative Study.* Cambridge, MA: Harvard University Press, 1985.

Pearson, M. N. "Spain and Spanish Trade in Southeast Asia." *Journal of Asian History* 2 (1968): 109–129.

Pestana, Carla. *The English Atlantic in an Age of Revolution, 1640–1661.* Cambridge, MA: Harvard University Press, 2007.

Pestana, Carla. "English Character and the Fiasco of the Western Design." *Early American Studies* 3.1 (Spring 2005): 1–31.

Pestana, Carla. *Protestant Empire: Religion and the Making of the British Atlantic World.* Philadelphia: University of Pennsylvania Press, 2011.

Philips, Edward. *The New World of English Words.* London, 1658. EEBO.

Pincus, Steven C. A. *Protestantism and Patriotism: Ideologies and the Making of English Foreign Policy, 1650–1668.* Cambridge: Cambridge University Press, 1996.

Pocock, J. G. A. *Virtue, Commerce, and History: Essays on Political Thought and History, Chiefly in the Eighteenth Century.* Cambridge: Cambridge University Press, 1985.

Polanco Martínez, Fernando. "Las ciudades de la Nueva España en Motolinía y Thomas Gage." In *Villes réelles et imaginaires d'Amérique Latine: Actes des Premiéres journées américanistes des Universités de Catalogne 19 et 20 mai 2000,* ed. Pierre-Luc Abramson, Marie-Jeanne Galera, and Pierre Lopez. Perpignan: Université de Perpignan, 2002: 63–76.

Pollman, Judith, and Mark Greengrass. Introduction to part 4, "Religious Communication: Print and Beyond." In *Religion and Cultural Exchange in Europe, 1400–1700,* ed. Heinz Schilling and István György Tóth. Cambridge: Cambridge University Press, 2006: 221–235.

Popkin, Richard H. *The Third Force in Seventeenth-Century Thought.* Leiden: Brill, 1992.

Preston, Joseph H. "Was There a Historical Revolution?" *Journal of the History of Ideas* 38 (1977): 353–364.

Purchas, Samuel. *Purchas His Pilgrimage.* London, 1626. EEBO.

Purchas, Samuel. *Purchas His Pilgrimes in Five Books.* London, 1625. EEBO.

Quijano, Anibal. "Coloniality of Power: Eurocentrism and Latin America." *Nepantla: Views from South* 1.3 (2000): 533–580.

Radway, Janice. "What's in a Name?" *American Quarterly* 51.1 (1999): 1–32.

Raman, Shankar. *Framing "India": The Colonial Imaginary in Early Modern Culture.* Stanford: Stanford University Press, 2002.

Ramsey, James. *Bloudy Newes from the East-Indies.* London, 1651. EEBO.

Ransom, Amy J. "Warping Time: Alternate History, Historical Fantasy, and the Postmodern *Uchronie Québécoise.*" *Extrapolation* 51.2 (Summer 2010): 258–280.

Rattansi, Pyarali M. "Paracelsus and the Puritan Revolution." *Ambix* 11 (1963): 24–32.

Reid, Anthony, and Jennifer Brewster. *Slavery, Bondage and Dependency in Southeast Asia.* New York: St. Martin's Press, 1983.

A Remonstrance of the Directors. London, 1632. EEBO.

Ritzenthaler, Mary Lynn, and Catherine Nicholson. "A New Era Begins for the Charters of Freedom." *Prologue* 35.3 (Fall 2003). http://www.archives.gov/publications/prologue/2003/fall/charters-new-era.html. Accessed 16 October 2016.

Rivers, Marcellus, and Oxenbridge Foyle. *Englands Slavery, or Barbados Merchandize; Represented in a Petition to the High Court of Parliament.* London, 1659. EEBO.

Robertson, James. "Cromwell and the Conquest of Jamaica." *History Today* 55.5 (May 2005): 15–22.

Rosenberg, Nathan, and L. E. Birdzell, Jr. *How the West Grew Rich.* New York: Basic Books, 1986.

Ross, Dorothy. "Historical Consciousness in Nineteenth-Century America." *American Historical Review* 89.4 (October 1984): 909–928.

Ross, Dorothy. "A New Look at Nineteenth-Century Historical Consciousness from the Modern/Postmodern Divide." *Modern Intellectual History* 9.2 (2012): 451–462.

Rubright, Marjorie. *Doppelgänger Dilemmas: Anglo-Dutch Relations in Early Modern English Literature and Culture*. Philadelphia: Pennsylvania University Press, 2014.

Ruescas, Javier, and Javier Wrana. "The West Indies and Manila Galleons: The First Global Trade Route." Paper presented at seminar The Galleon and the Making of the Pacific, Asociacio'n Cultural Galeo'n de Manila (Madrid), Manila, November 9, 2009. http://www.galeonde-manila.org/images/stories/The_West_Indies__Manila_Galleons_Ruescas__Wrana_-_Revised_March_2010_con_cabecera.pdf. Accessed 11 March 2015.

Rusche, Harry. "Prophecies and Propaganda, 1641 to 1651." *English Historical Review* 84.33 (October 1969): 752–770.

Said, Edward. "Globalizing Literary Study." In "Globalizing Literary Studies," special issue, *PMLA* 116.1 (January 2001).

Said, Edward. *Orientalism*. 25th anniversary ed. New York: Vintage Books, 1979.

Salisbury, Neal. "Red Puritans." *William and Mary Quarterly*, 3rd ser., 31 (January 1974): 27–54.

Sainsbury, W. Noel. 1825–1895. *The British Public Record Office and the Materials In it for Early American History*. Worcester, MA, 1893. Hathi Trust.

Sainsbury, W. Noel. *Hearts of Oak: Stories of Early English Adventure*. London: Bradbury, Evans, & Co, 1871.

Sanders, Julie. "Textual Introduction" in Julie Sanders, ed. *The Northern Lass*. In *The Complete Works of Richard Brome-Online*. Gen. ed. Richard Cave. http://www.hrionline.ac.uk/brome/. Accessed 21 September 2016.

Sanderson, William. *An Answer to a Scurrilous Pamphlet*. London, 1656. EEBO.

Sanderson, William. *A Compleat History of the Lives and Reigns of, Mary Queen of Scotland, and of her Son and Successor, James the Sixth*. London, 1656. EEBO.

Sanderson, William. *Graphice: The Use of the Pen and Pensil. Or, the Most Excellent Art of Painting*. London, 1658.

Sargent, Mark. "Thomas Hutchinson, Ezra Stiles, and the Legend of the Regicides." *William and Mary Quarterly* 49.3 (1992): 431–448.

Saslow, Edward. "Dryden as Historiography Royal: The Authorship of *His Majesties Declaration Defended*, 1681." *Modern Philology* 75.3 (1978): 261–272.

Scarry, Elaine. *The Body in Pain: The Making and Unmaking of the World*. Oxford: Oxford University Press, 1985.

Schille, Candy B. K. "'With Honour Quit the Fort': Ambivalent Colonialism in Dryden's *Amboyna*." *Early Modern Literary Studies* 12.1 (May 2006): 1–30.

Schivelbusch, Wolfgang. *Tastes of Paradise: A Society History of Spices, Stimulants and Intoxicants*. Trans. David Jacobson. New York: Vintage Books, 1992.

Schmidt, Benjamin. *Innocence Abroad: The Dutch Imagination and the New World, 1570–1670*. Cambridge: Cambridge University Press, 2001.

Schurz, William Lytle. *The Manila Galleon*. New York: Dutton, 1939.

Scott-Luckens, Carola. "Propaganda or Marks of Grace? The Impact of the Reported Ordeals of Sarah Wight in Revolutionary London, 1647–52." *Women's Writing* 9.2 (2002): 215–232.

The Second Part of the Tragedy of Amboyna: or, A True Relation of a Most Bloody, Treacherous, and Cruel design of the Dutch in the New-Netherlands in America. London, 1653. EEBO.

Seeman, Erik R. *Pious Persuasions: Laity and Clergy in Eighteenth-Century New England*. Baltimore: Johns Hopkins University Press, 1999.

Shapin, Stephen. "Pump and Circumstance: Robert Boyle's Literary Technology." *Social Studies of Science* 14.4 (1984): 481–520.

Shepard, Thomas. *Clear Sun-shine of the Gospel*. London, 1648. EEBO.

Sheppard, Jill. "A Historical Sketch of the Poor Whites of Barbados: From Indentured Servants to 'Redlegs.'" *Caribbean Studies* 14.3 (October 1974): 71–94.

Shetty, Sandhya, and Elizabeth Jane Bellamy. "Postcolonialism's Archive Fever." *Diacritics* 30.1 (2000): 25–48.

Shields, David. "Sons of the Dragon, or The English Hero Revived." In *Creole Subjects in the Colonial Americas: Empires, Texts, Identities,* ed. Ralph Bauer and Jose Antonio Mazzotti. Chapel Hill: University of North Carolina Press, 2009: 101–114.

Silverman, David J. *Faith and Boundaries: Colonists, Christianity, and Community among the Wampanoag Indians of Martha's Vineyard, 1600–1871.* New York: Cambridge University Press, 2005.

Singman, Jeffrey L. *Daily Life in Elizabethan England.* Westport: Greenwood Press, 1995.

Slater, Samuel. *A Rhetorical Rapture as Composed into a Funeral Oration.* London, 1658. EEBO.

Smith, Cassander. *"Washing the Ethiop Red": Black Africans and English Anti-Spanish Sentiment in the Early Atlantic World.* Baton Rouge: Louisiana State University Press, 2016.

Smith, John. *Advertisements for the Unexperienced Planters of New England, or Any Where.* London, 1631. EEBO.

Smolinksi, Reiner. "Caveat Emptor: Pre- and Postmillennialism in the Late Reformation Period." In *Milleniarianism and Messianism in Early Modern European Culture: The Millenarian Turn,* ed. J. E. Force and R. H. Popkin. Dordrecht: Kluwer Academic, 2001: 145–169.

Sontag, Susan. *Regarding the Pain of Others.* New York: Farrar, Straus and Giroux, 2003.

Sontag, Susan. "Regarding the Torture of Others." *New York Times,* May 23, 2004. http://www .nytimes.com/2004/05/23/magazine/regarding-the-torture-of-others.html?_r=0. Accessed 16 October 2016.

Steedman, Carolyn. *Dust: The Archive and Cultural History.* New Brunswick: Rutgers University Press, 2002.

Stevens, Laura. *The Poor Indians: British Missionaries, Native Americans, and Colonial Sensibility.* Philadelphia: University of Pennsylvania Press, 2004.

Stretton, Tim. "Widows at Law in Tudor and Stuart England." In *Widowhood in Medieval and Early Modern Europe,* ed. Sandra Cavallo and Lyndan Warner. London: Routledge, 1999: 193–208.

Stow, John. "Bishopsgate warde." In *A Survey of London: Reprinted from the Text of 1603,* ed. C. L. Kingsford. Oxford, 1908: 163–175. British History Online. http://www.british-history .ac.uk/no-series/survey-of-london-stow/1603/pp163-175. Accessed 24 November 2015.

Strong, Frank. "The Causes of Cromwell's West Indian Expedition. *American Historical Review* 4.2 (January 1899): 228–245.

Tardieu, Jean-Pierre. "Los negros de Hispanoamérica en la vision predestinacionista del inglés Thomas Gage (1648)." In *Culturas y escrituras entre siglos (del XVI al XXI),* ed. Alain Bégue, María Luisa Lobato, Carlos Mata Induráin, and Jean-Pierre Tardieu. Pamplona: Servicio de Publicacaiones de la Universidad de Navarra, 2013: 257–273.

Taylor, S. A. G. *The Western Design: An Account of Cromwell's Expedition to the Caribbean.* 2nd ed. London: Solstice Productions, 1969.

Tennenhouse, Leonard. *The Importance of Feeling English: American Literature and the British Diaspora, 1750–1850.* Princeton: Princeton University Press, 2007.

Thompson, Ayanna. *Performing Race and Torture on the Early Modern Stage.* New York: Routledge, 2007.

Thompson, Keith. *Religion and the Decline of Magic.* New York: Scribner's, 1971.

Thorowgood, Thomas. *Iewes in America.* London, 1649. EEBO.

Todorov, Tzvetan. *Fantastic: A Structural Approach to a Literary Genre.* Cleveland: Case Western Reserve University Press, 1973.

Tompkins, Jane. "'Indians': Textualism, Morality, and the Problem of History." *Critical Inquiry* 13.1 (Autumn 1986): 101–119.

Trevor-Roper, Hugh. "Mayerne, Sir Theodore Turquet de (1573–1655)." In *Oxford Dictionary of National Biography.* Oxford: Oxford University Press, 2004. http://www.oxforddnb .com/view/article/18430. Accessed 6 November 2015.

A True Relation of the Unjust, Cruell, and Barbarous Proceedings Against the English at Amboyna in the East-Indies. London, 1624. EEBO.

A True Relation of the Unjust, Cruell, and Barbarous Proceedings Against the English at Amboyna in the East-Indies. London, 1651. EEBO.

A True Relation of the Unjust, Cruell, and Barbarous Proceedings Against the English at Amboyna. London, 1665. EEBO.

Turner, Jack. *Spice: The History of a Temptation.* New York: Vintage, 2005.

Ulrich, Laurel Thatcher. *The Age of Homespun: Objects and Stories in the Creation of an American Myth.* New York: Knopf, 2001.

Ulrich, Laurel Thatcher. *Good Wives: Image and Reality in the Lives of Women in Northern New England, 1650–1750.* New York: Knopf, 1982.

Underhill, John. *Newes from America* (1638). Ed. Paul Royster. Electronic Texts in American Studies. Digital Commons, University of Nebraska-Lincoln. http://digitalcommons.unl.edu/etas/37/. Accessed 2 July 2015.

Vades-forte, Diego de [James Wadsworth]. *A Curious Treatise of the Nature and Quality of Chocolate.* London, 1640. EEBO.

Valdéon, Robert. "Tears of the Indies and the Power of Translation: John Phillips' Version of *Brevíssima Relation de la destrucción de las Indias. Bulletin of Spanish Studies* 89.6 (2012): 839–858.

Van der Welle, J. A. *Dryden and Holland.* Groningen: J. B. Wolters, 1962.

Venning, Timothy. *Cromwellian Foreign Policy.* New York: St. Martin's Press, 1995.

"The Vertues of Chocolate; the Properties of Cavee." Oxford: Henry Hall, 1660. EEBO.

Walker, Daniel. *Unclean Spirits: Possession and Exorcism in France and England in the Late Sixteenth and Early Seventeenth Centuries.* Philadelphia: University of Pennsylvania Press, 1981.

Wallerstein, Immanuel. *World-Systems Analysis: An Introduction.* Durham: Duke University Press, 2004.

Weaver, Jace. *The Red Atlantic: American Indigenes and the Making of the Modern World, 1000–1927.* Chapel Hill: University of North Carolina Press, 2014.

Webster, Charles. *Paracelsus to Newton: Magic and the Making of Modern Science.* Cambridge: Cambridge University Press, 1982; reprint, Dover, 2005.

Welles, Lemuel. *The History of the Regicides in New England.* New York: Grafton Press, 1927.

Werner, Sarah. "When Is a Source Not a Source?" *MLA Commons* 2015. doi:10.17613/M6PG6F. Accessed 15 August 2016.

White, Hayden. "Introduction: Historical Fiction, Fictional History, and Historical Reality." *Rethinking History* 9.2/3 (June/September 2005): 147–157.

Williams, Edward, and John Ferrar. *Virgo Triumphas, or, Virginia in Generall.* London, 1650. EEBO.

Wilson, Peter. "Perceptions of Violence in the Early Modern Communications Revolution: The Case of the Thirty Years War, 1618–1648." In *War and Violence in the Media: Five Disciplinary Lenses,* ed. Athina Karatzogianni. Hoboken: Taylor and Francis, 2013: 13–29.

Winslow, Edward. *The Glorious progress of the Gospel amongst the Indians in New England.* London, 1649. EEBO.

Winn, James Anderson. *John Dryden and His World.* New Haven: Yale University Press, 1987.

Wojcik, Jan. "John Dryden's Interest in Prophecy." In *Poetic Prophecy in Western Literature,* ed. Jan Wojcik and Raymond-Jean Frontain. London: Associated University Presses, 1984: 81–93.

Woolf, Daniel. "From Hystories to the Historical: Five Transitions in Thinking about the Past, 1500–1700." *Huntington Library Quarterly* 68.1–2 (March 2005): 33–70.

Woolf, Daniel. "Sanderson, Sir William (1586–1676)." In *Oxford Dictionary of National Biography.* Oxford: Oxford University Press, 2004. http://www.oxforddnb.com/view/article/24630. Accessed 16 September 2016.

Wright, Stephen. "Jessey, Henry (1601–1663)." In *Oxford Dictionary of National Biography.* Oxford: Oxford University Press, 2004. http://www.oxforddnb.com/view/article/14804. Accessed 16 September 2016.

Zakai, Avihu. "Thomas Brightman and the English Apocalyptic Tradition." In *Menasseh ben Israel and His World,* ed. Yusef Kaplan, Henry Méchoulan, and Richard H. Popkin. Leiden: Brill, 1989: 31–44.

Zorrilla, Roćio Olivares. "Chiapas a través de los viajeros del XVII: Aspectos narrativos e historia descriptiva en Thomas Gage y Antonio de Espinosa." In *Homenaje a Alejandro de Humboldt: Literatura de Viajes desde y hacia Latinoamérica, Siglos XV–XXI.* Oaxaca: Universidad Autónoma Benito Juárez de Oaxaca, 2005: 234–241.

INDEX